WOLE SOYINKA

CRITICAL STUDIES ON
BLACK LIFE AND CULTURE
(VOL. 15)

GARLAND REFERENCE LIBRARY
OF THE HUMANITIES
(VOL. 732)

CRITICAL STUDIES ON BLACK LIFE AND CULTURE

Advisory Editor
Professor Henry-Louis Gates

Charles T. Davis
Black Is the Color of the Cosmos

Margaret Perry
The Harlem Renaissance

Josephine R.B. Wright
Ignatius Sancho (1729–1780), an Early African Composer in England

Richard Newman
Black Index

Allan Austin
African Muslims in Antebellum America

Alan P. Merriam
African Music in Perspective

Alan Dundes
Mother Wit from the Laughing Barrel

Jeffrey C. Stewart
The Critical Temper of Alain Locke

Romare Bearden and Carl Holty
The Painter's Mind

George Campbell
First Poems

John M. Janzen
Lemba, 1650–1930

William Robinson
Phillis Wheatley and Her Writings

Sam Dennison
Scandalize My Name

Irma E. Goldstraw
Derek Walcott

Obi Maduakor
Wole Soyinka: An Introduction to His Writing

Eddie Meadows
Jazz Reference and Research Materials

Linda Rae Brown
Music, Printed and Manuscript, in the James Weldon Johnson Memorial Collection of Negro Arts & Letters, Yale University

Ishmael Reed
God Made Alaska for the Indians

Betty Kaplan Gubert
Early Black Bibliographies, 1863–1918

WOLE SOYINKA

AN INTRODUCTION TO HIS WRITING

OBI MADUAKOR

Garland Publishing, Inc.   ◆   New York and London   ◆   1986

Selections from *A Dance of the Forests* and *The Road* are reprinted by permission of Oxford University Press. Selections from *A Shuttle in the Crypt* are reprinted by permission of Hill and Wang. Selections from *Season of Anomy, The Man Died, Ogun Abibiman,* and *Ake: The Years of Childhood* are reprinted by permission of Rex Collings Ltd and Brandt & Brandt. Selections from *Idanre and Other Poems, The Bacchae* of Euripides, *Madmen and Specialists,* and *Death and the King's Horseman* are reprinted by permission of London Methuen and W.W. Norton & Company, Inc. Cambridge University Press has granted permission to print selections from *Myth, Literature and the African World.* The pictures on pages 110 and 111 are from *Ifa: An Exposition of Ifa Literary Corpus,* and are reprinted by permission of University Press Limited. Selections from *The Interpreters* are reprinted by permission of Andre Deutsch and Holmes & Meier.   Design by Alison Lew

© 1987 Obi Maduakor

Library of Congress Cataloging-in-Publication Data

Maduakor, Obi.
  Wole Soyinka : an introduction to his writings.

  (Critical studies on Black life and culture ; v. 15)
  Includes index.
  1. Soyinka, Wole—Criticism and interpretation.
I. Title. II. Series.
PR9387.9.S6Z77   1987   822   86-29434
ISBN 0-8240-9141-8 (alk. paper)

Printed on acid-free, 250-year-life paper

Manufactured in the United States of America

CONTENTS

PART FOUR: THE LITERARY ESSAYS

PREFACE

This book is the product of the author's long-standing
interest in Soyinka's works. It is written to meet certain
challenges posed by Soyinka's writings to students of literature. My contact with students in the years that I have been
involved in university teaching has shown that Soyinka is
often called "difficult." The areas of complaint concern
Soyinka's approach to his subject matter, his technical
innovations and, at times, obscurities, his use of mythology, the worldview proffered in his works, and his use of
language. This book seeks to introduce the student to
Soyinka's writings by attempting to clarify some of these
areas.

To this end, the book attempts a comprehensive coverage of most of Soyinka's works that have appeared in print
to date. Part One is devoted to the poems. The works
discussed include Soyinka's three books of verse: *Idanre
and Other Poems* (1967), *A Shuttle in the Crypt* (1972), and
Ogun Abibiman (1976).

Part Two is devoted to Soyinka's two novels, *The Interpreters* (1965) and *Season of Anomy* (1973), and to his
childhood autobiography *Ake*, subtitled *The Years of
Childhood* (1981). Each novel is discussed under some key
topics that are likely to exercise the curiosity of students.
The essay on *The Interpreters*, for example, is organized
around the following headings: "the narrative technique,"
"some major minor themes," "the interpreters," "the content of the pantheon," and "language." There are seven
subsections in the chapter on *Season of Anomy*, the high-

lights of which include sections on the novel's mythic and social background, the Cartel, the ideological motif, the theme of quest, nature, religion and ritual, language and narrative technique, and a postscript on characterization. Part Three views Soyinka as a dramatist. This section is devoted to the metaphysical plays which pose the greatest challenge to the students in terms of their themes, technique, and structure. These plays include *Dance of the Forests* (1963), *The Road* (1965), *Madmen and Specialists* (1972), *The Bacchae of Euripides* (1973), and *Death and the King's Horseman* (1975).

I have called these plays "metaphysical" in recognition of (a) their preoccupation with the theme of death, (b) their abstract and intellectual content, (c) their use of juxtapositional and elliptical techniques, and (d) Soyinka's deliberate insertion of their action within a worldview that is specifically African. This is a worldview of ritual in which order and harmony are mandated upon the imperatives of cosmic law. Each play is discussed under the following topics: dramatic technique, dramatic structure, theme, characterization, and language.

Part Four assesses Soyinka's achievement as a literary critic. It analyzes Soyinka's literary essays, most of which have been collected by Soyinka himself in *Myth, Literature and the African World* (1976). The ideas of the very early essays are reworked into the framework of the later volume, giving Soyinka himself a consistency of viewpoint in his assessment of African writers and their works. This chapter is organized into four parts with the following subheadings: (a) "Incidental Essays" in which the very early essays ("The Future of African Writing" (1960), "From a Common Backcloth" (1963), and "And After the Narcissist?") are discussed; (b) "The Ritual Essays" in which the seminal essay, "The Fourth Stage" (1969) and its later variants ["Morality and Aesthetics in the Ritual Archetype" (1976) and "Drama and the African World-View" (1976)] are discussed; (c) "Ideology or Social Vision" in which the two essays on the religious and secular dimensions of works of social vision are analyzed; and (d) "Controversies" in which we evaluate Soyinka's reactions to his critics especially the Chinwezu School and the Marxist radicals from the Ife-Ibadan axis.

INTRODUCTION

MYTHOPOEISIS AND COMMITMENT

The American readers of this book would do well to remember that in Africa, as in much of the rest of the third world, literature is generally perceived as a cultural institution whose production and reception are held to be deeply implicated in the destiny of the continent and its peoples. For just as in Asia and Latin America where the phenomenon of writers playing prominent roles in the public affairs of their countries and the process of historical transformation of their societies have been popularized and legitimized by such figures as Mao Tse-Tung, Rabidranath Tagore, Pablo Neruda, and Ernesto Cardenal, so have the example and influence of poet-presidents like Agostinho Neto (Angola) and Leopold Sedar Senghor (Senegal), in Africa, consecrated the bonds among literature, culture, and politics. A Norman Mailer cutting capers as a lame-duck mayoral candidate in New York City is a world away from the cultural norm in the third world in which writers are sometimes not only heads of state but also parliamentarians, bureaucrats, ambassadors, guerrilla combatants, and, in the satirical coinage of a young Nigerian poet, "politrickians."

This tradition of the third-world writer as a promoter of explicit social, political, and moral values crucial to the survival of his or her society and a champion of freedom, dignity, and justice for the majority of his people—a major writer like Borges, who sided publicly and steadfastly with oligarchs and dictators, is a minority phenomenon, a rarity even—can best be understood if the reader of this book recognizes that in Africa and most of the third world the writer belongs to a social group variously called the intelligentsia, the literati, the educated elite, whose role and visibility in society are markedly different from that of their counterparts in the "first world." For if, in the words of the English colonial novelist, Joyce Cary, the writer in the West is "doomed to be free," the third-world writer, whether or not he voluntarily and conscientiously accepts the role, is often "doomed" to be a spokesman for his race, his continent, his culture, or specific social groups and classes in his society like women, urban workers, or rural peasants. Even when they go into voluntary or enforced exile, it is almost unknown for third-world writers to choose the implacable renunciation of the claims of country, culture, and family which the embittered James Joyce, on choosing to go into exile, spat out with his triad of "exile, silence and cunning."

Like his West African fellow writers such as Chinua Achebe, Mongo Beti, Mariana Ba, Ousmane Sembene, Ayi Kwei Armah, Ama Ata Aidoo, Femi Osofisan, Festus Iyayi, and Niyi Osundare, like virtually every other writer and critic of literature in his society, Wole Soyinka belongs to this highly self-conscious group of literati yoked by social and historical circumstances to a direct, prominent role in the historical process. However, within this norm, Wole Soyinka has worked out a distinctive form of political engagement and a peculiar paradigm of the social role of literature, which not only somewhat set him apart from most of the other West African writers but also invite comparisons with, first, the fate of the writer in apartheid South Africa and, second, the axiomatic aesthetic individualism of Western writers. It is perhaps useful to expatiate briefly on each of these two points.

Among contemporary West African writers, it is perhaps only the Canerounian, Mongo Beti, and Wole Soyinka who, similar to the standard experience of many writers in South Africa, have so relentlessly and perhaps effectively taken up the role of the writer as a publicist against repression, tyranny, and injustice that they have drawn to themselves the full wrath and vindictiveness of the state. For his troubles Mongo Beti has been forced into more or less permanent exile from his homeland, while Soyinka, for *his* dare, has drunk fully from the bitter cup of his socio-political commitment: almost three years in detention during the Nigerian civil war (1967-70), most of it in solitary confinement, and during a period of widespread anomie in the years of turbulent electoral politics in Nigeria in the early 1980s, an undeclared war of attrition with the security police and paid would-be assassins of some of the professional political warlords. Against this background of idealistic, if often desperate activism, Soyinka has fully deserved the extensive public recognition he enjoys among his countrymen beyond the widest dreams of other writers and intellectuals. To most of the former he is a selfless, courageous, and uncompromising advocate of social justice and individual freedom, while to a few contrary spirits among both left-wing and right-wing skeptics, he is a quixotic neo-romantic who uses popular causes for staging in the public arena with what are, in reality, gratuitous, private self-dramatizations.

The idiosyncratic and often solitary expressions of Soyinka's socio-political commitment find something of an analogue in the assertive aesthetic individualism of both his conception of the function of literature in African society at the present time and the actual paradigms of commitment discoverable in the protagonists of his major works in the quintessentially *Soyinkan* imaginative universe in which they are made to act. For unlike most of his confreres in the canon of commited African literature, Soyinka has tenaciously turned away from overt didacticism and a realist conception of character and action. Except in the satires and light comedies among his plays and the satirical vignettes of occasional verses among his poetry, Soyinka's proclivities have not been for the obvious themes and the typical conflicts and dilemmas of contemporary social experience in black Africa. It is perhaps in those writings based on major events and realities of contemporary Africa like the trilogy on the Nigerian civil war, *A Shuttle in the Crypt, Season of Anomy,* and *Madmen and Specialists,* that we get an inkling of how Soyinka's artistry defines itself in a mythopoeic anti-realist propensity. An elaborate substructure of myth, ritual, and symbolism transforms these works, which derive from history, "banal" history, into haunting, apocalyptic creations of the imagination. Their characters and the worlds in which they move evoke both bafflement and a deep disquiet in affective response. And moreover, the mythic substructure, the symbolic and ritualistic framework are never really thematically clarified; rather they are cumulatively elaborated in hieractic action, emblematic mime, an epiphanic image, passages of incantatory speech or prose description. Typical, although unduly "notorious" among such structures of symbolism and ritual archetype, is the elaborate dramatic conceit of "As" in *Madmen and Specialists*. His mind loosing its moorings in an expedient rationality which proves slippery before the provocative, taunting irrationalism of the Old Man, the specialist asks with increasing frenzy: "Why As? What is As?" He may well have been articulating the reader's or audience's own bafflement! "As," the cult and the deity, preside over what Soyinka sees as the perenniality—"As was, is and ever shall be?"—of evil, especially that brand of evil which, in the name of a contemporary or presently fashionable orthodoxy, *at all times throughout history*, has rationalized and justified social cannibalism, man preying on man. Readers will, however, look in vain for the provenance of this cult and deity outside the constituted mythopoeic world of Soyinka's fertile, searing imagination within which, moreover, their significations are less to be elicited by rational exegesis than by total, sympathetic, and affective embrace.

"As" then may be taken as being representative of the difficulties posed for interpretation by the constituents of Soyinka's mythopoeic world: many entities, conceits, and figurations belong to that order of the products of the mind which Kant called *noumenon*—things that are produced by the mind but cannot be known or perceived by the senses. Sometimes indeed, the *noumenal* in the Soyinka mythopoeia is a joke, a deliberately private conundrum which Afro-Americans might call "signifying," as in the famous case of a non-existent physiological organ, the "drink lobes," about which one of the characters of Soyinka's first novel, *The Interpreters*, endlessly worries. The principle operating here seems to belong to the impulse which made Borges write *The Book of Imaginary Beings*: literature is born of the imagination; it ought always to push imagination even beyond its own unknown limits. This is perhaps what is implied in Soyinka's own term for his mythologizing tendency—"hermeticism."

The gods and avatars of the Yoruba pantheon who figure so prominently in the Soyinka imaginative universe are anything but noumenal, in the Kantian sense implied above, since the principles and phenomena of existence which they stand for are active instinctual forces in what Soyinka calls the "African world." Is Soyinka then a believer, a religionist? This question, which is ultimately redundant, is perhaps not unfair, given the deep sympathy lavished by the mythopoet on the gods and avatars, especially his chosen tutelary deity, Ogun. The relationship between the writer and the tutelary god, in fact, provides us with a key to unlocking the interest and enigma of the function of the gods in Soyinka's writings.

Ogun is the god of creativity, the principle of assertive, restless, exploratory will, the patron god of blacksmiths, carvers, hunters, and in a technological world, drivers and precision-tool machinists. Moreover, Ogun's complement of attributes is contradictory and dualistic, a destructive blood-thirstiness being the obverse of his positive, creative side. Soyinka's self-projection into the attributes of this god, and by extension the projection of the protagonists of most of his major plays into approximations of the Ogun archetype is a recognition of the contradictory, paradoxical nature of the creative principle in life.

The other Yoruba *orisa* encountered in Soyinka's writings stand for the same pattern of signification that enlarges our apprehension of the regulative principles of life, particularly within the cosmic framework of man's terrestrial existence. There is Obatala, the god of creation itself, a principle of spiritual purity, of patience, forbearance, and the moral necessity of suffering and ascetic self-control. There is Sango, the sky god, the medium of electrical energy and scourge of criminals and felons. Together with Ogun, Sango is the most notable survivor of the middle passage and the cultural genocide of the slave plantations; his cults thrive today in many New World cultures from Brazil to Cuba to Trinidad. There is also Orunmila, the oracular god of wisdom, the presiding spirit of those capable of a prescient probing into the unknown, the unanticipated. His companion and foil, Esu, the trickster god of chance and indeterminacy, is the most ubiquitous deity in the pantheon, and no wonder since he is also the principle of contradiction and ambiguity, which, as we know only too well, pervade all of existence.

Many critics, especially radical, left-wing critics, have described Soyinka's mythopoeic tendency, his obsession with the cosmic scale of values and significations in the dramas of the gods, as just so much sophisticated obscurantism, a kind of questionable neo-traditionalism capable of distracting from the urgent tasks and concrete historical realities of Africa's present period of rapid change and permanent crisis. Soyinka's response has been characteristically trenchant, a veritable 'Ogunnian' riposte: mythopoeisis is not necessarily against progress, not inherently retrogressive; the pantheon and its deities and their significations are for change that is *rooted* in Africa's unique, valid forms of conceptualizing experience and apprehending the self, they are for progress that is informed by the paradoxes and, ultimately, the imponderables of life and reality.

It would be misleading to leave the impression that Soyinka's writings contain only allegory, myth, and ritual, that the protagonists conceived in archetypal terms in his major works come off as abstract ciphers in a rarefied world of *noumenon* and *meta-nature*. Even the most casual acquaintance with his works cannot fail to notice the superbly observant and poetic strokes with which Soyinka is able to evoke, with vividness and lyricism, the mundane and the typical, the absurd and the risible expressions of *lived* experience in his society. In the end the Soyinka literary ambience is one of the skillful interfusion of reality and supra-reality, the ordinary and the metaphysical.

This book has sought to elucidate the variegated expressions of the fusion of mythopoeic richness with observant, poetic evocations of the real in Soyinka's writings. Dr. Maduakor has set himself a modest task, that of providing a critical guide into this dense, challenging, and enchanted world of Soyinka's writings without going into the intricacies of the complex significations they indicate. Dr. Maduakor has done a marvelous job of this task and his effort can only be described as a labor of love and dedication to the Soyinka canon and to literature. Because of the assiduity and clarity with which he has executed this task of elucidating the complex web of ideas and modes, of sensing and intuiting into experience the underpinnings of Soyinka's works, Dr. Maduakor has produced a work that both students and teachers of Soyinka's writings will find welcome and useful.

Biodun Jeyifo
Department of Literature in English
University of Ife
Nigeria

This book is dedicated to my mother Angelina, my brother Vin, my sister Susan, and my uncle M.C. Awgu.

PART ONE

THE POEMS

△ △

LYRICS OF AGONY (I):
THE SHORTER POEMS OF *IDANRE*

ON SOYINKA'S POETRY IN GENERAL

S oyinka is a poet who loves to celebrate the tribulations
of experience rather than the joy of innocence. The
painful birth of a soul and that awareness or self-knowledge that is begotten of experience—these are the situations
that appeal to his poetic imagination. In the poem "Luo
Plains,"[1] for example, the Kenya of the era of post-Mau
Mau rebellion, newly independent, is acclaimed as an
"eagle sentinel" begotten of "cactus." Soyinka's poetic
imagination is formed early by the knowledge that "hot
sterilizing pads sealed the cord at birth."[2] Consequently,
the music of humanity tends to be sad in his ear so that
meadows and landscapes of "locus amoenus" (a pleasant
spot) rarely feature in his poetry. What we have is the
splitting of the pod out of which emerges the new man or
the new soul:

> In the blasting of the seed, in the night-birds'
> Instant discernment, in the elemental fusion, seed
> To current, shone the godhead essence. (p. 64)

This passage is meaningful in its proper context, but it
illustrates (a) the process of artistic creation as Soyinka
conceives it, (b) the amount of labor that goes into the
making of a Soyinka poem, (c) the corresponding amount
of effort that is expected of the reader before that poem can
yield its meaning to the painstaking seeker, and (d) the

tactile ruggedness of Soyinka's poetry. In terms of item (a), the completed poem is the new "godhead essence," just as the gradual unfolding of meaning in a Soyinka poem is also suggested by that metaphor. The perils of experience are apparent from the poem's images of labor.

Even the coming of dawn is not gratuitous, as the poem "Dawn" shows. Dawn has to be *born*, that is, it has to undergo a painful emergence. Similarly, the activities of birth and death and love are accompanied by their attendant rituals. The individual who survives the ritual testing or the winged beast ("Around Us, Dawning") who dares the cosmos and returns safe to earth is celebrated as a hero. This is the basis of the celebration of heroic strength and the heroic will in Soyinka's poetry.

This tragic vision extends to the operations of natural phenomena. Rain storms are violent, but since they, too, form part of nature's ritual for its own renewal, they are also potent. Soyinka extends his perceptions of experience and phenomena into a dimension that is archetypal. The coming of dawn and the fall of rain enact patterns in the archetypes of rebirth and renewal. Ritual symbols thus feature in Soyinka's poetry. This poetry does not lend itself to too literal an interpretation as it frequently leaps into the unknown, the unfathomable, and the mystical in its quest to complement the visible with the invisible.

Soyinka's tragic imagination is linked to the tragic experience of his personal muse, Ogun, often extolled by Soyinka as the origin of the tragic spirit in Yoruba mythology and as the first tragic actor since his successful invasion of the dark irrational forces that inhabit the gulf of transition. The details of Ogun's labors in the abyss of transition are explained at length in chapters eleven and twelve of this book.

Ogun's spirit broods over Soyinka's poetic activities, coloring the poet's imagination with his tragic heritage. He is the god "aflame with kernels" in the first poem ("Dawn") of *Idanre and Other Poems* (1967), Soyinka's first book of verse. The main poem narrates the major events in the Ogun mythology while even the shorter poems are also permeated with the god's influence. Ogun features as a shuttle in Soyinka's prison poems, *A Shuttle in the Crypt* (1972), while *Ogun Abibiman* (1976) pays tribute to the god as the restorer of rights.

I have used the term "lyrics of agony" to designate Soyinka's poetry of experience. Implied in that terminology is the agony of the experience within the poem itself and the agony of interpretation; for Soyinka's poetry involves both the poet himself and the reader in a process of experiencing. Its tone is mournful, meditative and tragic, and its mood is dark.

Soyinka's poetic method is necessarily a function of his view of experience as a complex and multidimensional phenomenon. If experience is not unilinear as he often claims,[3] it is not enough to inscape it; it must also be *instressed*. The poet of an eclectic cast of mind seeks out not merely the surface value of experience but also its internalized dialectics, attempting to weld the two together in a precarious dance of fusion:

> A dynamic relationship which consists of an internalized dialectic of phenomena and perception—this is the poetic province whose occupants most readily stress and reward my intellect.[4]

Poetry born of this imagination cannot be purely descriptive or purely narrative; it is evocative and suggestive and communicates through allusions and insinuations, not by facile statements. The allusive method is compounded in the case of the long poem *Idanre* by the impaction of images. The various facets of experience collide at the very core of the initial stimulus. The favorite method in *Idanre* is to situate impacted images in a poise of action:

> As the First Boulder, as the errant wheel
> Of the death chariot, as the creation snake
> Spawned tail in mouth, wind chisels and rain pastes
> Rust from steel and bones, wake dormant seeds
> And suspended lives. I heard
> The silence yield to substance. (p. 65)

In the shorter poems, however, there is more counterpointing than impaction:

> Lakemists
> On her shadeless dugs, parched
> At waterhole. Veils. Molten silver
> Down cloudflues of alchemist sun . . .
> A lake's grey salve at dawn? (p. 13)

The poet has here presented to us his impressions of a
scene, but he has not done so in a formal grammatical
statement. What he does is to merely fling images at us in a
haphazard fashion: "lakemists," "veils," "molten silver."
To properly locate these images narratively in their context
the reader must act as co-creator with the poet. There are, of
course, some poems in *Idanre and Other Poems* which plot
meaningful narratives, for example, "In Memory of Segun
Awolowo," "The Hunchback at Dugbe," and "Dedication." But most of the poems adopt the method of collocat-
ing words and images without the copula of logical enun-
ciation.[5] But it is not words and images merely that are so
collocated; normal word order is rearranged and sentence
sense rendered incomplete by design, thus giving rise to
disjointed syntax:

> As who would break
> Earth, grief
> In savage pounding, moulds
> Her forehead where she kneels. (p. 25)

But the purely narrative poems are hard nuts to crack
because, at one point in the story, Soyinka deliberately
toughens the verse by introducing abstract and intellectual
experience into the narrative. This is the case with the
otherwise an easygoing poem, "The Hunchback at
Dugbe," until the episode of the devil injects a metaphysical strain into the story to frustrate our enjoyment of it. At
other times it is not an intellectual experience but a mythic
one that complicates our comprehension of the poem. This
is the case, for example, with "Death in the Dawn" which

is interrupted by Soyinka's vision of the unknown and the occult:

> burdened hulks retract,
> Stoop to the mist in faceless throng
> To wake the silent markets—swift, mute
> Processions on grey byways. . . . (p. 10)

and again (in "In Memory of Segun Awolowo"):

> They make complaint
> Grey presences of head and hands
> Who wander still
> Adrift from understanding. (p. 15)

One more source of difficulty is the researched rigor of Soyinka's imagery. Poetry does not come to him straight like leaves to a tree as Keats claims;[6] he picks his words meticulously as required to carry the burden of experience. This verbal sensitivity results in over-researched images which often startle by their ingenuity rather than by their appropriateness. In an otherwise simple poem, "A Cry in the Night," night is incapable of offering solace to a woman mourning the loss of a stillborn child; so the bereaved mother continues to appeal to the heavens for mercy. But those appeals are said to be "barren" because no mercy would ever come from heaven. The image of barrenness is slightly self-conscious. It sticks out from its context rather than being integrated within it. In another poem, "To One, In Labour," the ants' labor in building the anthill is said to be analoguous to the sexual labor in the making of a child.

To an uninitiated reader, Soyinka's modernist and neometaphysical technique is bound to be obstructionist. Roderick Wilson claims that it leads to complexity and confusion,[7] and the Chinweizu school of critics charge Soyinka with indulging in metaphysical obscurities for their own sake.[8] Soyinka's poetry requires the same kind of mental alertness that we have been accustomed to focus on the poetry of Donne and that of the neometaphysicians, Pound and Eliot. He resembles these in the dynamism of his mind, the resourcefulness of his intellect, and in the habit of yoking together heterogeneous ideas and concepts.

Soyinka's reply to his critics indeed recalls Eliot's defence of his own equally metaphysical verse: "Complex subjects sometimes elicit from the writer complex treatments,"[9] and again:

> We must stress the language, stretch it, impact and compact it, fragment and reassemble it with no apology, as required to bear the burden of experience and of experiencing.[10]

There is a thaw in syntactical turgidity in Soyinka's subsequent poetry. The impaction of images is rare in *A Shuttle in the Crypt* and in *Ogun Abibiman*. The range of his imagery continues to be eclectic; his language is still abstract, but the verse retains a texture that is generally more accessible than in *Idanre*.

THE POEMS OF "THE ROAD"

The principle of arrangement of the "shorter poems" of *Idanre* owes something to Ogun as has already been noted. The titles of the various subheadings take their cue from the god's mythological attributes. The poems of "The Road" pay homage to him as the god of the road; those of "Lone Figure" recall his destiny as a "lone deity," and the poems "Of Birth and Death" recall Ogun's paradoxical personality as the embodiment of creative and destructive essences. The poems of birth and death anticipate the fourth and fifth sections. Birth is directly linked to the poems of the fourth section, "For Women," which is devoted to growth and to the emergence of life; and death is the subject of the poems of "Grey Seasons." The poems of the final section, "October '66," have links with Ogun as the god of war. These attributes of the god's receive further emphasis in the main poem *Idanre*.

The poems of "The Road" are heralded by the image of dawn, the hour of travel both by land and air. Dawn features in nearly all the poems of this section. Dawn is the time when the god of the road lies in wait for travellers. But

Soyinka has not limited himself to the role of dawn in the Ogun mythology; he evokes dawn's painful emergence in the first poem, "Dawn." The operational concept is that the coming of dawn (or day) is a form of birth. When night (female principle) copulates with the sun (masculine principle), dawn is born. The copulation is the "celebration of the rites of dawn." The masculine aggressiveness of the sun is suggested through objective correlatives such as the action of the palm as it "breaks" earth or "spikes" the guard of palm fronds or pierces "high hairs of the wind." Because that action is intended as a comment on the sun-god's masculine assertiveness, both the palm and the sun-god share a common attribute—they are both "lone intruders." The sun's kernel is paralleled by the palm's "blood drops." The kernel is the sperm of the sun-god whose phallus is erect ("aflame").

Night as a female essence is assimilated into the figure of another maternal principle, the sky, which is seen as a female bull ("tearing wide/The chaste hide of the sky"). Soyinka's mind constantly seeks out parallels and analogies between images and amalgamates them into new wholes. Thus, the action suggested in the poem's dynamic images is also sexual: breaking, spiking, piercing, stealing, and tearing.

The unnamed "lone intruder" in the poem, "Dawn," assumes his proper identity as sunrise in the companion poem "Death in the Dawn."

> Let sunrise quench your lamps, and watch
> Faint brush pricklings in the sky light.

Dawn is the hour of hope, of rebirth, of vibrant energy and pleasurable sensations. The burdens that weigh down the soul at night recede ("burdened husks retract"). The opposite of dawn's hopeful aspirations is suggested by the approach of night. (See the poem "Night," in which the poet is weighed down by the unpleasant sensations evoked by the approach of night). However, dawn summons the fated individual to his tragic destiny. That is why the cautious traveller does not insist on going on a journey when the signs are unpropitious:

The right foot for joy, the left, dread
And the mother prayed, child
May you never walk
When the road waits, famished.

The last stanza of the poem introduces the paradox of technological civilization. Man has perfected modern means of travel which earn him a quick despatch to death:

But such another wraith! Brother
Silenced in the startled hug of
Your invention.

This stanza is addressed to the inventer of the "startled hug" (the white man).

The threatening possibilities of death neutralize the joy of air travel for Soyinka ("Around Us, Dawning"). He admires the expertise that has fashioned the airplane, but what about the total disaster that threatens if the sun explodes? The poet's cautious admiration for the technological feat that has fabricated the airplane is reflected in his other nomenclatures for the machine: "beast" and "bold carbuncle." If death is imminent, then the passengers are mere "martyrs" wreathed with "red haloes." The eddying and whirling motions that accompany the "beast's" take-off are captured in the musically orchestrated closing lines:

I am light honed
To a still point in the incandescent
Onrush, a fine ash in the beast's sudden
Dessication when the sun explodes.

The next poem, "Luo Plains," begins with the juxtaposition of apparently unconnected images which seek unsuccessfully to register the poet's impressions of Nairobi airport viewed from the air at dawn. The first stanza depends for its impressions on intuition: Other planes have landed at and taken off from the same airport. This air traffic appears to be what is evoked in "comet tails" and "egrets." Stanza two relies on pure perception: the poet

observes the lakes around Luo Plains which are shrouded
in mists. What is meant by "shadeless dugs" is not clear,
but as fertility symbols the "dugs" are parched even though
they are so close to "waterholes." "Veils" in the second
stanza is a synonym for "lakemists." When perceived at
the break of day, the mists look like "molten silver." From
this stanza therapeutic imagery creeps into the poem. The
lakemists are medicinal restoratives ("salve") for a Kenya
gradually recovering from the ravages of guerrilla warfare
(the Mau Mau terrorism). The idea of political independence is suggested in the word "dawn" in the third stanza.
"Spears" is a metaphor for the might of the colonial army,
but since that might wanes as the new nation gains its
independence, that might is passing through a "sunset"
phase. Even though Kenya's independence was won at the
battlefield, she has learnt to forgive her aggressors. The
point of stanza four is that Kenya is re-establishing contact
with the outside world now that independence has been
fought for and won. "Cactus" suggests the sacrifice paid
for independence, and independence won at the battlefield
is the "eagle sentinel" born of cactus.

The next poem, "In Memory of Segun Awolowo," is
more accessible than "Luo Plains." It is an elegy on the
death of Segun Awolowo who died in a motor accident
along the Lagos-Ibadan road in 1962. When the accident
occurred the victim's father, Chief Obafemi Awolowo, a
leading Nigerian politician, was serving a jail sentence for
treason. This double tragedy has driven "The last flint
deepest/In the heart of patience." This particular fatality is
blamed as usual on Ogun, the god of the road:

> The fault
> Is His of seven paths whose whim
> Gave Death his agency.

But the dead themselves ("the grey presence of head and
hands") are as amazed as the poet himself. They cannot
understand the reason for the victim's untimely death. The
poet is compelled by his own grief to involve the dead in
his mourning.

THE POEMS ON "LONE FIGURE"

The poems of the section entitled "Lone Figure" deal with the death and suffering of lonely individuals most of whom are conceived as martyrs. The first poem speaks of the untimely death of a political or religious martyr called the "dreamer": his ideas were revolutionary, challenging the views of the establishment in the political or religious sector, but he has not lived in vain because his words have taken root in the minds of his converts. Society may be presently unripe for his revolutionary ideas, but in time his teachings will be heeded to:

> Next year is reaping time
> The fruit will fall to searchers
> Cleansed of mould
> Chronicles of gold
> Mourn a fruit in prime.

The dreamer of the poem is deliberately invested with Christ-like attributes. He suffered on the cross like Christ, and like him his death has not been in vain. The images of Calvary that concretize his Christ-like characteristics include crown, cross ("Lord of the rebel three"), thorns, a mesh of nails and of flesh. The ultimate triumph of his ideas is suggested in the assertion that his "words" have flowered freely. The full harvest of his teaching is reaped after his death. The fruits fell to searchers cleansed of their one-year rust or mould, and the fruits are "chronicles of gold," mourning the untimely death of the martyr. In the third stanza the teachings of the dead hero have attracted a large following. His ideas and words, imaged as fruit, have bent the boughs to earth, which implies that the ideas have spread to the grassroots of the population and have attracted many converts, giving the church a sprirtual succor. One suspects that the dreamer is indeed Christ himself so that the poem becomes an ode on the spread of Christian religion to the four corners of the earth. Soyinka invests religious concepts and ideas with the imagery of seedling and harvest.

The hunched lunatic of Dugbe market at Ibadan is

another lone figure. His hunched back is a burden vividly imaged as an anthill; but why is the lunatic himself viewed as "a child's entangled scrawl"? Probably because his dirty and tattered rags make him appear as a caricature scrawled by children in their drawing-book.

Eldred Jones' reading of the episode of the devil in the poem can hardly be improved upon.[11] The hunchback is crushed out of existence by a cement-mixer truck; but he has only been transformed into a higher plane where ugliness or beauty does not mean much. Although the hunchback is dead, his memory lives still at Dugbe market. His large penis and his jingling buttock (he wears a bell on his waist) will remain part of the permanent landscape of Dugbe market.

The next poem "The Last Lamp" mourns the death of another figure, this time a woman of exceptional ability (although the poem is silent on exactly what that ability is). This woman is the light of her community, which is described, because of its ignorance and, one suspects, viciousness, as "crooked doorways." The woman is but a pale incision on her community's skin of night, and so her light did not last long nor did it illuminate the entire neighborhood; and when she dies her community resumes its state of night. Her extinction is sufficiently suggested with images of death: "dye" (a pun on die) and "shroud." Her *withdrawal* from the scene of social activity is made obvious in the second stanza, where the overall image is that of an abandoned homestead:

> Her shadow
> Now indrawn from dance
> On the silent eaves
> Gathers close about her.

Lamp is one image that suggests the woman's role as the light of the world. Its origin is biblical as is the image of "oil." The woman was a lamp lit in the wilderness and sustained by oil. But the woman's services to her community were not appreciated—the community was not patient with her and denied her peace.

"Easter" calls to mind another archetypal lone figure,

Christ, who was earlier recalled in "The Dreamer" and is indeed designated in the present poem as "the dreamer." "Dreamer" is Soyinka's euphemism for an idealist. The poem contrasts the meaning of Easter with the festive euphoria that greets the occasion among the present-day celebrants. Easter should be an occasion for spiritual reckoning or mortification of both body and soul which ought to lead to rebirth or regeneration, but most people see Easter only as a festive moment when children wave palm-fronds. The sense of euphoria is aptly suggested by the image of odor ("frangipane") transmitted by wind.

The first stanza suggests the quiet passing away of Easter merely as a celebrative moment whose lessons are lost upon the celebrants:

> This slow day dies, a wordless wilt
> Shades of silence reaping
> Soft frangipanes.

When the occasion is over, man settles down to a life of sinful routine:

> bosoms
> Too welcoming fold later chills
> Take death to innocents.

And since this is the case, the poet suggests that inanimate nature is more god-fearing than man and therefore more acceptable to God:

> Kinder these hard mangoes, green drops
> At the ear of god-apparent, coquettes
> To the future decadence.

The voice we hear at the end of the poem, the voice represented by "I," is the voice of the poet himself or his alter ego raging at so much decadence and crime (the present decay is but a faint reflection of the decadence of the future). The reference to "one bough" in stanza six is an allusion to Christ sacrificed on the cross so that many may be saved.

This verse is abstract; it transmits its meaning only by the overall mood of its imagery, not through literal or line-by-line interpretation.

THE POEMS "OF BIRTH AND DEATH"

The theme of the poems of the third section, "Of Birth and Death," is evident enough from the sectional subtitle. The poems speak of birth and death, and of the extensions of their respective connotations: life, growth, youth, growing old and dying. The first poem, "Koko Oloro," is a light-hearted appeal for nature's benevolence as spoken by a child persona. The simplicity of the verse form reflects the naiveté of the speaker.

The second poem ("Dedication") is Soyinka's prayer for his daughter, Moremi. The occasion is probably a naming or an "outing" ceremony during which the child is formally presented to the community as a new addition. The eldest member of the community is called upon to invoke blessings on the child. The poem begins on this note of invocation. The elder speaks in riddles and proverbs, hence the affinity which the poem's language bears with the language of traditional poetry. In a reply to the Chinweizu school of critics, Soyinka noted that the form of traditional poetry is not simplistic narrative but a densely packed matrix of reference: "The stark linear simplicity of translations should never be permitted to obscure the allusive, the elliptical, the multi-textured fullness of what constitutes traditional poetry." [12] "Dedication" shares this multitextured allusiveness.

The poem heaps blessings upon the child through the four elements: earth, air, water, and fire, this last element being represented by the sun. The first two stanzas invoke the blessings of earth upon the child, but they invoke them in an indirect manner by introducing the motif of envy. The point of these two stanzas is that the child will be "earthed," that is, be rooted in earth as an offspring of mother earth. She will draw strength from earth as the yam tuber buried in earth plumbs the deep for life. Then follows an analogy between the earthing and other things that draw strength from earth such as underground springs, the

roots of the baobab, and the homestead (hearth). The idea
of earthing means that the child will be fruitful. Soyinka
returns to this concern in the closing sections of the poem
where rainwater is evoked as an image of fertility.

Earth's beneficence is introduced through the motif of
envy. Dung (an extension of the image of earth) does not
crush the gecko when it falls from the rafters but sustains it;
in like manner, earth will sustain the child. Stanza three
invokes the blessings of air upon the child. This stanza
terminates in a proverb which asserts that the hoe that roots
up the forest ploughs a path for the squirrels.

Stanza four is a prayer for long life: "Be ageless as dark
peat" and "Long wear the sun's shadow." The force of the
second image ("sun's shadow") derives from the fact that
only one who is alive can see his shadow in the afternoon
sun. The next blessings invoked on the child will affect her
moral character. The concoction for a bold tongue is
brewed with pepper and that for tenderness with dew. With
her scorpion-arched tongue the child will spit a straight
return to danger's threat. This means that the child will be
fearless like the tail of the scorpion before any danger that
threatens her virtue, and yet, when the occasion arises, she
will be as tender as the dew. Aspects of the palm, Soyinka's
favorite fertility symbol, provide images for the invocation
of fecundity, beauty, and tenderness and amiability on the
child. Her scorpion-arched tongue will shield her like the
flesh of palm nuts held skyward in thorns nestling like
cuspids; while the oil of the palm supplies the potion for
beauty and tenderness; and the wine is milk for her breasts
("your podlings"). That wine is also honey which will
sweeten the child's life. Other symbols of fertility and
beauty evoked are camwood, chalk, and antimony. These
are constant elements in Soyinka's arsenal of fertility and
cosmetic images. Their function is more strongly felt in
Season of Anomy where Iriyise is decked out with them.[13]

"Dedication" looks forward to "For the Piper Daughters," the main poems in this section that celebrate life and
invoke blessings on women. The poet is sensitive to any
overtures that might lead to the violation of female honor
in the two poems. Moremi, in "Dedication," is encouraged
to "spit straight return to danger's threats" and the Piper

daughters are urged to repulse the cozening priest. This latter poem is Soyinka's prayer for some young women whom he found to be sincere, open, and friendly in their dealings with him. Love itself is not quite excluded from this relationship, for there is sexual innuendo in the confession: "this, your revelation/Unmasks past seemings." The poet urges the girls to continue to be sincere and open even in their old age. He invokes upon them the blessings of longevity and fecundity. They should

> Dance glad anguish of the mother rites
> Unravel seeds, the stranger essence
> Sprung from your goodness.

Eldred Jones interprets the allusions to "date," "linnet," and "pearl" as follows: "Every good beautiful creation comes with its protection."[14] And so, to the date is given a stone; to the linnet height, and to the pearls depth.

"A Cry in the Night" is the first poem to introduce the motif of death. The inscription beneath the title provides clues to the situation that has occasioned the poem. A mother is mourning the loss of a still-born baby. Her sorrow is suggested in the image which pictures her stone face as a tragic monument sculpted by grief. The woman's sorrow is compounded by her loneliness for she mourns her loss alone. Nature, we are told, does not share her grief:

> No stars caress her keening
> The sky recedes from pain.

But the use of the pathetic fallacy here is different from its general application; for it is in reaction to that grief that the stars withhold their light so that total darkness exacerbates the woman's condition.

"Scars" in the next stanza might refer to other misfortunes of childbirth the woman might have suffered, but the implication of "scars" and "scales" is not clear. The "tender stalk" hastily earthed in the closing stanza is the still-born child, and the mother is imaged here as a stricken snake dragging across the gulf of sorrow.

"A First Deathday" recollects the death of Soyinka's

sister, Folasade, who died on her first birthday when
Soyinka was nearly ten. This occasion was the first time
Soyinka saw someone die. The episode is fully narrated
in Soyinka's childhood autobiography, *Ake* (1981).[15] Folasade was an *abiku*; she had foreknowledge of her mission as
an *abiku*, and when the time comes she runs bridal to her
spouse, Death, thus mocking her brothers and sisters who
naively triumphed upon the wails of her birth.

The *abiku* theme links this poem directly to the poem
that treats the same subject, "Abiku." *Abiku* is the "wanderer child who dies and returns again and again to plague
the mother" (p. 28). An *abiku* rejects all the rituals of
appeasement meant to make her stay with the mother. She
boasts of her ability to thwart the efficacy of all propitia-
tion rituals: "I am the squirrel teeth, cracked/The riddle of
the palm." The *abiku* theme is worked into the concept of
cyclical repetition symbolized in the image of the tail-
devouring snake:

> I'll be the
> Suppliant snake coiled on the doorstep
> Yours the killing cry.

"To My First White Hairs" articulates man's fear of
death. The poet's grey hairs bear testimony to the passage
of time as the poet himself approaching the hoary phase,
which is a stepping stone to death. And since this is so, he
dismisses the dignity conferred by the grey hairs as "sham
veneration." He is unable to recognize them as signs of
wisdom either; for, all in all, he is trapped in the "webs" of
death.

The poem's mood is sombre. The rhetoric of the opening lines seeks in vain to disguise the gravity of the subject.
Man is forever alarmed at the prospect of his inevitable
confrontation with ultimate reality, death.

This reality cannot be rationalized or be subjected to
scientific scrutiny, says the next poem, "Post Mortem."
Post mortems can reason out the causes of individual
deaths, but no post mortem can fathom out the secret of
death. Perhaps the best thing for man to do is to reconcile

himself to the reality of death; so, the poem concludes, let us love all things of grey: grey slabs, grey scalpel, grey sleep and grey images.

THE POEMS ON WOMEN

Love is the theme of the poems on women—frustrated love, fruitful love, broken and patched-up relationships between men and women. The first poem "Song: Deserted Markets" is the love song of an African Prufrock in Paris. The poem articulates the nocturnal agonies of a stranger who spends loveless nights in Paris. It is addressed to Paris only in so far as that city symbolizes hopeless passion or unanchored love. And yet there is love in Paris, for some lovers spend the night in a surfeit of love (this abundance of love is imaged as a flowing stream: "Runnels of rain/ seeds fill your gutters"); but for the frustrated male persona who speaks in the poem it is "a long night of pain" which is unrelieved by dawn ("Dawn hastens in vain").

Roderick Wilson misread this poem miserably in his recent essay on Soyinka's poetry.[16] Part of his problem is the erroneous inclusion of the inscription below the poem's title into the rubrics of the title. The inscription "To a Paris Night" is not even a subtitle but a clue to the poem. Most of the poems in the volume are accompanied with such interpretative clues. The poem is unambiguous in its evocation of frustrated passion. The "long night of pain" that puzzles Roderick Wilson is the pain of frustrated love, the agonies of a man hopelessly in search of love. The line "a night for a life" in the fourth stanza is not ambiguous if it is understood as a metaphor for the dark night of the soul. The lover is passing through this dark night rather than enriching his life in love. The "seeds" indeed are not literal. They refer to the male and female "seeds" washed down the drain with contraceptives; and "ebony grain" defines the color of the alienated lover.

The next poem, "Psalm," operates on the basis of an analogy between harvest and the process of birth, and between a stalk of maize and a woman. Behind this analogy is the traditional concept of land as woman. As a hymn on

fecundity, the poem exploits the parallel between biological gestation and land husbandry. Land husbandry culminates in harvest or seedling season; so can the husbandry of
a woman's womb culminate in a different kind of harvest:

> the seeds have ripened fast my love
> and the milk is straining at the pods.

The phrase "ever-eager thought" in the second stanza is a
metaphor for the fire of passion. Passion can be sober
("chaste") only after the woman's virtue ("her corn-stalk
waist") has been ruined. In the third stanza, the germ of life
deposited within the woman's womb becomes her lover's
"swaddlings of . . . gratitude"; these "swaddlings" stir
within the woman's "plenitude" (womb). They are referred
to in the fourth stanza as the "quickening consciousness/
sealed in warm mis-shapenness"; and the life that results
therefrom is the "bright stream from unbroken springs/
threads of ever linking rings." In the seventh stanza land
and woman merge into one entity: the woman's "sanctity"
(womb) is sealed in earth" from whence emerges seed in
both biological and vegetational connotations: "sealed in
earth your sanctuary/yields to earth." The prenatal con-
tractions of the womb are "a mystery of pulses." The poet
contemplates this mystery as well as the new life which it
precipitates.

> and a mystery
> of pulses and the stranger life
> comes to harvest and release
> the germ and life exegesis
> inspiration of your genesis.

"Her Joy Is Wild" is one of the few poems in the book
that take their cue from a happy emotional relationship
between man and woman. It speaks of the uncontrollable
joy of a mother who has been happily delivered of a child.
But this is a birth with a difference. The sex of the baby
fulfills the hopes of the mother; and so she can tie her
womb: "This is the last-born; give me/A joyful womb to
bind." But the persona who speaks in the poem (the poet

himself probably) views the woman's happiness with some degree of irony, mocking the woman's lack of foresight. How can she decipher the future which is like a "nut" encased in a shell? The shift in meaning between the connotation of the image of kernel or nut in the first stanza and what it signifies in the last is noteworthy. "Nut" suggested in "rind" in the first stanza is a metaphor for sexual expectations that are about to be fulfilled: "Your strong teeth will weaken/If you nibble the rind." But the word "nut" in the last stanza is an image for the future which is enclosed in a shell. Because the woman has no foresight, she is said to be "maimed on her vision of the blind." The poem is artfully silent on what the woman's shortsightedness consists in.

In "Black Singer," a black American woman empties her soul of its racial burden in a song she sings at night. The poem's imagery establishes a parallel first between the circuitous movement of the stems of the vine coiled round their support and the gentle undulations of the rhythms of the song in the furrows of night and then (and this is the poem's major conceit) between the woman's throat and a vase. The song emanates from her throat with a regularity and a consistency that recall the flow of wine from a vase: "a votive vase, her throat/poured many souls as one." Darkness is a proper backdrop for the woman's ritual song: "how dark/The wine became the night"; but the imagery of darkness also defines the theme of the song: it is a lament, an elegy that mourns the tragedy of the black race; and so the song is "dark" as a token of the deeper wounds of the black race which have no chance of being healed either now or in the future. The last two lines picture the woman's song as a lonely ambassador in a world indifferent to the sufferings of her people:

> Song, O Voice, is lonely envoy
> Night a runnel for the wine's indifferent flow.

In the next poem, "Bringer of Peace," peace is restored to a troubled soul through the maternal concern of a woman symbolized as light rain. The speaker's self-destructive rage (a masculine persona) is imaged as "fire." This image

recurs in a slightly modified form in the second stanza as
the "hiss of ashes" and the "thirst of embers." But in the
last stanza the man's rage becomes more agitated and turbulent, even uncontrollable. Two images capture its
temper at this stage: "python's throes" and "bowstring's
nerve." The poem reads "straight" in stanzas one, two, and
four. The third stanza introduces a Soyinka freak into the
poem, that is, the deliberate attempt to toughen his lines
even when it is not necessary to do so. Whose is the "fire"
mentioned in the first line of this stanza—the peace-mak-
er's superior moral strength, or is it a continuation of the
fire image in the preceding stanzas? Both readings appear
to be plausible. The woman's superior moral strength
keeps the man's rage in check ("inclose"), or the man's rage
is an expression of a more disturbing turmoil that is
within. "Sift" in the last stanza is probably a misprint for
"shift." The woman attacks the man's rage with a superior
fire power (maternal tenderness) which seeks at every turn
to comprehend the root of the man's rage.

   With "To One, in Labour," we come to Soyinka's most
ingeniously contrived poem. The process of gestation is
here analogous to the collaborative industry of the ant
citizenry in building the anthill (otherwise called "a cathedral" or "mud spires"). The mud regurgitations reach their
paroxysm at the point when the anthill is born. In this
process of birth, the poem postulates, both the ants and
their queen are in "labor". The ants do the building and
the queen replaces the old builders with new ones.

   The operative image is the conceit that views gestation
itself as a "Queen insealed/In the cathedral heart" of the
anthill. This image is contrived but it is visual and, to a
certain extent, effective in so far as its frame of reference is
to be restricted to the maternity functions of the ant-queen,
that is, conception, gestation, and delivery. She is rendered
pregnant by the male ants who die soon after mating; and,
when she unburdens herself of her pregnancy, she gives
birth to other ants who grow to become her lovers. But if
the imagery is to be extended also to the process of human
biological gestation, as the title of the poem suggests, the
poem fails to sustain its logic. The imagery cannot sustain

the application of the ants' mode of procreation to the human procreative processes. The ants mate with the mother ant, but humans do not.

The poem succeeds as an ode to the ant world as an industrious community. It pays homage to the process of organized labor, for example, the industry of the male ants in building the anthill and in impregnating the ant-queen, and the industry of the queen in bringing forth new builders. It is from these three-dimensional aspects of labor the architectural, the sexual, and the procreational, that the pun on "labor" becomes meaningful.

The architectural images erect vivid pictures in the mind. Anthills in Africa do indeed look like cathedrals, so that the images "mud spires/Thrust inviolate against colonnades/of heartwood" effectively evoke their cathedral awe and the mystery of their baroque architecture.

"In Paths of Rain" is both a prayer for fruitfulness and a reflection on the happy result of a successful sexual union between man and woman. Life, Soyinka assumes, can emerge even from the crevices of rocks when those grooves are watered by rain. Even so, prays the poem's male persona, may life emerge from moments of wild sexual gratification. The poem expresses the emotions of a man whose conjugal love-making has not always yielded fruit:

> The last despairing pause, birth-teasing
> Yields dues on precipice, to love,
> Reassurance, and strangled seeds
>
> Unleashed, exult,

and there is the uncomfortable suggestion that the woman has not always responded to the lover's overtures, so that the "instants of wild-fox fires" are not frequent, but, when they do occur, they are rare in the sense of being highly prized. The low tempo of sexual fulfillment is implied in the lines "sly lights from your night redress/My darkness." The woman's coldness towards her lover launches the man into a dark night of the soul often symbolized in Soyinka's poetry by rage (see, for example, the poem "Bringer of

Peace"). However, a captive tenderness is emerging from "deep wells of denials" and the renewed relationship is also yielding fruit; and seed is the emblem by which the success of the union is measured. The poem ends with an interplay of images of creation extended into myth as is usual with Soyinka in his charged moments:

> Roots of rage [are] held to a lucent stance
> Glow-swarms lightening
>
> High thorn-bushes. Clean vistas-
> Flecked mica after rain, plankton in antimony
> Off rain-washed shores.

"By Little Loving" is the lament of a lover who has learned from a painful experience never to give all the heart away. The theme of love links this poem to the rest of the poems in this section. The aggrieved speaker in the poem has learned to conquer pain and to keep floods of passion at bay by refraining from a total commitment in love. He has kept his feet from the path of love by not dreaming of love. He managed once to protect himself from the "ruptured wheel/of blood" by retiring from society. But the discipline and self-control that protected him from the agonies of love are now giving way, and the poet regrets this new development. Love's agonies he calls "accidents of flesh" which he hails as "man's eternal lesson." The pains of love are vividly projected in the fourth stanza:

> Enough, I swore, the wear
> Of pulses, stretch of flesh hunger hourly howled.

The speaker claims to have attained some emotional salvation after he has turned away from love and embraced its opposite, hate: "I know redemption in the truth of hate." But this confession is deceptive: he has not really found peace through withdrawal, for memories of his past love haunt him daily. And when he finally let loose the emotions he has sought to suppress, it led to his death. The half line "phoenix of each pyre forestalled" implies that he did not resurrect from his ashes as would the phoenix.

THE POEMS OF GREY SEASONS

The poems of "Grey Seasons" mark the culmination of "grey" symbolism in Soyinka's poetry. The color "grey" is rich in associations for him. Grey is associated with age and ageing, with moments of sadness ("grey hour"), and with death. It is the color of the road as an agent of death ("grey by-ways") and of the gods who inflict death on mortals through the agency of the road ("grey presences").

The trend of grey symbolism that has been building attains its climax in the poems of "Grey Seasons." The first poem, "I think it rains," transforms rain, usually an image of life and hope in Soyinka's poetry, into one of despair. The first stanza recalls in a general statement the traditional function of rain as a life-force symbol. It is rain's function to assuage the thirst of a parched tongue, says the stanza, and set it free from the forces that bind it to the dry roof-tops of the mouth. A tongue, metaphorical or literal, so resuscitated will bear fruit (knowledge) in its due season:

> I think it rains
> That tongues may loosen from the parch
> Uncleave roof-tops of the mouth, hang
> Heavy with knowledge.

But there is a particular rain that recalls other emotions (for example, purity of sadness). This is the rain that is associated with grey seasons. The generalized focus of the statement "I think it rains" contrasts with the particularity of the observation:

> I saw it raise
> The sudden cloud, from ashes. Settling
> They joined in a ring of grey; within,
> The circling spirit.

This particular rain evokes disturbing emotions subtly suggested in the image of "ashes." The ashes stirred up by the rain form a ring of grey as they settle. The ring of grey imprisons the human spirit which normally should soar in flight. Punctuational devices straighten the syntax of line two above. What is within the ring is the circling spirit.

Stanzas three and four expand the moods evoked by the rain: despair, some uncomfortable intimations or foreboding, purity of sadness, unhealthy desires described as "dark longings." The image of baptism in the fourth stanza emphasizes the deliberate inversion of the normal connotations of rain in this poem. Rather than renewing the soul, this particular rain inspires thoughts of evil. The meaning of "Sear" in this context is ambiguous. Are the longings being purified by the "fire" of the cruel baptism? The general mood of the poem implies that there is nothing purificatory in "Sear." If anything, the dark longings are reinforced by the rain.

The conjugal imagery in the last stanza derives its force from the traditional concept of earth as woman and of rain as its fertilizer. But the key image is rock, used here as a metaphor for the inherent tendencies (and burdens too) of the mind made manifest by the moods of the rain. The poem is a good example of the way a poetic emotion can be harnessed to an objective correlative. The objective correlative here is rain, which has been made to stir up other emotions ("purity of sadness" and "dark longings").

The passage of time symbolized by grey hairs has brought the subject of the poem "Prisoner" to the "hoary phase" called "grey season" in the poems of this section. The direction of the poem is not easily decipherable. The first line, "Grey, to the low grass cropping," alludes to the grey hairs of a man who is ageing fast. The grey hairs are wisps of smoke in the next line, and since they anticipate the end of a man's life journey, they are "heavy." But it is not clear how they can be "elusive of thin blades" or "curl inwards to the earth." That they breed "grey hours" is obvious. The grey hairs called "sad mocking/Threads" in stanza two anticipate the inevitability of old age ("the wise grey temples we shall build/To febrile years"). After the first two stanzas the poem falls apart. The third stanza takes up a new experience disguised in esoteric imagery. What is being intimated through the evocation of nature's turbulence is not made clear, but one suspects that it is death. Disturbances in nature are distant reminders ("intimations") of the inevitability of death. But the reality itself is unmistakable when our physical conditions have themselves testified to the conquest of time. This awareness is the most painful reminder of the inevitability of death. The personal evidence of the reality torments the poem's persona. If man has been made prisoner to pains and fears, he is even a more miserable prisoner in the face of sorrow. Man is then a prisoner to vain fears and hopes.

"Season" examines the two ages of man: Youth and old age correspond, respectively, to spring, the season for sowing, planting and growth, and autumn, the season for reaping and harvesting. The poem begins with an aphorism that reminds us of the interrelatedness of the two seasons: One leads inexorably to the other and either is indispensable:

> Rust is ripeness, rust,
> And the wilted corn-plume.

The wilted corn-plume is "rust," but this condition precipitates ripeness or harvest. The poem goes on to discuss each condition or season. It begins with the season of youth (spring) when lovers mate and moves in the second stanza to the season of harvest when the youths of the first stanza have spent their energy:

> Now, garnerers we
> Awaiting rust on tassles, draw
> Long shadows from the dusk.

"Shadows" and "dusk" introduce the omens of death into "rust," while dusk and rust exemplify a functional application of the device of internal rhyme. The statement "Laden stalks/Ride the germ's decay" recalls the poem's opening aphorism, made more emphatic elsewhere in the statement: "growth is greener where/Rich blood has spilt."[17]

The tone of the poem "Night" is sombre and lugubrious, like the tone of nearly all the poems of "Grey Seasons." Night brings with it a heaviness of feeling and unsettling sensations of foreboding and uneasiness that cause the poet some emotional and psychic discomfort; and in stanza three the action of Night on the poet is physical: his energies are sapped as by a sexual action. In the first stanza the poet contrasts his heavy heart with the light-hearted frolics ("mercuric") of the clouds. In the second stanza, Night, now a jealous woman, eclipses the sea's own luminosity as well as the vibrant activities of the waves. In stanza four the poet speaks of the shadow cast by Night on vegetable nature and of himself as being completely envel-oped in Night. The complete immersion deepens the un-pleasant sensations evoked by the approach of Night. And in the final stanza, the poet appeals to Night to protect him from the dangers of Night (from the ghosts, witches, and thieves that prowl the night). The poem offers a good opportunity for the study of Soyinka's diction; it is a re-searched and learned diction; for example, he uses such words as mercuric (sprightly and volatile), exacerbation (aggravating), crescent (moon-shaped peak), incessant (con-tinuous), fluorescence (shining, luminosity), serrated (fur-rowed), suffusion (enclosure), sensations (feelings).

The poem is indeed a celebration of the birth of Night, and should in this regard be contrasted with "Dawn," which is a celebration of the birth of Dawn.

"Fado Singer" captures Soyinka in a rare instant of inspiration. The range of the poem's system of imagery confirms it; it begins with the terrestrial and extends into the cosmic. The poem acknowledges the strange and awful powers of fado music as played by Amalia Roderiguez. The melody evokes sensations of a painful pleasure capable of transporting the listener into unknown regions. And yet that tragic melody, the painful pleasure itself is man's companion (and therefore comforter) in his journey into life and death.

Roderick Wilson[18] was unable to appreciate the dyna-mism of the poem's emotional logic and thus dismissed its imagery as being inorganic. What unites the images is logic of emotion. The poem is made up of a series of apostrophes acclaiming both the musician and the power of her music. And one way by which the impact of the music is underscored is the constant effort on the part of the poet to relegate its essence into the cosmic realm:

[You] pluck strange dirges from the storm
Sift rare stones from ashes of the moon, and ride
Night errands to the throne of anguish.

"Pumice" in the first stanza exploits the sense of painful
hypnosis:

My skin is pumiced to a fault
I am down to hair-roots, down to fibre filters
Of the raw tobacco nerve.

In the second stanza the poet has taken off into the unknown:

I wander long
In tear vaults of the sublime

And because the emotions and moods evoked by the music
are painful, the player is called "Queen of night torments."
The idea of pain implied in "torments" and "grief" (stanza
two) prepares us for the imagery of physical pain inherent
in "sutures" (surgical stitches):

Queen of night torments, you strain
Sutures of song to bear imposition of the rites
of living and of death.

The poet breaks down ultimately under the tyranny of
the song:

too much crush of petals
For perfume, too heavy tread of air on mothwing
For a cup of rainbow dust
Too much pain, oh midwife at the cry
Of severance . . . too vast
The pains of Easter for a hint of the eternal.

Of importance is the light thrown by these lines on the
meaning of "Easter," an insight that illuminates the poem
"Easter" in the section entitled "Lone Figure." Easter, the

poem implies, is the pain suffered by a ritual protagonist
for the promise of rebirth ("a hint of the eternal").

In the closing stanzas the poet wishes to be liberated
from the tyranny of the fado music. In the effort to escape,
he evokes further the powerful impact of the music in
cosmic and apocalyptic images:

> I would be free from headlong rides
> In rock reams and volcanic veins, drawn by
> > dark steeds
> On grey melodic reins.

THE OCTOBER POEMS

"The October Poems" were inspired by the civil disturbances that rocked the foundations of Nigeria in the sixties
and which led to the civil war that lasted from 1967–1970.
They deal, therefore, with war and its savagery. What
emerges is a powerful condemnation of violence and the
destruction of human lives that is mandatory in war situations. Soyinka's attitude to war is decipherable from his
delicately modulated tone of irony. In the first poem
"Ikeja, Friday, Four O'clock," earth is thirsty, but what can
assuage her thirst is not wine or water but a surfeit of
human blood. The poem was occasioned by Soyinka's encounter at the Ikeja Airport with a convoy of military
trucks conveying troops to the war front. These trucks, he
reflects, are but gourds for earth to drink from. The ill-fated
troops have lost their human identity and are perceived
only as apparitions or as a

> mirage of breath and form
> Unbidden offering on the lie of altars.

At the war front, the soldiers sacrifice their humanity to
their bestial instincts, becoming "a crop of wrath when
hands retract and reason falters." The humanity of the
miracle of loaves and fish is contrasted with the inhumanity of "lead."

"Harvest of Hate" is predicated upon a mythic world-

view in which the death of the king spells disaster for his
people. Nigerian leaders are killed by young army officers,
and so the land is stricken. This phenomenon is transliter-
ated in the third stanza in the statement:

> The child dares flames his fathers lit
> And in the briefness of too bright flares
> Shrivels a heritage of blighted futures.

But Soyinka's metaphor for the killings is hatred. Nature
suffers a reversal of its normal cycle because men have
hated: "So now the sun moves to die at mid-morning." A
wind of hate has frustrated all life impulses. Soyinka's
favorite life symbols such as palm and oil suffer a negation
of their roles: "The fronds of palm are savaged to a bristle"
and "rashes break on kernelled oil." The picture of universal disaster depicted in the poem is rendered pathetic by the
pastoral reminiscences of the closing lines:

> There has been such a crop in time of growing
> Such tuneless noises when we longed for sights
> Alone of petals, for muted swell of wine-buds
> In August rains, and singing in green spaces.

The next poem, "Massacre, October '66," has sparked
much controversy in the course of which the poem itself
has been forgotten. The Chinweizu group of critics has
castigated Soyinka for borrowing images from an alien
landscape in mourning the victims of the October 1966
massacre. What really matters is the poet's ability to put to
adequate poetic advantage the images he has borrowed in
order to deprecate the bitterness and folly of civil strife.
Soyinka harnesses autumn to his poetic needs. As the season of incipient decay, autumn is an appropriate metaphor
for the moral decay that gave rise to the massacres. But the
relevance of autumn goes beyond mere moral callousness;
it also connotes death. This transition is effortlessly effected through a physical vehicle, "dying leaves": "I swam
in an October flush of dying leaves." The poet is able to
merge various levels of meaning into one image. Through
subtle juxtapositions and echoes, the images leap from

their literal sense to a symbolic level. "Dying leaves" juxtaposed with "gardener's labour" limit that labor at first
sight to its purely horticultural context. But when in stanza
five the dying leaves are transposed to human skulls, the
gardener's labor shifts from the aesthetic to a fatalistic
connotation. Death itself becomes the gardener; at this
point the poet makes obvious what has earlier been hinted,
that is, the equation between autumn and death:

> The oak rains a hundred more
> A kind confusion to arithmetic of death:
> Time to watch autumn the removal man
> Dust down rare canvases.

The acorn has within itself a mechanism that qualifies it as
an apt metaphor for the violence of war. When the "shell"
explodes, the outer covering falls off. The acorn shell leads
by association to a military "shell":

> each shell's detonation
> Aped the skull's uniqueness.

Details of the setting in the opening stanzas need some
clarification. The poet is swimming in a lake in Tegel close
to a church. Oak trees stand on the premises and a gardener
is busy trimming the lawn with a mower. The church
windows are reflected on the lake's surface, hence the statement:

> Through stained-glass
> Fragments on the lake I sought to reach
> A mind at silt-bed.

The cuttings from the gardener's labor fly about the mower's engine-head, littering the wind. They resemble the
splashes made on the lake by a racing motorboat ("painted
craft"):

> Swept from painted craft
> A mockery of waves remarked the idyll sham.

"Civilian and Soldier" dramatizes a war-time encounter
between a civilian and a soldier, who represent, respectively, humanity and brutal force. The soldier administers
lead while the civilian dispenses bread. But the poem
makes it clear that the soldier's brutality is not of his own
making; it is forced upon him, and this is his "plight."

"For Fajuyi" is an elegy on the death of Colonel Adekunle Fajuyi, first Military Governer for Western Nigeria
during the military regime. Fajuyi came to power after the
January 1966 coup. He was Soyinka's ideal soldier, a true
nationalist and a dedicated socialist, who died with
General Jronsi in the countercoup of July 1966. The short-
lived regime of Fajuyi was a sign of hope for the people of
Western Nigeria. That brief period of hope is the subject of
the encomium in the first stanza:

> Honour late restored, early ventured to a trial
> Of Death's devising. Flare too rare
> Too brief, chivalric steel
> Redeems us living, springs the lock of Time's
>   denial.

A man of Fajuyi's integrity is not easily come by. Hence
the poet extols him as "a mystery kernel" thrust out from a
miserly earth that sprouted to a miracle of boughs. But it
takes the "stress of storm" to elicit the sterling qualities
latent in Fajuyi. The poet laments his death, but that death
is also a source of inspiration. Thus, he speaks of Fajuyi
being recreative as the sun's energies. Fajuyi has come to
his journey's end; but he has left a name behind. Images of
durability ("gold," "beam") register the permanence of his
achievement; and these are contrasted with their opposites,
weeds. "Weeds" is Soyinka's euphemism for the people
who killed Fajuyi and the regime they put in place of his.

Fajuyi is the prototype of the "pilgrim feet' in Soyinka's
writings, the lone wanderer or seeker. These are fictional
characters as Eman as well as historical figures such as
Victor Banjo, Christopher Okigbo, and Soyinka himself (a
one-time prisoner). In *A Shuttle in the Crypt*, where he
speaks of his own prison experience, Soyinka calls himself
a lone wanderer:

Feet of pilgrims pause by charted pools
Balm seeking.

In "Malediction," the last short poem in the volume,
Soyinka rains down a curse on a woman who rejoiced at a
time when "the human world/shared in grief's humility."
The woman, says the poet, will be herself the victim of this
pattern of inhuman joy, so that when others rejoice, she
will become the target of misfortune. The poet calls on
nature to unsex her, and, if she has already procreated, asks
that she never know the joy of motherhood. The language
of the poem is remarkable for its verbal play. The tongue-
twisting alliteratives are self-consciously pedantic:

those lips
crossed in curse corrugations
thin slit in spittle silting
and bile-blown tongue
pain plagued, a mock man plug
wedged in waste womb ways
a slime slug slewed in sewage.

Notes

1. Wole Soyinka, *Idanre and Other Poems*, (London:
Methuen, 1967), p. 13. Further references are to this edition.

2. Wole Soyinka, "And After the Narcissist?" *African
Forum*, Vol. 1, No. 4 (Spring 1966), p. 53.

3. See Soyinka's unpublished reply to the Chinweizu criticism of his poetry, entitled "Neo-Tarzanism: Aesthetic Illusion," unpublished manuscript, p. 17.

4. "Neo-Tarzanism: Aesthetic Illusion," p. 20.

5. Herbert Marshall McLuhan, "Tennyson and the Pictur-
esque," in Eugene McNamara, ed., *The Interior Landscape: The Literary Criticism of Marshall McLuhan* (Toronto: McGraw-Hill, 1969), p. 144.

6. Letter to John Taylor, in M. H. Abrams et al., eds., *The Norton Anthology of English Literature*, Vol. II (third edition, 1974), p. 708.

7. Roderick Wilson, "Complexity and Confusion in Soyinka's Shorter Poems," in James Gibbs, ed., *Critical Perspectives on Wole Soyinka* (Washington: Three Continents Press, 1980), pp. 158–69.

8. Chinweizu et al., "Towards the Decolonization of African Literature," *Transition*, Vol. 9, No. 48 (April/June, 1975), pp. 29–32.

9. John Agetua, "Interview with Wole Soyinka," in *Six Nigerian Writers* (Benin City: Bendel Newspapers Corporation, 1975), p. 46.

10. "Neo-Tarzanism: The Aesthetic Illusion," p. 20.

11. Eldred Jones, *The Writing of Wole Soyinka* (London: Heinemann, 1973), p. 110.

12. Wole Soyinka, "Neo-Tarzanism: The Poetics of Pseudo-Tradition," *Transition*, 48 (April/June 1975), p. 39.

13. See chapter one of *Season of Anomy* (London: Rex Collings, 1972), pp. 7–8, and the third stanza of the poem "Seed" in *A Shuttle in the Crypt* (New York: Hill and Wang, 1972), p. 56.

14. *The Writing of Wole Soyinka*, p. 116.

15. Wole Soyinka, *Ake: Memories of Childhood* (London: Rex Collings, 1981), pp. 95–98.

16. Roderick Wilson, "Complexity and Confusion in Soyinka's Shorter Poems," in *Critical Perspectives on Wole Soyinka*, p. 160.

17. *Idanre and Other Poems*, p. 65.

18. "Complexity and Confusion in Soyinka's Shorter Poems," p. 158.

2

────────────── △ △ ──────────────

LYRICS OF AGONY (II):
THE LAMENTS OF THE SHUTTLE

The link between the shorter poems of *Idanre* and Soyinka's second book of poetry, *A Shuttle in the Crypt*
(1972), is provided by the Nigerian Civil War (1967–1970)
and the events that precipitated it. Coming at the end of the
sequence of shorter poems, the October elegies mark a shift
from the poet's preoccupation with privatist fantasies to an
obsession with public themes. In a way, the social upheavals of the sixties introduced a public voice in Soyinka's
poetry.

Soyinka was opposed to war in principle; he condemned
the massacre of the Ibos in the North, and welcomed the
January 1966 military coup as an event motivated by a
"genuine revolutionary zeal."[1] When the war broke out
following the secession of Biafra, he tried without success
to reconcile the two parties in the dispute, the federal
government and the Ibo "nation" in eastern Nigeria. He set
up a neutral body called The Third Force made up of the
original architects of the January coup and some socialist
elements in the country. The Third Force was opposed to
the Biafran secession; it was strongly in favor of a united
Nigeria whose affairs were to be managed by men of proven
ability and integrity. The social anomy of the war years was
a good opportunity for the Third Movement to seize power
at the center and set up a socialist regime in the country.
The attempt failed, and, for his activities in Biafra, Soyinka
was imprisoned. The failure of the revolutionary objectives
of the first coup and of the Third Movement is lamented in

two poems in *A Shuttle* ("Conversation at Night with a Cockroach" and "And What if Thus He Died?").[2]

A Shuttle in the Crypt is a collection of poems supposedly written in prison. Their form is still raw, their language loose in parts, and their texture occasionally porous. Most of the poems were originally scribbled on the inside of cigarette packs or in between the pages of books smuggled into prison. The jottings were later recopied and bundled to the publisher with little revision. Soyinka intends their raw form to remain a living testimony of the "course trodden by the mind."[3]

The poems have no narrative focus, nor has the poet the leisure to indulge in metaphysical conceits for their own sake as in *Idanre and Other Poems*. The poems are emergency measures to stay the season of a mind. Soyinka calls them "mouse-eaten thoughts peeled from time's corpses," "Cobweb hangings on the throne of death/In solitude."[4]

Of particular interest are the incantations called "animystic spells," the rantings of a demented psyche. The only way the poet could assure himself of his own existence was through the reality of his own sound: "Utter words, order moods if thought will not hold."[5] The animystic spells are the soul's speech with itself, verbalizations of the nightmares and hallucinations that invade the mind. These hallucinations appeared quite frequently to Soyinka in his cell:

> Locked and barred from a more direct communion, a human assertiveness has reached me through the cosmos, a proud inextinguishable Promethean spark among dead bodies, astral wraiths, failed deities tinsel decorations in barren space. Sign, probe and question I accept you, incandescent human dare. Extension of my restless eye and mind I claim you and absorb you. I transmit you, pore of my skin, electronic core of my will, prowl . . . prowl.[6]

The poems' basic conceit is reflected in the very title of the volume. The poet identifies himself with a shuttle and sees his prison underworld as a crypt. The shuttle bears the

same moral and psychological attributes as Soyinka's god,
Ogun. It is a secretive seed, shrine, kernel, phallus and well
of creative mysteries, and a restless bolt of energy. The
implication is that Soyinka, shut up in the abyss of the
crypt, is undergoing the same ordeals as Ogun in the abyss
of transition, and if Ogun survived the terrors of the abyss,
so may we expect his protege, Soyinka himself to survive
his trials in the abyss of the crypt. Soyinka thus evokes
Ogun:

> Ogun, comrade, bear witness how your metal
> [prison chains] is travestied.[7]

The story of Soyinka's own ritual testing and of his survival of the agonies of that ritual is poignantly told in
Chimes of Silence.

But what gives the shuttle its uniqueness is not necessarily its capacity for survival but the ability to "re-create"
itself in the very act of creation. In this regard, the shuttle
recalls Ogun as the god of creativity. Finally, the shuttle-
crypt metaphor gives value to Soyinka's tragic view of
artistic creativity. This view relates the origin of artistic
creativity to a sense of unease. The Nigerian poet, Christopher Okigbo, upholds this view when he calls his own
poetry "a cry of anguish . . . the thunder of splitting
pods."[8] The world itself came into existence, argues
Soyinka, from the anguish of the gods. The divine fiat
which materialized into what is known as the world was
God's own strategy for overcoming his own loneliness.
Pluto escaped the terrors of his own loneliness by engaging
himself in meaningless pastimes:

> There being nothing worse to do, Pluto tried to dis-
> cover tunnels even from the dead netherworld into
> deeper bowels of Void.[9]

Imagining himself as the sole creator in the home of death,
Soyinka sees a parallel between himself and God, and between himself and Pluto. Like these, he will escape his own
loneliness through creation:

I create, I re-create in tune with that which shuts or
opens all about me. Dawn or dusk. Darkness or light.
Concrete bars and iron gates.[10]

The volume is made up of five sections and an Epilogue.
These include *Phases of Peril, Four Archetypes, Chimes of
Silence, Prisonnettes,* and the satirical sketches entitled
Poems of Bread and Earth. Of these the first three are
central to the shuttle's experience.

PHASES OF PERIL

Phases of Peril opens with the poet's invocation (in the
poem "Roots") of his own willpower, his ancestral gods,
his personal god (Ogun), and the benevolent forces of nature to lend him spiritual succor in his hour of trial. All
these forces are subsumed under the word "roots." The
central metaphor is one of a sea journey on a terrain (the
Nigerian body politic) flooded with hate's dark waters. The
poet and a few voices of conscience called "pilgrims" sail
on the corrupt waters in search of a safe anchor and pure
fountain:

> Roots, be an anchor at my keel
> Shore my limbs against the wayward gale
>
> Reach in earth for deep sustaining draughts
> Potencies against my endless thirsts
>
> Your surface runnels end in blinds, your courses
> Choke on silt, stagnate in human curses.
>
> Feet of pilgrims pause by charted pools
> Balm seeking. Dipped, their thirsty bowls
>
> Raise bubbles of corruption, sludge
> Of evil, graves unlaid to tears or dirge.

The bulk of the poem is a prayer to these "roots" to sustain
the poet and purge the land of streams of tainted seepage.
The entire invocation is musical; its inspiration is traditional poetry, especially the chant sung before a shrine or
an oracle by the priest as he invokes the god's protection on

behalf of a group of warriors or adventurers at the time of their setting out. Soyinka lends rhythm to his verse by arranging his lines into rhyme-oriented couplets.

"Conversation at Night with a Cockroach" is slightly narrative. The events that led to the outbreak of the Nigerian Civil War are recalled, including the first military coup of 1966 and the massacre of the Ibos in the North. For Soyinka, the first military coup was a necessary intervention. He said, as already noted, that "the basic motivation was of a genuine revolutionary zeal." In "Conversation" he sees the military intervention as an action "heat-drawn by fire/of truth." It was for him "The first fire-arc of regenerative eyes/Lowered beneath the rotted roots." Its purpose was "To force impurities in the National weal/Belly up," and to "free our earth/Of distorting shadows cast by old/ And modern necromancers." The cockroach in the poem is an arm of the "old necromancers." As a symbol of evil and the enemy of all revolutionary initiatives, the cockroach impaired the healthy objectives of the coup with secretions from its ducts:

> Saw teeth, dribbling a caress
> Of spittle on the wound, you nibbled trust
> From the heart of our concerted bond.

After this complaint, the cockroach appears, unruffled, to make his declamation. Why revolution? Why ever the desire to change the body politic?

> Rock not our neat foundations
> With futile quarrying.

The shuttle next recalls the victims of the massacres in the North:

> Not human faces, hands, were these
> That fell upon us, nor was death withheld
> Even from children, from the unborn.
> And wombs were torn from living women
> And eyes of children taken out
> On the points of knives and bayonets.

After the massacre, after the lament of the victims, the cockroach has the last word:

> All was well. All was even
> As it was in the beginning.

This is the beginning of the "Philosophy of As," which is fully expounded in the absurdist stage of *Madmen and Specialists.*

The language of the next major poem in *Phases of Peril* ("When Seasons Change") is esoteric as a private experience is merged into a public one. Like "Conversation at Night with a Cockroach," "When Seasons Change" laments the failure of both the first coup and the Third Force to effect a change in the nationalweal. This failure is the subject of the poem's fourth stanza:

> Yet this progression has been source
> For great truths in spite of stammering
> Planes for great buildings in spite
> Of crooked sights, for plastic strength
> Despite corrosive fumes of treachery.

But the season has also changed for the poet as an inhabitant of the crypt. Thus, the phantoms and the ghosts evoked by his mind (pure material bodies) commingle with hopeful aspirations of aborted revolutionary movements called "purity of ideals." Both are now "time's spectres," and they fleet through the mind as visible objects:

> They thread their way through rocks
> And creviced growths, old, silent vapours
> What seek ye, cloud weeds in air?

The mind soars in flight, the poet says, to conjure up these apparitions. But there are moments when these daydreams are interrupted by reality as, for example, the outbreak of a storm:

> Hailstone summons on the dovecot roof
> The drums are here again.

This phenomenon is summoned to attest to the poet's misfortunes (the failure of the "purity of ideals"), so he tells the rains to "Shed your hard tears." The rains have roused earth from its lethargy. And yet the rains later metamorphose into a metaphor for human hopes and disappointments:

> The blows of battle and the scars, old fences
> And the guarded opening of a gate
> Old welcomes, the heat of comradeship
> And cold betrayal, old sacrifices
> The little victories and the greater loss.

At the end of the poem, the poet characterizes his musings and daydreams. They are

> Shrouds of Seasons gone, peeled
> From time's corpses, mouse-eaten thoughts
> You flutter upon solitude in winds
> Armed in shrapnels from the shell of vision.

The remaining poems in this section are of a minor key. The spider image in "A Cobweb Touch in the Dark" emphasizes the magnitude of the poet's loneliness. In a situation where darkness is tangible and silence absolute, even a weird creature like the spider is a welcome guest. In "I Anoint My Flesh," the poet has attained a state of nirvana. In "To the Madmen Over the Wall," he credits lunatics with supersensory intuitions:

> I fear
> Your minds have dared the infinite
> And journeyed back
> To speak in foreign tongues.

FOUR ARCHETYPES

The archetypes are metaphors for the poet's destiny as a victim of injustice. Sometimes an event in the Nigerian Civil War drama is provided with an analogue from history or literature. For example, Hamlet is such an analogue for

Victor Banjo's vacillations at a moment when the situation
required a decisive strike. The use of archetypes as a poetic
device has enabled the poet to address his readers directly
through the voice of a persona. Furthermore, he universal-
izes his experience through that strategy, thereby using
"As" to signify the recurrent pattern of human stupidity.

The story of the first archetype (Joseph) is taken from
the Bible.[11] Joseph was a servant in the household of Poti-
phar, the captain of Pharaoh's security guards. His wife attempted to lure him to her bed, and when all her strategies
failed, she accused Joseph of attempting to violate her
honor. Joseph was immediately clamped into prison without trial. In this regard, Soyinka's imprisonment is another
case of an imprisonment without trial like Joseph's. However, the Biblical Joseph resigned himself to his fate, but
Soyinka is a "cursing martyr" who renounces "the saintly
vision":

> Indeed I was not Joseph, a cursing martyr I,
> No Saint—are Saints not moved beyond
> Event, their passive valour turned to time's
> Slow unfolding? A time of evils cries
> Renunciation of the saintly vision
> Summons instant hands of truth to tear
> All painted masks.

Joseph was endowed with the gift of prophecy and the
interpretation of dreams. The creative artist is also an interpreter of dreams. Thus the poet calls Joseph "the old
ancestor":

> We,
> All whose dreams of fire resolve in light
> Wait upon the old ancestor in pursuit
> Of truth, and to interpret dreams.

But it is the passive instinct in the face of the need for
awful daring that is castigated in the second archetype,
Hamlet. Joseph and Hamlet belong to the category of
"failed prometheans" in Soyinka's aesthetic philosophy.
Joseph sacrificed a sense of injustice to his saintly vision

and Hamlet, to his penchant for metaphysical specula-
tions, whereas, for Soyinka, what redeems man's authentic
being is the capacity for engagement:

> Man can only grasp his authentic being through con-
> frontation with the vicissitudes of life.[12]

and again

> To act, the Promethean instinct of rebellion, channels
> anguish into a creative purpose which releases man
> from a totally destructive despair, releasing from
> within him the most energetic, deeply combative in-
> ventions which without usurping the territory of the
> internal gulf, bridge it with visionary hopes.[13]

The situation of Hamlet is then not applicable to Soyinka,
the true progenitor of the original protagonist of the abyss.
While the poet identifies himself with the other archetypes,
he distances himself from Hamlet by the use of the pro-
noun "he," rather than the self-identifying "I." What relevance, then, does this Hamlet have to the war situation that
inspires the poems? The poem's Hamlet is Victor Banjo,
the Commander of the expeditionary forces of the Third
Force, which invaded the Midwest in the early days of the
war. Victor Banjo's Third Force and its failure to make a
decisive sally into Lagos were very much in Soyinka's mind
while he was in prison. He often reminisced on the misfortunes of Victor Banjo's vacillations:

> What kept him? What kept him in Benin while the
> naked underbelly of Lagos lay helpless in its gross
> inert corruption, waiting to be pierced?[14]

In the third archetype, Gulliver, Soyinka paints a picture
of his real alter-ego. Gulliver was humane, long-suffering,
law-abiding and accommodating but would never compromise his principles of justice. The particular episode that
brings out these qualities in Gulliver is his role in the war
between the Lilliputians and the Blefuscudians. In a single
act of valor, Gulliver immobilized the entire fleet of the

enemy kingdom and thus won victory for the Lilliputians.
But the Lilliputian Emperor was not satisfied with moder-
ate victory, he was bent on using Gulliver's strength to
achieve total victory over the enemy. He nursed territorial
ambitions over the Blefuscudian empire and wanted to use
Gulliver's strength to achieve this purpose. For Gulliver,
however, war was fought for a purpose and when that
purpose is achieved with minimal casualties on both sides,
war should cease. Gulliver's observations on the Emperor's
territorial ambitions underscore his moral scruples:

> His majesty desired I would take some other opportu-
> nity of bringing all the rest of his enemy's ships into
> his ports. And so unmeasurable is the ambition of
> princes that he seemed to think of nothing less than
> reducing the whole empire of Blefuscu into a prov-
> ince, and governing it by a viceroy; . . . by which he
> would remain sole monarch of the whole world. But I
> endeavoured to divert him from this design by many
> arguments drawn from the topics of policy as well as
> justice: and I plainly protested that I would never be
> an instrument of bringing a free and brave people into
> slavery.[15]

This point of view is recalled in Soyinka's poem in the
following lines:

> I could not choose but serve
> I took their measure in the depth
> Of sea-beds, galley-slave to claims
> Of bread and salt. I brought the enemy fleet
> To port, and pressed a reasoned course
> Of temperate victory. It did not suffice
> I pledged reversion of my strength
> To arbitration; they pledged extinction of their kind.

Gulliver's refusal to accommodate the Emperor's territorial
ambitions earned him the anger of the monarch. But before
the Emperor had time to put into execution the evil plans
he hatched against Gulliver, he (Gulliver) crossed over to
the side of the Blefuscudians.

Like Gulliver, Soyinka was a veteran critic of war fought
for no other purpose than to assuage the territorial ambitions of a rapacious mafia. The Nigerian Civil War was for
him a war of "solidity" rather than "unity," for it was not
accompanied by a "re-definition of social purpose."[16] He
played the role of mediator in the conflict and established
the Third Force as a way of neutralizing the energies of
both parties in the conflict. Unlike Gulliver, Soyinka did
not escape punishment but was clamped into prison for
holding illegal consultations with the rebels.

Soyinka's link with the fourth archetype, Ulysses, is
subtle. James Joyce's Ulysses was a wandering Jew, a "key-
less" citizen, cuckolded and jolted by intrigue but supremely resourceful and perceptive. He was modelled on
Odysseus, the great war general who lost his way on a homeward voyage after the end of the Trojan War. What unites
the two heroes (Homeric and Joycean) is the motif of peregri-
nation. Odysseus traversed the Mediterranean coastline in
search of his son (Telemachus), his wife (Penelope) and his
kingdom (Ithaca). Ulysses roamed through Dublin and its
environs in search of his adopted son (Stephen Daedalus)
and his wife, Molly. Soyinka's role as a creative artist with a
social vision necessarily involves him in a quest: the search
for the ideal of justice and an equitable social order for his
country. This aspect of the explorer in the poet is treated in
full in *Season of Anomy* (1972);[17] and there is an allusion in
the poem "Ulysses" to all others who are involved in it,
especially the army majors of the first coup:

> oh how
> We surf-wrestle to manure the land at ebb!
> How golden finally is the recovered fleece?
> A question we refuse to ask the Bard.

The poet indeed alludes to the upheavals that led to the
Biafran revolution in the images of storm, wind, and rain
at the beginning of stanza two.

A more fundamental form of quest is evoked in the poem
to which the Homeric or Joycean parallel functions as an
analogue: the quest for the essence of the self in the territory of the mind. The internal quest is aptly symbolized in

the poem by an external correlative for the mind, an abyss. In his prose confessions, Soyinka speaks in his own voice:

> I cannot circle indefinitely in the regurgitations of my mind alone. It is evil.[18]

The poet speaks of himself as a "heritage of thought," condemned to "haunt the music of the mind." His descent into the netherworld of the mind is briefly glimpsed in the following lines:

> I grow into that portion of the world
> Lapping my feet, yet bear the rain of nails
> That drill within to the archetypal heart
> Of all lone wanderers.

Solitude, his greatest torment, becomes a boulder rooted in the soils of the mind in order to enable the reader to realize its magnitude:

> On minds grown hoary from the quest
> Rest, rooted even in the turmoil agency
> A boulder solitude amidst wine-centred waves.

And one strategy of assuring himself of his continued existence as a material object in space is the therapy of sound:

> And, lest I lose the landmarks of my being
> Pocked the air with terse, echoing rounds
> Drumtap feelers on the growth of leaves.

All quests are bedevilled by perils or the Scylla and Charybdis of experience. Images at the beginning of stanza four suggest the poet's awareness of the obstacles and perils of Odysseus. There is a Homeric echo in the images of swine, straits, and rocks:

> It turns on quest cycles, to track a skein
> Of self through eyeless veils, stumble on warps
> Endure the blinds of spidery distortions, till

Swine-scented folds and caressing tunnels
Come to crossroads at the straits, between
Vaginal rocks.

CHIMES OF SILENCE

Chimes of Silence represents the climax of the shuttle's personal purgatory in the abyss of the crypt. Its organization is ritualistic, and its basic metaphor is one of a journey, that is, a rite of passage. The poem's structure thus enacts the death and rebirth pattern basic in rites of passage. In "Bearings," the shuttle and his co-sufferers are already immobilized in the crypt. In "Procession" and "Last Turning," he approaches the stage of ritual death which actually takes place in "Recession," while the last two poems, "Space" and "Seed," are reserved for the motif of rebirth. "Hunt of Stone," which intervenes between "Recession" and "Space," is only a diversionary interlude in the experience.

The poem's ritual structure is a deliberate conceit for Soyinka who sees his own agonies in the crypt as a re-enactment of Ogun's trials in the abyss of dissolution:

> When man is stripped of excrescences, when disaster and conflicts . . . have crushed and robbed him of self-consciousness and pretensions, he stands in present reality at the spiritual edge of this gulf, he has nothing left in physical existence which successfully impresses upon his spiritual or psychic perception. It is at such moments that transitional memory takes over and intimations rack him of that intense parallel of his progress through the gulf of transition, of the dissolution of his self and his struggle and triumph over subsumation through the agency of the will.[19]

The first poem, "Bearings," is a "topographical preface" to the body of *Chimes of Silence*. Here the shuttle surveys the landscape of his prison underworld. There is the Wailing Wall, which echoes with the babblings of penitent inmates. Next is the Wall of Mists, which harbors female inmates. Soyinka uses the word "mist" to underscore the ghostly appearance and murmurings of the apparitions that inhabit this location. The third location is Amber Wall over which the sun rises. Through this wall, the shuttle discovers a hunter (a boy) hot on the trail of a mango. The boy addressed as "breath of the sun" and as "a royal being" is an image of freedom for the beleaguered shuttle. The boy is "an open/Noon above the door that closed." But the poet suggests that his incarceration is not without its advantage—it is another lesson of experience. He is thus richer than the royal sun:

> I would you may discover, mid-morning
> To the man's estate, with lesser pain
> The wall of gain within the outer loss.

Purgatory is the region reserved for hardened criminals, lunatics and lifers. It is here that a Stygian taskmaster metes out punishment to criminals. Vault Centre is the shuttle's own cubicle.

But the poet tries occasionally to neutralize the threats of death through self-mockery and parody. The proceedings in the prison yard are converted into theatrical antics. The inmates of the Wailing Wall where prayers are heard are treated, for example, as a church congregation and the cell itself as a cathedral ministered unto by vultures and crows:

> Vulture presides in tattered surplice
> In schism for collection plates, with
> Crow in white collar, legs
> Of toothpick dearth plunged
> Deep in a salvaged morsel.

On the cathedral walls are "stained-glass wounds" rather than windows. The whole of Purgatory is a subterranean theatre featuring Pluto, the King of the underworld in the person of Polyphemus the "cicatriced tower of menace."[20] Polyphemus comes to his own here as the "priest of the

rites of submission."[21] All opposition is quelled; all recalci-
trant criminals are subdued:

> Hero of the piece, a towering shade across
> The prostrate villain, cuts a trial swathe
> In air, nostalgic for the thumbscrew
> Rack and nail extractors.

Other actors on the stage are the establishment surgeon
who supplies "wet timbres to the dry measures of the
Law," and "a cardboard row of gaolers, eyelids/Of glue—
the observation squad." The stage props consist of the
following items:

> Bench for a naked body, crusted towel,
> Pail of antiseptic yellow to impart
> Wet timbres to the dry measures of the Law.

The stage shifts to the upper regions of ether in Vault
Centre where the antics of sun-gleaners are inscaped. The
wood pigeons and the egrets in their arcs and figure eights,
their death-dives and love-duets, form a sharp contrast
to the poet immobilized in the vault centre of night.

If "Bearings" is merely prefatory, the ritual proper begins with "Procession," a poem in which the poet mourns
the death by hanging of five men serving life sentences:

> What may I tell you of the five
> Bell-ringers on the ropes to chimes
> Of silence.

The movement of the five convicts in a procession to their
grave operates as a metaphor for man's journey from life to
death. The poet plays on the word "passage" in the second
part of the poem to emphasize the sense of "passage" as
death and its meaning also as a continuing process in an
on-going ritual. For the five hanged men the rite is over,
but for the poet it is still continuing; and so he can pause in
Part II to take a surrealistic leap into the world of childhood inhabited by old women working on the loom. In

Part I of the poem the poet laments his inability to help his
fellow-travellers on the road to death who fell by the way-
side. In Part II he diverts our attention from the stench of
infested earth by a look into the past:

> See where they pass
> Our old women of the loom, and they bring
> On silent feet echoes in moult of earth
> Indigo shawls filled with burns of night.

In "Last Turning," the poet returns to the theme of death
as the end of man's journey here on earth. Death is welcomed as a liberator, as a form of new life, a rebirth in
which all contradictions cease. If man's life here on earth is
encumbered by weeds, in death he comes to "time's or-
chard." This metaphor of fulfillment is carried forward in
the observation: "'on beds of vines/Press lenten hands."
The most outstanding image for the obstacles on man's
life-journey is "jagged peaks." For many, "the peaks' fine
needles have embossed/Missals on the heart." The poet sees
the death of those who fall on the hillside as a ritual
sacrifice for his own survival:

> And your companion dead, fallen
> On hillside, all were steps on the ascent
> Parts to the sum of seekers' questions
> Sandals on milestones.

In "Recession," the shuttle dies a symbolic death in
preparation for his final rebirth. The poem is based on the
Hindu concept of *Mahapralaya. Mahapralaya* is the great
apocalypse which, in Hindu metaphysical thought, is des-
tined to end all things; but this apocalypse comes about
only as a necessary imperative of a cyclical dialectic. That
is, *Mahapralaya* is not the end of life but merely one of the
necessary processes for its renewal. It is in this regard that
Soyinka has utilized the concept in the poem.[22] In "Recession," the shuttle passes through a stage of night, followed
by an entry into regions of light:

cliffs of clay have walled the human pass
a lifelong fall of ash has sealed the straits
now flares the savaged ember
now lifts the pinioned egret through the pass.

In "Bearings," walls are images of enclosure, inhibiting the aspirations of the human spirit toward self-fulfillment. After the ritual sacrifice in "Recession," the shuttle (now an egret) has transcended the limitations of concrete and iron bars.

The final poems of the section, "Space" and "Seed," work out the motif of rebirth. In "Space," the shuttle is represented as Noah's dove sent out from the ark to test the firmness of the new world.[23] The image is a little forced since the shuttle's ordeal in the crypt is hardly a universal disaster like Noah's flood. Soyinka here uses the dove as a symbol of freedom, and he uses birds consistently in the poem as a symbol of that freedom which the shuttle seeks.

"Seed," the last poem in *Chimes of Silence*, is an emblem for the phase of the new life and self-fulfillment awaiting the shuttle. The shuttle has come to the "hour of kernel-baiting." The change in tense marks the movement from darkness into sunlight. "I waited on the sonorous sift/Of ashes," laments the shuttle. But having come to the hour of kernel-baiting, he says, "I speak in the voice of gentle rain."

The poem "Hunt of the Stone," placed between "Recession" and "Space," is a brief digression from the poem's ritual topography. The myth behind the poem is explained in the head and footnotes to the poem. Soyinka calls himself Sango's stone (the magical elixir) hunted by priest–scavengers for its magical potency. The allusion to Sango is not out of place, for Ogun and Sango are two Promethean deities in the Yoruba pantheon whom the poet has consistently used as metaphors for heroic will (and therefore for himself). The ideal fusion is that which combines the essences of the two gods. *Idanre* and "Chimes of Silence" are two poems in which Soyinka has presented himself as the symbol of that fusion. In the present poem he has used the term, "priest-scavenger," to denote his _es, the mind-butchers who were responsible for his imprisonment. These, like Sango's priests, rush to exploit the misfortunes of a stricken hearth, but their hands, the poet affirms, shall close in emptiness:

> They shall hold,
> Nought but husks of the seed of passage, though
> They sift in ashes of eternity. The shuttle-eel
> Shall their nets escape though they cast
> In waters of the Deluge.

PRISONNETTES

Poetry as a concentrated statement sustained by a subtle interplay of images ceases to exist the moment we come to the end of the first three groups of poems in *A Shuttle in the Crypt*. These poems are the product of a fevered imagination; their language is taut, their texture compact. A theme or a motif is taken up and treated as an expanded metaphor. In "Roots," Soyinka calls upon the pathfinder to the underworld to "lead/My feet to core, to kernel seed." In "Four Archetypes," he uses Joseph, Hamlet, Gulliver, and Bloom as objective correlatives for his own personal predicament as a political prisoner. In *Chimes of Silence* he works out his own salvation through the metaphor of a ritual journey. These technical devices have helped Soyinka to discipline his emotions and tighten his verse while at the same time lending sophistication to the exploration of his emotions. There is a lightness of touch in the handling of theme and language in the *Prisonettes* (under which category we include the poems of bread and earth) which is disconcerting but understandable if one assumes that the *Prisonnettes* were actually written in prison. Soyinka calls these poems "lyrical breezes,"[24] short and light enough to remain in the head until the poet has had the opportunity to put them down on paper. Their language is prosaic; their insights fragmentary. There is no attempt to explore the various implications of an image or symbol. "Live Burial," for example, is made up of unconnected episodes in the poet's daily ritual as a tenant of the crypt. One of these is an official medical report on the prisoner's health:

> Bulletin:
> He sleeps well, eats
> Well. His doctors note
> No damage
> Our plastic surgeons tend his public image.

This episode is lifted straight from the prison notes unmediated by the discriminating judgment of what Coleridge calls the "secondary imagination":

> He sleeps well, eats well, is allowed
> to see his own doctor.[25]

Another poem in "Live Burial" originates from a casual recollection of the hangman's tricks for relaxing his nerves after he has completed a hanging assignment:

> The ghoul:
> Flushed from hanging, sniffles
> Snuff, to clear his head of
> Sins—the law
> Declared—that morning's gallows.[26]

"Flowers for my Land" attempts an exploration of a poetic image: the nation, for example, is called a garden of decay where bones of slaughtered youths sprout to accuse the leaders. Other images include flowers as the sacrificed youths of the land, mountain flowers as bombs falling from the sky, the bursting buds as the sound of booming guns and bombs, garlands of scavengers weighing heavy on human breasts as the nation's cross in a time of civil war. But the flow of images is interrupted by the intrusion of one of Soyinka's prison pastimes:

> I traced
> A dew-lane on the sun-
> flower leaf; a hailstone

Burning, blew
A trap-door on my lane for falling through.

The "Animystic Spells" are incantations or "mantras,"
verbalizations of Soyinka's mental hallucinations. They
have value as the speech of the soul with itself:

Around this rockface, self
Encounters self.

The spells make no pretensions to meaning; they are heroic
cries that reassure the poet of his own existence. The poems
have pathos and a seriousness of tone which rescue them
from triviality. The language is occasionally mythopoeic
and the lines rhythmic. Poetry is here what Okigbo calls
"catatonic pingpong":

First you must
Walk among the faceless
Their feet are shod in earth
And dung
Caryatids in anterooms of night's inbirth.

Death
Embraces you and I
A twilight cone is
Meeting-place
The silent junction of the grey abyss.[27]

When Soyinka treats poetry as an extended image, he
achieves concentration (and, of course, sophistication) in
the exploration of his emotions. His tone is controlled
because his anger is subdued by the power of the image to
suggest rather than assert. Therein lies the success of the
two poems in the "Epilogue" on the death of Victor Banjo
and Christopher Okigbo, both of whom the poet regards as
the heroes of the Biafran revolution.

He wondered in a treasure-house
Of inward prices, strove to bring
Fleeting measures of time

To tall expressions, to granite arches
Spanned across landslides of the past.

We return to the perennial question: can the prisoner become a poet?[28] The high quality of a majority of the poems in *A Shuttle* is proof that he can, but only in so far as the prison experience itself is an emotion recollected in tranquillity. But if the prisoner insists on offering the prison experience as living art, the attempt is likely to lead him into lyrical effusions rather than seasoned poetry.

Notes

1. Wole Soyinka, *The Man Died* (London: Rex Collings, 1973), p. 147.

2. For more information on the Third Force, see chapter 23 of *The Man Died*. In *Season of Anomy*, Ofeyi, the hero of the novel, made some effort to achieve the ideals of The Third Force.

3. Wole Soyinka, *A Shuttle in the Crypt* (New York: Hill and Wang, 1972), p. vii.

4. *A Shuttle in the Crypt*, p. 17.

5. *The Man Died*, p. 187.

6. *Ibid.*, p. 252.

7. *Ibid.*, p. 40.

8. Christopher Okigbo, *Labyrinths* (London: Heinemann, 1971), p. xiv.

9. *The Man Died*, p. 255.

10. *Ibid.*, p. 258.

11. Genesis 39:7–23.

12. *The Man Died*, p. 87.

13. Wole Soyinka, *Myth, Literature and the African World* (Cambridge: The University Press, 1976), p. 146.

14. *The Man Died*, p. 174

15. *Gulliver's Travels*, Part I: A Voyage to Lilliput, in *The Norton Anthology of English Literature*: Vol. I (Third Edition), p. 1,952.

16. *The Man Died*, p. 181.

17. For more information on this subject see my essay, "Soyinka's Season of Anomy: Ofeyi's Quest," *International Fiction Review*, Vol. 7, No. 2 (Summer 1980), pp. 85–89.

18. *The Man Died*, p. 223.

19. *Myth, Literature and the African World*, p. 149.

20. *The Man Died*, p. 125.

21. *Ibid.*, p. 126.

22. For more information on "Mahapralaya," see my essay, "Conquering the Abyss of the Crypt: Survival Imperative in Soyinka's Shuttle," *World Literature Written in English*, Vol. 16, No. 2 (November 1977), pp. 250–251.

23. Genesis 8:6–12.

24. *The Man Died*, p. 250.

25. *Ibid.*, p. 67.

26. An account of this story is contained in *The Man Died*, p. 205.

27. The Animystic poems are discussed in detail in my article, "Soyinka's Animystic Poetics," *African Studies Review*, Vol. XXV, No. 1 (March 1982), pp. 37–48.

28. Taking the prison poems of Dennis Brutus as an example, Bahadur Tejani argues vehemently that the prisoner cannot become a poet. See his essay in *African Literature Today*, No. 6, pp. 130–144.

△ △

3

EPICS OF ENERGY:
IDANRE AND *OGUN ABIBIMAN*

S oyinka said in 1966 that Leopold Senghor's long poem
Chaka is rendered effete by Senghor's indifference to the
literary possibilities of the aesthetics of action. It is as if
for Senghor "poetry is not in itself a force for violence or
an occasional instrument of terror," wrote Soyinka. The
poem's celebrative tone, the author's passive stance, is even
contradicted by the poet's subject, the character of Chaka
himself. Soyinka traces the weaknesses in Senghor's artistic
method in this particular poem to their source, to Senghor's insensitivity to the principles of genuine creativity
(the paradox of artistic creativity) which has prevented an
omnidirectional perception of experience. Senghor's one-
dimensional vision breeds "narcissistic" art. The true artist
thrives on his recognition of the permanence of flux, of the
existence of contradictions in the heart of matter. Senghor's
poem is celebrative, static and passive, whereas it is the
function of true art to reveal the damnation as well as the
salvation, the savage as well as the beautiful. "That it
combats fear by the revelation of beauty is undoubtedly one
of poetry's functions."

His own god, Ogun, Soyinka insists, embodies the true
artistic sensibility, and he offers this god to Senghor as the
true artistic spirit:

> In explication of the real problem of Senghor in the
> interpretation of *Chaka*, which cannot be solved by
> the poetic self-identification, the essence of Ogun the
> Yoruba god of war and the creative principle, proba-

bly offers the best assistance . . . Primogenitor of the
artist as the creative human, Ogun is the antithesis of
cowardice and Philistinism, yet within him is contained also the complement of the creative essence, a
bloodthirsty destructiveness. Mixed up with the gestative inhibition of his nature [is] the destructive explosion of an incalculable energy.[1]

In another essay, "The Fourth Stage," the energies within
the god, Ogun, are said to be as violent as volcanic erup-
tions. Ogun, aroused, recalls in his fierce masculine vitality
the "explosion of the sun's kernel" or "the eruption of fire
which is the wombfruit of pristine mountains," for no less,
no different were "the energies within Ogun whose ordering and control through the will brought him safely
through the tragic gulf."[2]

Soyinka has immortalized the energies of his god in two
epic poems, *Idanre* (1967) and *Ogun Abibiman* (1976),
which are remarkable for their celebration of savage
strength. Ogun emerges here as the revolutionary archetype, the god "Who goes for[ward] where other gods/Have
turned."[3] In *Idanre* he is situated in the context of Yoruba
mythology where he distinguished himself as the protagonist of the abyss and as both the hero and the monster at the
Battle of Ire. In *Ogun Abibiman* the god's mythic attributes
receive a contemporary interpretation. Samora Machel's
decision in 1976 to declare Mozambique at war with the
white minority regime of former "Rhodesia" regards Ogun
as the warlord, for he is the god who commands the liberation forces of all Abibiman, abetted by his historical counterpart, Chaka.

The language of the two poems is heroic, the tone, epic,
and their emotions and attitudes, motivated by the aesthetics of action.

In *Idanre* Ogun visits earth in order to fertilize her, for he
controls, as the god of harvest, the rhythm of the seasons.
His descent implies harvest, and his withdrawal heralds
drought and scarcity. On this particular visit he is accompanied by his acolyte, the poet himself seeking creative
inspiration. His other exploits in the context of Yoruba
mythology are recounted in the course of the poem; and the

journey itself is a symbolic re-enactment of the god's passage through the abyss of transition.

The abyss is a thick undergrowth of matter and nonmatter that separates the realm of the gods from the abode of men. Originally, it was a metaphor for human or divine estrangement as a result of sin, but Soyinka has incorporated the abyss into his cyclic conception of existence whereby death (psychic, aesthetic, material, and metaphysical) is inevitably followed by rebirth (regeneration, renewal, growth). Ogun's task in the primeval epoch was to hack his way through the undergrowth in order to construct a bridge by which contact between man and god was reestablished. He had to clear that path in order to resume the human essence of his own totality. That journey, as has been noted, has become integrated into the language of the seasons and is also undertaken as a form of penance for a previous error. Because of its seasonal connotation, the journey is properly preceded by an eruption of a cosmic deluge. In the first stanza of the poem's opening section, "Deluge," imagery, diction, and rhythm aspire evoke an atmosphere of marmorean loftiness:

> Gone, and except for horsemen briefly
> Thawed, lit in deep cloud mirrors, lost
> The Skymen of Void's regenerate Wastes
> Striding vast across
> My still inchoate earth.[4]

The motive force in this stanza is concentrated in the active participles, "Gone," "lit," and "lost." They compel attention by their emphatic position in the stanza (at the beginning, middle or end of the lines in which they occur), and they suggest action. The actors are "primal giants and mastodons," heroic personages whom Soyinka addresses as "the Skymen of Void's regenerate Wastes." Their gigantic limbs traverse the cosmos, the Skymen are still "Striding vast across/My . . . inchoate earth." The landscape is still reeking with spoils of war. There is only a brief "thaw" in the gelded rage of the warring horsemen. Nature also participates in the rage for action; she is in a state of "fevered distillation," for Ogun's descent to earth is preceded by a

cosmic deluge. This deluge is unleashed on earth only
when the instrument that has sealed up the bottled energies
of the sky has been unscrewed. The instrument itself, the
"corkscrew," etches sharp affinities with the combatant
giants, for it is "flaming" even as they themselves are still
flaming out with the anger of war. With the release of the
rain-suffused energies of the cosmos, "roaring vats of an
unstoppered heaven deluge/Earth in fevered distillation":

> The flaming corkscrew etches sharp affinities
> ....
> When roaring vats of an unstoppered heaven deluge
> Earth in fevered distillations, potent with
> The fire of the axe-handed one.

The "axe-handed one" is Sango, the Yoruba god of lightning and electricity. His presence disappears in the first
section of the poem, for the narrative is primarily an epic of
Ogun. Soyinka indicates in the notes to the poem that
Sango's essence is absorbed into the personality of Ogun
and that the poem is in its early sections a celebration of the
fusion of Ogun and Sango:

> Today Ogun of the metallic lore conducts Sango's
> electricity. The ritual dance of the fusion is seen some-
> times during an electric storm when from high-ten-
> sion wires leap figures of ecstatic flames.[5]

The "ecstatic flames" are sparked by the "axe-handed one."
Still, in conformity with Ogun's active energies, the fire is
"potent".
    Rain reeds are no less potent with energy, for they are
"violent" and "tremulous in fire tracings/On detonating
peaks":

> And greys are violent now, laced with
> Whiteburns, tremulous in fire tracings
> On detonating peaks. Ogun is still in such
> Combatant angles, poised to a fresh descent
> Fiery axe-heads fly about his feet.

Ogun is entrenched firmly, then, in the opening stanzas of the poem in a landscape of epic action. Sango is the first victim in this section of Ogun's heroic energies:

> He catches Sango in his three-fingered hand
> And runs him down to earth.

Earth is the beneficiary of those creative energies:

> And no one speaks of secrets in this land
> Only, that the skin be bared to welcome rain
> And earth prepare, that seeds may swell
> And roots take flesh within her, and men
> Wake naked into harvest tide.

All these images of war, of conflict in "Deluge," which are reminiscent of the primal war in most mythologies are indeed metaphors for the rain cycle in nature. Soyinka has allowed his epic imagination to get the better of him. He speaks of "my still inchoate earth." But the earth has not just been created. "Deluge" states that Ogun is the god of the rainy season and Sango of lightning and thunder and that, when it rains and thunders, the gods of rain and thunder, Ogun and Sango, are on duty.[6]

In section II, "And After," Ogun has landed on Earth to fertilize her and to energize the inhabitants of that universe. Earth, the immediate beneficiary of the harvest tide, is symbolized in the maternal image of Oya. Oya operates as the symbolic receptacle of the harvest-tide:

> At pilgrim's rest beneath Idanre Hill
> The wine-girl, dazed from divine dallying
> Felt wine-skeins race in fire-patterns within her.

Oya is not only a symbolic representation of mother Earth; she is also a bartender ("wine-girl"), the victim of a motor accident, a wife of Ogun and later of Sango. As an ex-wife of Ogun and Sango, Oya shares the attributes of both deities. Ogun's sperm ("wine-skeins") are electric currents (Sango's essence) racing through her in "fire-patterns".

Oya is ruled by a kind of internal tide. Physically, she is not wholly purged of the impulse toward motion inherited by Ogun. In stanza three of "And After," she is an eel meandering effortlessly in the waters: "She swam an eel into the shadows." But the human side of her personality (she is half-human, half-divine) was fated to taste the ashes of death in a motor accident. In one lightning instant of elemental action ("The sky cracked half-ways"), Oya became "a greying skull/On blooded highways." Combining his new agency over thunder and lightning with his traditional role as the guardian of the road, Ogun acted and Oya suffered:

> Vapours rose
> From sudden bitumen and snaked within
> Her wrap of indigo.

The snake image has a special relevance to Ogun, for the snake is an important totemic element in his worship; it signifies the "doom of repetition." In this particular instance, the image evokes intimations of an eternal torment which culminates in death. The idea of death is further suggested with the image of darkness in "bitumen" and "indigo." In the stanza that immediately follows, it strikes an immediate key:

> Darkness veiled her little hills poised
> Twin nights against the night, pensive points
> In the leer of lightning, and sadness filled
> The lone face of the wine-girl.

The issue of transference of energy is all important in this section. This transference Soyinka designates as the "dance of fusion." Ogun is the supreme essence of motion, and the reactivation of essences has been his inheritance since his successful invasion of the sleeping monsters of the chthonic realm on the night of transition. While on earth, he has taught "the veins to dance, of earth of rock/Of tree, sky, of fire and rain, of flesh of man/And woman." His mere presence in nature reactivates dormant energies. The dead "who by road/Made the voyage home" (that is, vic-

tims of road accidents) rise up from their grave to pay
homage to the god of the road:

> Ogun, godfather of all souls who by road
> Made the voyage home, made his being welcome
> Suffused in new powers of night.

Stanzas twenty to twenty-five evoke in surrealistic language what Soyinka has called "apocalyptic visions of
childhood and other deliriums." These deliriums are no
digressions but visions fully integrated into the poem's
ideological framework; they endorse one of the poem's
leading concepts: the doom of repetition. The repeating
cycle in this instance is one of conflict. The apocalyptic
passages etch a graph of conflict stretching from the cosmos down through the history of man. In the opening lines
the engagement is primarily cosmic:

> Vast grows the counterpane of night since innocence
> Of apocalyptic skies, when thunderous shields clashed
> Across the heights, when bulls leapt cloud humps and
> Thunders opened chasms end to end of fire:
> The sky a slate of scoured lettering
> Of widening wounds eclipsed in smoke.

Down the line the whirling incandescent stone of conflict
has traversed the heavens to plague mankind. The human
side of the cosmic conflict is heavily emphasized towards
the closing stanzas of the apocalyptic passages:

> Whorls of intemperate steel, triangles of cabal
> In rabid spheres, iron bellows at volcanic tunnels
> Easters in convulsions, urged by energies
> Of light milleniums, crusades, empires and revolution
> Damnations and savage salvations.

These battles recall the cosmic conflict in the opening lines
of *Idanre* and the human conflict in "The battle" section of
the poem. They remind us, of course, of Atunda's role as
the architect of tragic conflict in Yoruba mythology.
    The special keynote of the apocalyptic passages is the

delineation of action. In the first passage the cosmic bull pierces the clouds with its humps as it galvanizes itself into action. The apocalyptic impact is enhanced by precise visual and auditory images. The thunderous shields still re-echo, and the bulls with mountain humps are vividly realized—a rare achievement by Soyinka in visual description. The auditory and the visual converge in line four where the cosmic chasm yawns open as thunderous cannonades of fire ignite the skies. The entire section on childhood vision retains its self-conscious apocalyptic intonation. The following stanza continues the catalogues of tumultuous action:

> Nozzles of flames, tails of restive gristles
> Banners of saints, cavalcades of awesome hosts
> Festival of firevales, crush of starlode
> And exploding planets.

The climactic evocation in the apocalyptic passages about the vortex of destructive energies in nature recalls the whirling motion of the gyres in Yeats's "The Second Coming." And, in true Yeatsian logic, a second coming was indeed expected at this particular point in *Idanre,* for "the world was choked in wet embrace/Of serpent spawn, waiting Ajantala's rebel birth." Ajantala is *Idanre's* "rough beast." Soyinka calls him a "monster child, wrestling pachyderms of myth." In the Notes to *Idanre* he is described as

> Archetypes of rebel child, iconoclast, anarchic, anti-clan, anti-matriarch, virile essence in opposition to womb-domination.[7]

Ajantala's double in the poem is the traitor-god Atunda (referred to in Section III as the "Boulder"), who represents the diversity principle in Yoruba mythology. About Atunda, Soyinka writes in "The Fourth Stage":

> Myth informs us that a jealous slave rolled a stone down the back of the first and only deity and shattered him in a thousand and sixty-four fragments. From this first act of revolution was born the Yoruba pantheon.[8]

The tragic fragmentation of the godhead essence is narrated in "Pilgrimage":

> Union they had known until the Boulder
> Rolling down the hill of the Beginning
> Shred the kernel to a million lights.
> A traitor's heart rejoiced, the god's own slave
> Dirt-covered from the deed.

"Pilgrimage" recounts Ogun's pilgrimage to the rockhills of Idanre, believed to be the terrestrial domicile for the god and described in the Preface as "a god-suffused grazing of primal giants and mastodons, petrified through some strange history, suckled by mists and clouds."[9] The rocks of Idanre remind Ogun of Atunda's errant wheel, the fateful instrument of fragmentation, and he wept:

> On the hills of Idanre memories
> Grieved him, my Hunter god, Vital
> Flint of matter, total essence split again
> On recurrent boulders.

After Atunda's revolutionary initiative in disintegrating the original godhead essence, there is not just one god but many gods. That action liberated man from divine tyranny; he may choose to follow one of the gods or no god at all. Therefore, Ogun is aggrieved that "Control had slipped/ Immortal grasp." The "cupped shell of tortoise" in stanza three of "Pilgrimage" is the original form of the Orisa-nla Oneness, the first and only deity before the fragmentation. It is what has been referred to in stanza five as the "Vital/ Flint of matter" or "total essence" which has been split on "recurrent boulders."

The stanza beginning with "This road have I trodden in a time beyond/Memory of fallen leaves" alludes first to the Beginning, to the time of Ogun's first passage through the gulf of transition and, then, to other subsequent journeys he had made to earth both as a pilgrimage and as an atonement on the altar of the rocks of Idanre, "the rocks of genesis," for his unwitting massacre of his own men at the Battle of Ire. Since this journey is undertaken "annually," Ogun's pathway is a "Mobius" orbit signifying the "doom

of repetition." The journey through transitional chaos is
the subject of the first part of "The Beginning" (stanzas 1–
7), and the rest of this section right up to the whole of
Section V, "The Battle", is devoted to the story of Ogun's
erroneous massacre of his own men under the influence of
palm-wine. Sections IV and V are then diversionary reminiscences on Ogun's exploits both as "path-finder" and as
a monster. Section VI, "Recession," returns the narrative to
the present.

Section IV, "the Beginning," takes us back to the origin,
to the womb of time after the creation of the pantheon
when the primordial deities newly created, Orisa-nla, Orunmila, Esu, Ifa, were plagued by the "anguish of severance"
because "a mere plague of finite chaos/Stood between the
gods and man." Of all these gods, it is Ogun alone who
mustered the courage to descend to earth to do battle with
the "immense chaotic growth which had sealed off reunion with man."[10] For this reason, Soyinka extols Ogun
in "The Fourth Stage" as

> The first actor . . . first suffering deity, first creative
> energy, the first darer and conqueror of transition.[11]

This side of the Ogun legend is briefly touched on in two
asides in Section IV:

> To think, a mere plague of finite chaos
> Stood between the gods and man
>
> And this plague he gave the heavens
> I will clear a path for man.

The legend is positively suggested in the line "His fingers
touched earth-core, and it yielded." The fabrication of
Ogun's weapon for the conquest of separation is the subject of stanza five. "The Fourth Stage" narrates the story as
follows:

> The artifact of Ogun's conquest of separation, the
> "fetish," was iron ore, symbol of earth's womb-ener-
> gies, cleaver and welder of life. Ogun, through his

redemptive action, became the first symbol of the alliance of disparities when, from earth itself, he extracted elements for the subjugation of chthonic chaos.[12]

Ogun is in his element as the god of war in "The Battle" (Section V). All the apocalyptic trends that have been building through the poem come to a climax in this section. The quiet, casual tone of the opening stanzas is the more ironical because of the havoc they foreshadow:

> A rust-red swarm of locusts
> Dine off grains
> Quick proboscis
>
> Find the coolers
> Soon the wells are dry.

In the second of these two passages, Ogun is a thirsty elephant with a giant proboscis eager to suck dry the wells of human life. "Rust," which appears in the first passage, is frequently associated in Soyinka's poetry with death. "Rust is ripeness," writes Soyinka in "Season,"[13] a poem largely devoted to the gyre-like interrelationship in human life between the cones of death (rust) and those of life (ripeness). As a decaying crust of iron, rust recalls Ogun's status as the god of the "metallic lore." Ogun is "The Iron One", the god of iron, and "the first . . . technician of the forge."[14] Iron is his symbol of destruction. In "The Battle," iron is immediately recalled in the image of sword and axe. In stanza eleven of this section, Ogun's sword is "an outer crescent of the sun" which no eye can follow. In stanza fifteen, his "butcher's axe" hacks men to pieces. The first stanza of the passage under discussion establishes a parallel between Ogun and a horde of locusts. Like the god, the legion of iron-winged locusts are swooping, deadly to men and things.

Ogun emerges in the entire section as a possessed deity tuned to the dance of death: "his hands cleave frenetic/To the jig!" As "His sword possesses all," a host of butchered humanity falls:

> There are falling ears of corn
> And ripe melons tumble from the heads
> Of noisy women.

The death harvest here is a continuation of the grain image in the first stanza of "The Battle." The "whorls of intemperate steel" suggested in the image of the crescent-shaped sword (stanza eleven) have come full circle in this battle scene:

> A lethal arc
> Completes full circle
>
> Unsheathed
> The other half
> Of fire
>
> Incinerates
> All subterfuge
> Enthrones
> The fatal variant

The carnage unleashed by Ogun is a "fatal variant" of the tragic cycle inaugurated by Atunda.

Section VI ("Recession") is a quiet reflection on the theme of destiny. In the previous section ("The Battle"), Ogun has massacred his own men through a predestined error. For we are told that since that first Boulder (Atunda) had dared to roll down the hill of Beginning, men's lives are fated to be split again on recurrent boulders. Ogun's massacre of his men is part of the tragic cycle inaugurated by Atunda, but it is a cycle that has enabled nature to renew itself. Man is able, as a result of that cycle, to "ignite our several kilns" so that mankind can "glory in each bronzed emergence." Atunda is celebrated then as the hero of the revolutionary spirit and the author of the diversity principle, which affords an opportunity to both man and god to be the thing that each wishes to be. Not Ogun but Atunda is the primogenitor of change:

> Rather, may we celebrate the stray election, defiant
> Of patterns, celebrate the splitting of the gods

Canonization of the strong hand of a slave who set
The rock in revolution.

You who have borne the first separation, bide you
Severed still; he who guards the Creative Flint
Walks, purged spirit, contemptuous of womb-yearn-
ings
He shall teach us to ignite our several kilns
And glory in each bronzed emergence.

All hail Saint Atunda, First revolutionary
Grand iconoclast at genesis—and the rest in logic
Zeus, Osiris, Jahweh, Christ in trifoliate
Pact with creation, and the wisdom of Orunmila, Ifa
Divining eyes, multiform.
Evolution of the self-devouring snake to spatials
New in symbol, banked loop of the 'Mobius Strip'
And interlock of re-creative rings, one surface
Yet full comb of angles, uni-plane, yet sensuous with
Complexities of mind and motion.

Soyinka's metaphor for unity in diversity is the "Mobius
Strip" defined as

a mathe-magical ring, infinite in self-recreation into
independent but linked rings and therefore the freest
conceivable (to me) symbol of human or divine (e.g.,
Yoruba, Olympian) relationships.[15]

The reference to the Olympian pantheon in this passage
explains the allusion to Zeus in the third stanza above. Zeus
is but one deity in the Greek pantheon, Osiris but one deity
in the Egyptian divine canon; and Jahweh but one in the
Hebrew pantheon. Christ is linked with God the Father
and God the Holy Ghost in a trifoliate pact with creation
in Christian mythology. The principle of individuation
and separation is traced in Yoruba mythology to the grand
iconoclast, Atunda.

The "Mobius" metaphor is a Western concept, but its
African equivalent is the image of the self-devouring snake
which, in traditional Yoruba society, is regarded as Ogun's

emblem because of his eternal condemnation to the doom
of repetition. Says Ogun himself in "Pilgrimage":

> This road have I trodden in a time beyond
> Memory of fallen leaves, beyond
> Threat of fossil on the slate, yet I must
> This way again. Let all wait the circulation
> of time's acrobat, who pray
>
> For dissolution.

The compulsory effort of a snake to make both ends of its
body embrace each other will reshape it into coils of concentric rings. These coils can be metaphysically interpreted
as the "Mobius" orbit for recurrence or as routes for the
eternal cycle of karma. But Soyinka finds a contradiction in
the "Mobius" metaphor itself, since the concentric rings
harbor a "kink" at the center, which has provided the
Atundas of the world with a centrifugal escape from destiny.

The poem concludes in Section VII with a postscript
image of dawn, symbolized by harvest. When Ogun has
withdrawn into the heavens, harvest comes, responsive to
the biddings of dawn. Harvest is his legacy for mankind,
his reparation for the injuries done to man. It is in this
section of the poem that "earth's broken rings" are genu-
inely healed by dawn's restorative sympathies. The pattern
of fevered distillation is repeated as nature is activated: "the
air withdrew to scything motion/Of his dark-shod feet." It
is the "season of mists and mellow fruitfulness":

> The first fruits rose from subterranean hoards
> First in our vision, corn sheaves rose over hill
> Long before the bearers, domes of eggs and flesh
> Of palm fruit, red, oil black, froth flew in sun bubbles
> Burst over twigs of golden gourds.

Critics have complained of complexity and confusion in
Soyinka's poetry. There are enough of these complexities
in *Idanre*. The reader is hindered by syntactical, and elliptical obstacles within the poem's structure. Soyinka has

taken too much liberty with poetic license. He ignores
punctuational aids and the proper positioning of operative
words within the structure of his lines which would have
clarified most of the syntactical obscurities. It is difficult,
for instance, to make sense out of the following stanza:

> Who, inhesion of desparate senses, of matter
> Thought, entities and motions, who sleep-walk
> Incensed in Nirvana—a code of Passage
> And the Night—who, cloyed, a mote in homogeneous
> gel
> Touch the living and the dead?[16]

The key word "celebrate" has been left behind in the preceding stanza. The stanza, thus, has no meaning as a self-
contained unit. Then, too, the passage is overloaded with
esoteric mysticism: "Incensed in Nirvana," "a code of passage," "a mote in homogeneous gel."

But these observations need not detract attention from
the poem's compelling rhythm and its savage strength.
Soyinka exploits words like Okigbo for their musical cadence. He betrays this inclination quite early in the poem:

> And greys are violent now, laced with
> Whiteburns, tremulous in fire tracings
> On detonating peaks.

And it is the impression he wishes the reader to leave his
poem with:

> And they moved towards resorption in His alloy es-
> sence
> Primed to a fusion, primed to the sun's dispersion
> Containment and communion, seed-time and harvest,
> palm
> And pylon, Ogun's road a 'Mobius' orbit, kernel
> And electrons, wine to alchemy.

Assonance, repetitions, and alliterations are constant elements in Soyinka's rhetoric. In the first example, "laced"
sparks off a musical harmony with "greys," and the re-

maining one line and half are orchestrated into an alliterative unit: "laced *with/whiteburns*, tremulous in fire tracings." The entire verse advances to a counterpoint of explosive consonants in the last line: "fire tracings/On detonating peaks." This counterpointing and the balancing of musical units within the line are responsible for the musical intensity of the most explosive stanza in the apocalyptic passages:

> Nozzles of flames, tails of restive gristles
> Banners of saints, cavalcades of awesome hosts
> Festival of firevales, crush of starlode
> And exploding planets.

In the stanza beginning "And they moved towards resorption," Soyinka's rhythm relies essentially on alliterative counterpoints:

> primed to a fusion
> primed to the sun's dispersion
>
> containment and communion
>
> palm and pylon.

Idanre must be viewed as the culmination of the symbol of Ogun. The god's masculine energy, his indomitable will is felt through nature and by nature throughout that poem. His whirling incandescent stone of conflict and energy agitates the cosmos and descends from thither to earth and can penetrate even into the womb of earth so that the veins of matter, the rocks, the ore were able to inscape themselves in a self-individuating dance. When Ogun is around, earth is "a surreal bowl/of sounds and mystic timbres."

By the time we come to *Ogun Abibimañ* (1976),[17] Ogun's masculine energy is spent; his possibilities as a poetic conceit are exhausted. This latter poem contains but a frail reflection, a faint echo of the passionate intensity, the cannonades of fire and thunder, that explode through *Idanre*. There is no place here for the metaphysical suggestiveness of the "Mobius" symbolism or the virtues of the diversity

principle or even the redemptive role of revolutionary hubris celebrated in *Idanre*. Soyinka has bowed to the pres-
sures emanating from the socialist-realist school of literary
criticism in harnessing the energies of his god in a south-
ward-bound liberation mission in Southern Africa. The
result is a poem in which his own private and personal
voice is subordinated to a public voice, and a work which,
even though it cannot be charged with insincerity, is devoid, at least in the first two sections, of passion. *Ogun
Abibiman* is not as emotionally engaging as *Idanre*. Soyinka
nearly fell into the trap that caught Senghor in *Chaka* by
failing to make his own poem a focus for the poetry of action.

For there is in *Ogun Abibiman* only a *will* for motion
and an *intent* to action. We hear of wars and rumors of war,
but there is no real confrontation. Section I is devoted to
Ogun's military preparations prior to the launching of the
great offensive. He ignores his duties as farmer and carver
and becomes the technician of the forge. Hoe and adze lie
in neglected corners, but at the forge glows the ore that will
be transformed into a sword.

In Section II Ogun's military intentions are sanctioned
by the great warlord of the Velds himself, Shaka, described
by Soyinka as "Africa's most renowned nation builder"
and as a "military and socio-organizational genius." From
the land of the dead, Shaka had intimations of Ogun's
military intentions from the rockhills of Idanre to the sa-
vannah of the South, and it reminded him, of course, of his
own military exploits in the area that is about to be invaded
by Ogun and his cohorts of black-browed infantrymen.
Ogun's mission and the terrible fearsome aspect of the god
appealed to Shaka. Ogun is for him a god appointed by
destiny to complete the task of total conquest of the black
nation south of the Sahara which he himself had initiated
in his prime. Thus, Shaka identifies himself readily with
Ogun's military explorations and provides the reader with
a most revealing attribute of the god:

I

Felt the rain of sand as nerve-ends
On my hairless head, and knew this tread—
Of wooded rockhills, shredded mists of Idanre,

The heart of furnaces, and pulsing ore,
Clang of anvils, fearsome rites of passage
Harvest in and out of season, hermit feet
Perfumed in earth and dung of all Abibiman—
Shape of dread whose silence frames the awesome
Act of origin—I feel, and know your tread
As mine.

These attributes have much in common indeed with
Shaka's career as an invincible warlord. "Where I paused,"
he boasted, "the bladegrass reddened./My *impi* gnawed the
stubble of thornbushes/left nothing for the rains to suckle
after."

The imaginary encounter between the two warriors is
celebrated in a climactic dance of violence written in
Yoruba. The English version reads:

Turmoil on turmoil!
Ogun treads the earth of Shaka
Turmoil on the loose!
Ogun shakes the hand of Shaka
All is in turmoil!

Ogun is commissioned by the most authoritative voice of
revolution in the precolonial history of Southern Africa to
carry the war of liberation to its logical conclusion, victory:

The task must gain completion, our fount
Of being cleansed from termites' spittle—
In this alone I seek my own completion.

And Shaka urges Ogun to be ruthless even as he himself
had been and as Atunda also was, for when man or god is
the agent of destiny he need not show remorse or recognize,
as Ogun did in *Idanre*, "the pattern of the spinning rock."

Section III is the poet's own rationalization of Ogun's
decision to embark upon a military campaign. It is not
vengeance, says the poet, that the god represents, not hate,
nor brute force, but justice, hope and the need for self-
fulfillment and self-realization for an oppressed people:

> Our songs acclaim
> Cessation of a long despair, extol the ends
> Of Sacrifice born in our will, not weakness
> We celebrate the end of that complaint
> Innocence of our millennial trees.

And to the prophets of dialogue, of that subterfuge otherwise known as diplomacy, to the great rhetoricians of "sightless violence" to whom Ogun might appear to be no more than a blood-thirsty anarchist, the prototype of Yeats's rough beast (or Soyinka's Atunda) who unleashes disorder upon nature, Soyinka recalls Yeats's ("Easter 1916") in which Yeats says that violence can beget a terrible beauty:

> When, safely distanced, throned in saintly
> Censure, the prophet's voice possesses you—
> Mere anarchy is loosed upon the world et cetera
> Remember too, the awesome beauty at the door of
> birth.

Soyinka had endeavored to sustain reader interest in this impersonal poem through twenty-two pages. He manages his lines with caution although occasionally the verse degenerates into doggerel in those passages where he strives for self-conscious wit. The word play in the following examples is amateurish:

> Dialogue chased its tail, a dogged dog
> Dodging the febrile bark
> Of Protest.

> Ogun is the tale that wags the dog
> All dogs, and all have had their day

> Hope

> Has fled the Cape miscalled Good Hope

Much of the poem's unsatisfactory flavor can be attributed to its occasional character. In those passages where Soyinka speaks in his own voice, self-manipulation tends to give way to passion.

Notes

1. Wole Soyinka, "And After the Narcissist?" *African Forum*, Vol. 1, No. 4 (Spring 1966), p. 59 (for all quotations).

2. Wole Soyinka, "The Fourth Stage," in *Myth Literature and the African World* (Cambridge: Cambridge University Press, 1976), p. 160.

3. Wole Soyinka, *Idanre and Other Poems* (London: Methuen, 1967), p. 72. Hereafter referred to as *Idanre*.

4. *Idanre*, p. 61. All quotations and references are taken from this edition.

5. *Ibid.*, p. 86.

6. At the beginning of the second part of *The Interpreters*, rainfall is treated in epic terms.

7. *Idanre*, p. 87. For more information on Ajantala, see Wole Soyinka and D. O. Fagunwa, *The Forest of a Thousand Daemons* (London: Thomas Nelson, 1968), pp. 106–115.

8. *Myth and Literature*, p. 152.

9. *Idanre*, p. 57.

10. *Myth and Literature*, p. 144.

11. *Ibid.*, p. 145.

12. *Ibid.*, p. 146.

13. *Idanre*, p. 45.

14. *Myth and Literature*, p. 141.

15. *Idanre*, p. 87.

16. Cited also by Gerald Moore, *Wole Soyinka* (London: Evans, 1978), p. 96, in illustration of Soyinka's strained and turgid language.

17. Wole Soyinka, *Ogun Abibimañ* (London: Rex Collings, 1976).

PART TWO

FICTIONAL AND
AUTOBIOGRAPHICAL PROSE

△ △

4

INTERPRETING
THE INTERPRETERS

THE NARRATIVE TECHNIQUE

The Interpreters has acquired a reputation as a difficult work. It was probably the first modernist novel published in English by a West African writer. Soyinka's experiments with time, his preference for a nonlinear narrative approach, the frequent interruptions in the story line, all recall the changes in British fiction in the first decades of the present century. Alan Friedman, in his study of the characteristic features of this fiction, uses the image of the cobweb to define its structure: "(the structure of) the novel gradually underwent a change: from the structure of a ladder to the structure of a cobweb." Speaking of the experiments with time and plot, Friedman adds:

> The rendering of time—the triumph of the story teller's art in every age—underwent extraordinary modifications. The present moment together with the layers of the past, all of time buried in consciousness, all of time available there, became fair game for any degree of manipulation that might help illuminate the new centre, the self. The fragmentation of the story-line which resulted from this unexampled freedom to move through time quickly became kaleidoscopic. The primary importance of plot ("the ladder") was called into question. Instead, the evocation of symbols to serve as centering nodes upon which meaning could condense, to give coherence and structure to

> the flux of the novel, became a useful but strange kind
> of network ("the cobweb radiating from the self") that
> offered to the replace the framework of the plot.[1]

Friedman is describing the experiments of Henry James, Joseph Conrad, and James Joyce, but his observations are also true of Soyinka's methods or even Armah's.

The Interpreters has no continuous and firmly-established story line; it has, instead, a series of apparently unrelated, and sometimes symbolic, episodes featuring the major characters. Soyinka abandons linear narrative in favor of labyrinthine movement. The narrative shuttles back and forth as it shifts its focus arbitrarily from the present preoccupations of the major characters to their pasts, back again to the present and, sometimes, to the future. The transitions from the past to the present are managed with minimal aid of traditional transitional "signatures"; the reader must rely on his own ingenuity to reconnect the broken ends of the narrative.

Details of action and scene are deliberately obscure; and we cannot rely on the interpreters to clarify issues for us, for these are generally ironic and ambiguous in their utterances. Characters' gestures, hints, innuendoes, and half-statements are more meaningful as modes of communication than informative statements. The "interpreters" themselves are young professionals and intellectuals, a self-conscious group who interpret developments in society and grope for self-understanding in a kind of self-analysis.

But the novel's experimental structure cannot be explained solely in terms of Western modernism. Soyinka's Western education has brought him into contact with modernist techniques; but this education has been enriched by his own cultural heritage. His allusion to the Yoruba gods has given his novel a profound mythological background. Its free movement through time might be connected with the intermingling of past, present, and future in the Yoruba concept of time. The novel's complex structure and its dense verbal texture reflect the personal idiosyncracies of its author and those of his patron deity, Ogun. Ogun is the god of complexity, of contradictions or ambiguity, as well as of uniqueness and experiment.

Still, in spite of its technical innovations, *The Interpreters* has not been unanimously applauded by readers and critics. The bone of contention is Soyinka's language and the manner in which his narrative is structured. The objections on these grounds are most vociferously articulated by the Sierra Leonian critic, Eustace Palmer:

> Verbal dexterity and linguistic sophistication almost become ends in *themselves*. Soyinka rejoices in his power over words but this power is not always related to meaning. . . . Then there is the problem of the novel's structure. It is surely extravagant praise to describe *The Interpreters* as "a well-conceived whole" or to suggest that the stage of narration gives the novel compactness of structure and a feeling of wholeness of conception. The dominant impression left by *The Interpreters* is one of a tedious formlessness.[2]

The manipulation of language may have been overdone, but style has its reasons. Where Soyinka has overindulged his power over words, it is with the deliberate intention of achieving a poetic resonance or seeking to express in words a mystical and sometimes surrealistic experience which is difficult to articulate. The charge of "formlessness" recalls the early unfavorable reactions to Joyce's experiments. In the case of *the Interpreters*, such critics ignore the network of criss-crossing themes, allusions, and images that hold the work together. The theme of creation, for instance, runs throughout the novel in Kola's serviette sketches, the *apala* dancer's performance, Egbo's poetic utterances, Sekoni's technological handwork at the Ijoha power station, and in Joe Golder's singing. These low-keyed allusions to creation assume a larger dimension in Sekoni's "Wrestler" and Kola's "Pantheon," works of unquestionable creative insights. They serve as the culminating focus for the theme of creation at the end of the novel.

Part Two of the novel takes up the themes and issues announced in Part One. Egbo's Osa commitments continue to engage the interest of the intellectual interpreters; the themes of choice and of apostasy recur; the albino of Part One re-emerges; and Egbo's romance with the un-

named undergraduate student approaches a climax. The
gathering that concludes Part One anticipates the party
that brings Part Two to an end. The novel is developed, as
Juliet I. Okonkwo has admirably summed it up, "on a
cyclic and almost static framework of revelation and re-
affirmation."[3]

As for the flashbacks that have caused Palmer so much
uneasiness,[4] their apparent illogicality has its justification
in the Yoruba concept of time: In the Yoruba worldview, as
Soyinka tells us so often,[5] the demarcations in time are not
absolute. The boundary lines between past, present, and
future tend to evaporate. Egbo's reminiscences force themselves into his consciousness even as he is engaged with the
preoccupations of the immediate moment. The movement
back and forth from the past to the present in the narrative
structure may be intended to emphasize the continuing
relevance of the claims of the past upon the living. The
enduring relevance of this claim is one of the lessons that
Egbo must learn. Egbo tends to reject the past, but he finds
himself "incessantly drawn to the pattern of the dead"
(p. 11).[6] Assuming that in the Youruba world-view time is
fluid, it is perhaps futile to look for temporal logic in
Soyinka's flashbacks. The flashbacks rather operate by
means of an associational logic. Images or personages cross
the mind of the characters and call up past moments in
their lives in which these images or personages have played
some role. The major flashbacks in the novel are provoked
by the associational connections of three major images:
water, woman, and Sir Derinola. In the opening scene of
the novel, there is an unexpected rainstorm, and as the rain
water gathers itself into a pool in Egbo's glass, his mind
runs back to a boat journey with the other "interpreters" to
an ancient property of his in the creek neighborhood of
Osa. At this point the journey itself is re-enacted, and as it
goes on Egbo re-reads his memories. He was fourteen when
he last saw his maternal grandfather, the warlord of the
creeks. The Osa dynasty holds an ambiguous promise for
Egbo: it stands for sterility in spite of its "dark vitality"
(p. 12); hence, Egbo is unwilling to go ashore when the
party arrives at the creeks.

Egbo's boat journey leads to Sekoni's homeward voyage from Europe, laden with high hopes of his ambitious engineering programs for his country; and Egbo's erotic excitement at the voluptuous bosom and buttocks of the *apala* dancer, whom he named "Owolebi of the squelching oranges" (p. 122) recall memories of his encounter with the nightclub "matriarch" Simi, who initiated him into the mysteries of sex. The story of the initiation is suspended at the end of chapter 4, only to be taken up again in chapter 9 (p. 123), where it is juxtaposed with Egbo's recent romance with the unnamed student.

The starting point for Sagoe's surrealistic daydreams in chapter 5 is Sir Derinola. Sir Derinola's ghost has haunted Sagoe from the club (p. 20). At Dehinwa's flat the ghost of the ex-judge looms large in Sagoe's imagination. A flashback takes us back to Sagoe's traumatic interview with the Board of the *Independent Viewpoint*, chaired by Sir Derinola. The movement in time brings to light other scenes and situations which are associated with both the national daily, the *Independent Viewpoint*, and the former chairman of its board of governors, Sir Derinola. This backward shift leads to a description of the offices of the *Independent Viewpoint*, which paves the way for Sagoe's exposure of the intrigues of the corrupt board.

The narrative is consistently structured on the framework of memory from chapter 5 until the middle of chapter 7. The attempt to anchor the story in the present by resuming in chapter 5 the Sagoe–Dehinwa story which was broken off at the end of chapter 2 breaks down under the impact of the waves of reminiscences that pervade Sagoe's consciousness. It is only after the middle of chapter 7 (p. 107) that the narrative returns to the present. The reader is still following the progress of Sagoe's day after the night rendezvous at the club. From the middle of chapter 7, Sagoe is gradually recovering from the throes of hangover although he is sober enough to attend Sir Derinola's funeral later in the afternoon. When we meet Sagoe again, after his brief interview with the albino in chapter 8, he is an "enfant terrible," performing superbly at Professor Oguazor's party.

The narrative is static in Part Two. Nothing happens that has not been anticipated in the earlier section. The albino's mystical experience of death and Noah's apostasy receive further attention and are incorporated into Kola's canvas. The "Pantheon" and Sekoni's "Wrestler" assume greater importance as works of art. The question of making a choice between Osa and his Foreign Office appointment and between Simi and the "stranger woman," continues to torment Egbo. The differences between the community of pseudo-intellectuals and the interpreters persist silently and routinely. Sekoni's exhibition and Joe Golder's vocal concert bring the story to its climax in an episode that reaffirms the severance of self from self and of self from the community.

The action of the novel is frequently internalized. Egbo's dilemma of choice is an inner drama; it is not reinforced by external correlatives. The conflict between the interpreters and the community of wit is not dramatized. The flash-backs in the novel are verbal externalizations of what goes on in the mind. There is generally no grand action in human terms. Nature is violent but nothing drastic happens in the realm of human community. The novel's cyclic structure reinforces the theme of non-event, of the absence of human initiative.[7]

SOME MINOR MAJOR THEMES

Egbo's Osa heritage is linked up with the theme of power. Egbo admits in chapter 1 that kingship in the Osa dynasty is a position of power: "Oh there is power, all right. Either way. Ally with the new gods or hold them to ransom" (p. 13). Over a hundred pages later, in chapter 12, he returns to this subject: "My rejection of power was thoughtless" (p. 182).[8] Kola takes up the question of power at the beginning of chapter 15, and he examines its various implications. For Egbo, the main consideration is political power, but Kola has a wider view of power: political, creative, and physical power—"he had felt this sense of power, the knowledge of power within his hands, of the will to transform; and he understood then that medium was of little importance, that the act, on canvas or on

human material was the process of living and brought him
the intense fear of fulfilment" (p. 218). When Sekoni explodes with a formidable creative power, he produces a
tensely sculptured art work, "The Wrestler," which was
inspired by Bandele's unusual manifestation of physical
power in a nightclub brawl. There is a sexual dimension,
too, to the theme of power in relation to Egbo, who is
endowed with almost superhuman sexual energy: "And
Egbo, astonished at his flesh, unbelieving that from somewhere within him could come again this new pylon of
power, in the same night, barely two hours after his first
initiation" (p. 125). Later in this episode, power is linked
with poetic intuition, for Egbo leaves the den of the gods
with a divine knowledge which he calls "a power for
beauty" (p. 127).

Apostasy is an issue that is raised quite early in the
novel, and it embraces both the interpreters themselves and
Lazarus' new apostle, Noah. Apostasy occurs here in the
context of revolutionary action and of religious conversion.
It is a figure of speech in the one and can be understood
literally in the other. The interpreters are "apostates" in
the sense that they are unfaithful to their own social convictions: They lack the moral courage of the ideal society
they envision. They recognize that the system is corrupt but
they acquiesce in it, lending "pith to hollow reeds" as Egbo
puts it. They recognize the need for change, but they are
unwilling to try to bring it about: "Too busy," Egbo said
in self-mockery,

> although I've never discovered doing what. And that is
> what I constantly ask—doing what? Beyond propping
> up the herald-men of the future, slaves in their hearts
> and blubbermen in fact doing what? Don't you ever
> feel that your whole life might be sheer creek-surface
> bearing the burden of fools, a mere passage, a mere
> reflecting medium or occasional sheet mass controlled
> by ferments beyond you? (p. 13)[9]

Noah's apostasy has a religious connotation, but both
Egbo and Kola differ in their interpretation of this apostasy. To Egbo, Noah is a straightforward Judas because he

is untouched by the flurry of religious activities that goes
on in Lazarus' church. "I cannot like the new apostle,"
Egbo said. "He looks submissive not redeemed. I find his
air of purity just that—air. There is no inner radiance in
the boy" (p. 177). Kola, on the other hand, sees Noah as a
false Christ because he submits himself meekly though
thoughtlessly to a Jesus role which is imposed on him by
Lazarus and his church. The difference between the interpreters' apostasy and Noah's is that Noah is not aware of
what he is, while the interpreters are social apostates by
choice. On Kola's canvas Noah represents the first apostate
in the Yoruba mythology, Atunda; but that role, according
to Egbo, is misconceived, for "Noah's apostasy is not the
wilful kind, it is simply the refusal to be, the refusal to be a
living being, like a moon" (p. 231).

The interpreters suffer from an oppressive sense of alienation and rootlessness. They are alienated from both the
academic and civil service arms of the establishment, and at
the end of the novel they are alienated from themselves.
Sekoni is the victim of the hostility of the system towards
genuine intellectual integrity. His death is a ritual sacrifice
to the demigods of the system on behalf of the interpreters.
Many critics[10] have commented on the psychological de-
fences the interpreters have erected for themselves against
the psychic disintegration that ruined Sekoni: Egbo retreats
to the loneliness of the rocks, and Sagoe makes verbal
excursions into the philosphy of "voidancy," a pun on the
idle activities of the intellectual.

Joe Golder's isolation on the stage is a dramatic representation not only of his own loneliness but of the general
position of the interpreters as alienated individuals. The
image of the lone actor performing on the stage has frequently served Soyinka as a symbol of divine and human
estrangement. His god Ogun, who is the "the first darer
and conqueror of transition," is also "the first actor";[11] and
in another context he writes:

> The spectacle of a lone human figure under a spot-
> light on a darkenend stage is . . . a breathing, living,
> pulsating, threatening fragile example of (the cosmic
> human condition).[12]

In *The Interpreters* Joe Golder represents such a spectacle:

> Some bones on that stage were bared, sandbags and transverses, collapsible platforms billowing black drapes on the two sides, two naked spots converging and Joe Golder. Beyond him, deep void and total dark, and Joe Golder. And outwards from the black edges of the moveable proscenium which framed him, an archaic figure disowned from a family album, Joe Golder sought the world in hope, the faceless, unfathomed world, a total blank for the man whose every note tore him outward. Joe Golder bared his soul, mangled, spun in murky fountains of grief which cradled him, the long-lost child (p. 245).

Alienation is one theme that links Simi, the seductive anima and sex goddess, by association to the interpreters. In spite of her overpowering physical charms, she is a tragic figure; her clammy eyes emit an aura of sadness (p. 257). Self-fulfillment for her can only come through sexual consummation. Her name means "drag me into (sexual?) well-being."

Art offers the interpreters a means of escape from the emptiness of their "creek surface" existence; each is to some measure an artist. Egbo is a mystic poet, and both he and Bandele are connected with the major artistic creations in the book: Kola's canvas and Sekoni's "Wrestler." Sagoe the journalist is also an essayist, and we learn from Kola that "Sagoe has a sort of seventh sense, a kind of creative antenna with which he pursues his vocation" (p. 228). Kola and Sekoni have at last attained self-fulfillment through art; the other interpreters achieve a sense of vicarious fulfillment in the masterly creations of these two major artists. The "Pantheon" or the "Wrestler" is not just the work of one man but a group achievement of the community of alienated interpreters. Art, as represented by the "Pantheon" and the "Wrestler" gives meaning to the life of the interpreters in contrast with the apostles of etiquette, the Oguazors and the Ayo Faseyis, who find fulfillment in social recognition. Art extends its promise of salvation to both the *apala* dancer and to Joe Golder. At the beginning

of the novel and at the end, both the lone dancer and Joe
Golder attain self-realization through the act of dance and
of song.

But in a sense, art is inadequate as a means of achieving
ultimate salvation, especially for the religious sceptics
among the interpreters. The world of art on Kola's canvas
points boldly to what is missing in their lives, that is,
religion, or the link between the human and the divine.
Sekoni offers early in the novel a clue to the image of the
bridge which occurs at the end (his stammer is eliminated
for easy reading):

> we must accept the universal dome because there is no
> direction. The bridge is the dome of religion and
> bridges don't just go from here to there; a bridge also
> faces backwards (p. 9).

It is not by accident that Lazarus, the major voice of religion after Sekoni, is the link. Noah cannot be the link
because he is faceless, neutral, passive, and negative.

Two mythologies meet on Kola's canvas: the Yoruba
myth of creation and the Biblical account of how the world
was repeopled after the Great Flood. Lazarus introduces the
biblical motif. He appears as "an arched figure rising not
from a dry grave, but from a primordial chaos of gaseous
whorls and flood-waters" (p. 132). Kola's contact with Lazarus and the overpowering vehemence of floods in the
novel encourage him to add a biblical dimension to the
canvas much to the dismay of his mentor, Egbo. Kola
modifies the original design for the "Pantheon" according
to his own creative intuition. Lazarus serves as the symbol
of the relationship between life and death because he has
experienced the worlds of the living and the dead. In both
the Christian and the Yoruba worldviews, death and life
are interrelated—death is only a gateway to a higher form
of life. For the Yorubas, especially, the dead are ever present
in the lives of the living. The integration of Lazarus into
the structure of the "Pantheon" is the stroke of a master
craftsman. Egbo recognizes the significance of Lazarus'
role, but he dismisses it as "an optimist's delusion of continuity" (p. 233). It is Sekoni (again) who has prepared us for

the correct response: "To make such distinctions disrupts the dome of continuity, which is what life is" (p. 9).

Egbo quarrels also with the just representation of the only Ogun we know in the novel: the Ogun who plays with knife and blood—"The moment that you say *to*, my knife will go in the neck of this ram. *To*, and a fountain of blood will strike the ceiling of this studio" (p. 225). Egbo has not manifested the positive virtues of Ogun's personality in his conduct and attitudes. He shrinks from the one commitment that would have redeemed him and his god; he is unable to accept his responsibility towards the unnamed undergraduate woman.

Though he is an artist, Egbo fails to recognize that an artist surrenders himself body and soul to the muse in the process of creation; for the "Pantheon" is as much a work on creation myths as a manifestation of the operation of the creative process itself. Inspiration comes in fits and starts as Kola struggles to trap moments of experience "with the primal slime of all creations" (p. 237). As he says, "my intimations of all these presences have been too momentary and they come in disjointed fragments" (p. 228). Kola's poor rating of his own artistic skills should be viewed with reservation. He is unquestionably a gifted artist and can say of the "Pantheon" in a less guarded moment that "it is weight. It will confound the senses, brow-beat objective responses" (p. 228). It is normal, of course, for an artist to underrate his own powers. Demoke of *A Dance of the Forests* was equally dissatisfied with his work on the totem although independent observers thought it was the kind of action that redeems mankind.

THE "INTERPRETERS" THEMSELVES

Soyinka used the term "interpreter" in a broad sense. Interpretation is, for him, the act of evaluating experience. The reader is himself a major interpreter as are the religious mystic, Lazarus, and his unworthy acolyte, Noah. However, the major interpreters in the book are the introspective, questioning intellectuals: Egbo, Kola, Sekoni, Bandele and Sagoe.

Egbo sees mystery in things; life for him is a ritual. The

Osa pilgrimage is senseless but necessary, for it establishes
an ambiguous link between him and his past. There cannot be a definite commitment to the past; it can only be
relived through ritual pilgrimages, for therein lies the
much-needed escape from the "creek surface." Nor can
there be a question of making a choice between the past
and the present; there is only his fear of drowning.

Egbo loves groves and sacred places where he can commune with the dark recesses of his psyche: "I truly yearned
for the dark. I love life to be still, mysterious" (p. 9), and
again near the creek: "Egbo put his hand in the water and
dropped his eyes down to the brackish stillness, down the
dark depths to its bed of mud" (p. 8). The dark he yearns for
includes the labyrinths of a woman's being. The sexual act
for him is like a descent into the dark; he relives its mysteries through a physical immersion into the womb of darkness. Images of darkness feature in Egbo's celebrations of
the mysteries of sex: "in darkness let me lie . . . in darkness
cry" (p. 127).

Egbo incarnates the darker aspects of Ogun's personality. He has the perception to assess the predicaments of his
fellow interpreters whom he calls a "company of alienates
. . . caught in a common centrifuge through the hurt of
gilded abstractions, full of flies, reaching for a long time-
whisk to brush away thought-smarts embedded in each
sting" (p. 221). With his gift of mind goes a weakness for
women and a morbid anguish of indecision. If Kola dares
not be truly fulfilled, Egbo would never be committed. He
finds himself defeated before the pride and self-confidence
of "the stranger girl" whom he branded "the new woman
of my generation" (p. 235). His inability to possess her
fully leaves him bitterly frustrated; the frustration spills
over into his relationship with Simi. Near the end of the
novel Egbo is a lonely man isolated by his friends and by
nature herself because of his failure to accept responsibility
for this baby of the undergraduate student. The crackles of
thunder remind him of Bandele's anger, and the rain refuses to soothe his sorrows:

> the clouds held the water, though he longed for the
> rain to fall, to break, even if the sky held firm, to break

> at least the earth beneath his feet into loose sands,
> liberate his skin from the fevered tingling into the
> running freedom of skin clarity, bared quartz in quick
> runnels, hearing his racing heart pound now slow but
> strong against staggered flagstones of threaded granite
> . . . but the rains stayed dry above him and the earth
> was mere wet clods against his futile kicks. (pp. 245–
> 246)

Kola is a dedicated artist, conscious of his limitations
and unsparing in his self-criticism. He is a modest ap-
praiser of his own abilities, for he is indeed gifted. He is at
the center of the novel within the context of the theme of
creation. He works on his canvas for fifteen months and
thus helps us to measure the temporal span of the novel's
action from the Cambana Club to Sekoni's exhibition. The
god represented on Kola's canvas provide the novel with
metaphysical depth. The bridge inserted on the canvas at
its completion is the symbol of what Soyinka elsewhere
calls the "gulf of transition,"[13] a pathway by which contact
is maintained between men and the gods and by which
peace and harmony are assured in both the human and the
divine worlds. Kola's bridge established "contact" in the
world of art as an ironic reminder of the "night of severance" in the human world. Kola the artist evaluates for the
reader the mood of the interpreters towards the close of the
novel:

> And Kola, who tried to see it all, who tried to clarify
> the pieces within the accommodating habit of time,
> felt much later, in a well-ordered and tranquil mo-
> ment, that it was a moment of frustration that what
> was lacking that night was the power to shake out
> events one by one, to space them in intervening stand-
> stills of the period of creation. (p. 244).

Sekoni's physical exit in the novel occurs in Part Two,
but it has been sufficiently foreshadowed as early as the first
chapter, in which his personality and temperament are so
strongly presented. Although his physical presence is brief,
his shadow dominates the novel because Sekoni has re-

incarnated himself in the lasting artistic monument he leaves behind. "The Wrestler" is the symbol of what his life has been all along—struggle. The imprisoned energy within him is expressed in two instances of powerful creations: the experimental power station of Ijioha and "The Wrestler".

At the beginning of the novel, religion is represented by Sekoni. His is the only religious voice to counter the blasphemous chatter of the other interpreters. In the second half of the novel, Sekoni's role as the voice of religion is transferred to Lazarus. Of all the interpreters, only Bandele benefits from Sekoni's sudden death and Lazarus' mystical experience of resurrection. Bandele's unyielding moral sensitivity gathers intensity throughout the novel. Sekoni's death and Lazarus' story of his resurrection from death bring home to Bandele the reality of death. Of his visit to Lazarus' church, Bandele said:

> I would not have been curious to hear Lazarus if Sekoni had not recently died. Deep inside me, I suppose that was why I came. (p. 181)

And about Lazarus and his story Bandele continues:

> I was curious. It gave me a strange feeling to sit opposite him at that table and hear him claim that he had died. (p. 181)

Towards the end of the novel, Bandele becomes the voice of religion and of moral conscience, replacing Sekoni, who is dead, and Lazarus, whom the interpreters distrust. Because he is their equal, Bandele's opinion carries far greater weight among his colleagues than Lazarus' testimony. Bandele's new role is strongly emphasized toward the end of the novel: "Bandele sat like a timeless image brooding over lesser beings" (p. 244). He is almost a god among men, a Jupiter hurling a verbal hammer of reprimand against those who have offended against the moral law. At one point in the novel his anger is the anger of nature herself, protesting against Egbo's failure to acknowledge his responsibility towards the helpless student he has impregnated:

> Egbo had walked nearly the length of the college,
> indifferent to the gathering of the mercury pall above
> him, the sudden dry crackles which electrified his skin
> as when his hair would rise along the arm in waves to
> a passing comb. They reminded him of the quality of
> Bandele's anger, a static current breaking clean har-
> mattan air, a quiet russle of antagonism. (p. 245)

For Kola, Bandele's uncompromising moral principles give meaning to his life; he has at least something to live for: his conscience. On Kola's canvas Bandele should represent Orisa-nla, the Supreme deity.

Sagoe is the most active critic of society among the interpreters. His journalistic career has brought him into contact with all segments of society; a sizeable cross-section of Lagos society is subjected to his bitter moral scrutiny: globe-trotting managing directors, corrupt corporation chairmen, inconsiderate and hypocritical university wits and even the mob itself. Sagoe's coverage of Lagos society is crowded into four chapters (5-8). The tone of his satirical strictures is passionate and ruthless. Of the barbarism of a murderous mob bearing down upon a youth suspected of theft, he says:

> It was not merely that he wanted the crowd to learn a
> lesson—it was doubtful if they were capable of that—
> but he had become used to a thinking which required
> the sharp, violent focusing of dormant problems. Like
> the casual barbarism of such a crowd, their treachery
> against those who were momentarily below them in
> daily debasement. (p. 115)

Lagos city itself is viewed against a background of filth and squalor which anticipates the moral and physical decadence of its people. Physical setting as an index of moral and physical decadence is suggested in the case of the canteen girl of the *Independent Viewpoint*; the odor of dish

water around the canteen is complemented by the stench
emanating from the girl's body:

> It was difficult to tell what gave the special quality to
> the smell in the canteen, there was the greasy water in
> which yesterday's lunch plates were soaked, or it could
> be the sweaty girl who served the staff in a stupor, a
> mere eighteen at the most, and her movements sug-
> gested a knee-deep wadding of sanitory towels. And
> she remained clogged all twenty-eight days of her
> cycle. Eyelids gelled to—it would appear—her navel,
> her only extraneous movement was to wipe her fore-
> head with an arm that revealed an armpit in alternate
> streaks of black and white, powder and grime. Her
> whitened face further confirmed a daily toilet of
> powder, never water. (p. 73)

Sagoe was at the height of his excitement at the Oguazor's party. The artificial company there acted as castor oil
to his psyche, resulting in a diarrhoea-like voidance.

THE CONTENTS OF THE "PANTHEON"

Chapter 16 opens with an inventory of the gods depicted
in the "Pantheon" as prefaced with allusions to the Yoruba
creation myth. The Yorubas believe that the world was
created by their supreme deity, Olodumare. The "flood"
and "fogs" of the beginning are the "watery marshy
waste"[14] that eventually became the earth after Olodumare
had decided to create the world. The "first messenger" is
the chameleon. Olodumare assigned the duties related to
earth's creation to his vice-regent Orisa-nla (Obatala)
whom he provided with the following materials for the job:
a bag containing loose earth, a five-toed hen, and a pigeon.
When Orisa-nla descended on the watery void, he placed
the loose earth on a convenient spot and let loose the hen
and the pigeon to scatter and spread the grains of sand on
the watery waste. This they did until what is known as "the
earth" was created. The hen is alluded to in chapter 16 as
"a fowl" and the loose earth as the "thimble of earth."

The allusion to "the first apostate" refers to the creation of the other gods in the Yoruba pantheon. Orisa-nla was supposed to have been the first and only deity. His slave-god, Atunda, jealously rolled a boulder on the back of his unsuspecting master and shattered him into fragments, each of which reformed itself into a god in its own right. Thus was born the Yoruba pantheon. Another version of the myth claims that Orunmila, the god of Wisdom, had been created before the fragmentation of the godhead essence in Orisa-nla. Orunmila "picked up and pieced together with devotion" the shattered fragments of the arch-divinity.[15] The "shell of the tortoise around divine breath" is the broken piece of the godhead essence that later reformed itself into a god. It is also an extension of the godhead essence in the arch-divinity shared by each succeeding deity in the pantheon. In his essay "The Fourth Stage," Soyinka designates Obatala as the "delicate shell of the originl fullness";[16] and in the poem *Idanre* he speaks of the fragmentation and the re-formation of the broken essence into a new divine whole in the following terms: "Piecemeal was their deft/Re-birth, a cupped shell of tortoise, staggered/Tile tegument."[17]

Before the earth was created, the gods descended on the watery waste by means of spiders' webs. The spider's web is probably what is meant by the "endless chain for the summons of the god." The "phallus of unorigin" is a creation motif, symbol of the creative potency of Olodumare and his agent, Orisa-nla; its female counterpart is the "sky-hole." But the allusions to the "endless chain" and to the "phallus of unorigin" may evoke the god of wisdom and divination, Orunmila. This god is endowed with special wisdom and foreknowledge of the origins of the world, of man and of the gods themselves, in consequence of which he is known as the oracle divinity. The summoning of the gods is a metaphor for divination, a process by which the wishes of the gods are ascertained. The gods, too, consult Orunmila for the details of their own destiny.[18] The "endless chain" is therefore the divination chain known in Yoruba as *Opele* (see Appendix 1)[19] and the "phallus of unorigin" is the phallus-shaped instrument of divination, the *Iroke* (see Appendix 2), and the sky-hole is the divination tray, the *Opon Ifa*, which is circular in shape (see Appendix 3). The Ifa priest invokes the spirit of *Ifa* by knocking the divination tray with *Iroke* to produce a sonorous sound.[20] But since the gods themselves consult Orunmila for the details of their own destiny, the phallus of unorigin pointing to the sky-hole suggests cosmic divination. The allusions in this passage evoke the attributes of Orunmila.

The "unblemished one" is Obatala, the god of creation. He was empowered by Olodumare to mold man's physical form, while Olodumare reserved for himself the task of breathing life into the human shapes. Obatala made cripples, albinos, and the deformed while he was under the influence of palm wine. He is directly addressed as the "unblemished god" in the "The Fourth Stage."[21]

The "lover of gore" is Ogun, the god of war, guardian of the road, the creative essence, explorer, artisan, hunter, god of iron and metallurgy. He massacred his own men in error at the battle of Ire. The myth of Ogun is told in Soyinka's essay, "The Fourth Stage," and in the long poem *Idanre*.

The "one who hanged and did not hang" is Sango, the god of thunder and lightning, and, formerly, the third King of Oyo. As the head of the Oyo Kingdom he was noted for his tyranny and cruelty. His authority was challenged by two powerful chiefs in his kingdom whom Sango tried to eliminate by forcing them into a military confrontation with each other. The stronger of the chiefs faced the king after subduing his opponent. Sango was, however, unable to take up the challenge; he hanged himself as a face-saving gesture, but he was apotheosized after his death as the god of thunder and lightning. His apotheosis nullified his suicide hence the saying "the king did not hang," which in Yoruba is *"Oba koso."*

The "bisexed one" is Erinle, an animal spirit who is believed to have two sexes. He was drowned in a river, which was then named after him.[22]

The allusions to the "parting of the fog and the retreat of the beginning" evoke Ifa, the god of divination and order. The "fog" is a metaphor for the unknown that can only be ascertained through divination. Divination or the process of knowing is referred to as "the retreat of beginning," for

the Yorubas believe that man's destiny is sealed at birth.
The role of Ifa as the god of divination is suggested in the
passage: "the eternal war of divining eyes, of the hundred
and one eyes of lore, fore and after vision." Soyinka sees Ifa
as separate from Orunmila. Orunmila is for him the "es-
sense of wisdom," while Ifa is the god of divination and
order.[23] However, most Yoruba scholars think of Orunmila
and Ifa as one and the same god.[24]

The words that immediately follow the phrase "fore-
and after-vision" introduce another god, Esu, the god of
chance. Esu, the god of chance and disruption, has a sickle
head (see Appendix 4). The war image in which Esu is
presented alludes to Olodumare's "war" and Orunmila
who with Esu thwarts the designs of both the gods and
mankind. Ogun's fatal error at the battle of Ire is believed
to have been the handwork of Esu.[25]

The "repulsive scourge riding purulent on noontides of
silent heat" is Sopona, the god of smallpox; and the "one
who stayed to tend the first fruits of the ginger earth" is
Ela. He is not endowed with any particular quality, but he
is believed to have been appointed by Olodumare to "orga-
nise earth's affairs and set things in their proper places."[26]
He is the god that sets things right. As Bolaji Idowu has
affirmed, the name Ela means "Safety" or "One who keeps
in safety," "Preservation," or "Preserver."[27] The festival of
the first fruits, especially that of the new yam, is called in
Yoruba Ela.

Two other gods mentioned in the book but not listed in
chapter 16 are Obaluwaiye (p. 50), the respectful name for
Sopona, and Esumare (p. 227), the god of the rainbow.

The "Pantheon" features the primordial deities only.
There are over a thousand gods and goddesses in Yoruba
myth, but only those who were with Olodumare at the
beginning of things are here represented.

LANGUAGE

Soyinka's language is dense, compact, and sometimes
eccentric, and the novel owes part of its appeal to its linguistic eccentricity, to the author's originality in his de-

ployment of words. The very first sentence requires an act of "interpretation" on the reader's part. "Metal on concrete jars my drink lobes," says Sagoe in a fit of subdued anger. The deliberate syntactical ambiguity begins to straighten itself out on a second reading when it becomes apparent that Soyinka refers to the effect on Sagoe's "drink lobes" of the scraping of a metal chair on a concrete floor. Such a sound is an especial irritant to someone who is intoxicated or in a state of meditation. The "drink lobes" pose their own semantic problem. Eldred Jones thinks of them as a "poetic rather than a physiological organ."[28] The lobes may allude also to the frontal lobes of the brain, and Sagoe might be thinking in terms of the effect of alcohol on the brain. When he is at the saturation point, alcohol transports him into a transcendent world much like the experience felt by religious mystics in moments of ecstasy. The sound of metal on concrete recalls him unwillingly to earth.

As an opening sentence, however, the strange expression is effective; its stark directness jolts the reader into a compulsory attentiveness. He must be on the alert all the time if he intends to keep up with the frequent juggling with words. And yet, in spite of the abrupt, casual tone of Sagoe's remark, the images are premeditated. The attributes of the Yoruba gods Ogun (metal) and Obatala (concrete or mud) lurk at the back of Soyinka's mind in the allusion to "metal" and "concrete." These deities are, respectively, the gods of creativity and of creation in Yoruba mythology. The indirect allusion to both gods in these images points to the theme of creation which is central in the novel.

A mystical aura hangs over language in general in the entire novel, which can be accounted for by the fact that the interpreters and even the narrator himself (the implied author) speak under possession. The language of the novel is the language of possessed artists. Egbo, Sagoe, Sekoni, Kola—all make their utterances in moments of possession. In Yoruba society, the oral performer or the actor on the stage is a man possessed, who very often surrenders his personality to the external forces whose mouthpiece he has become. In a possessed utterance, as Soyinka has noted, language is "highly charged, symbolic, mytho-embryonic," and words "are taken back to their roots, to their original poetic sources when fusion was total and the movement of words is the very passage of music and the dance of images." [29]

The critics who charge Soyinka with verbal mystification have not reckoned with the influence of Soyinka's native Yoruba language. In the Yoruba community, all human activities revert to ritual and ceremony. In *The Interpreters*, too, actions are frequently transformed into ritual and ceremony, from which they easily drift from their terrestrial settings to cosmic dimensions. The extension of actions to a perspective that is epical and ritualistic accounts for the charged poetry, the formal diction, and the ritual echoes we encounter not only in this novel but also in *Season of Anomy*. Sekoni's engineering dreams are epical; the *apala* dancer's response to drum music becomes a ritual dance; Egbo's lovemaking is meaningful only when the gods have been summoned to witness it; and rainfalls "deluge/Earth in fevered distillations."

The language in the passage on Sekoni's technological schemes at the beginning of the novel is mythopoetic; the personages that are evoked in that passage are primordial beings: "primeval giants," "brooding matriarchs," "mammoth rolls," and columns of rock which are "petrifications of divine droppings from eternity" (p. 26).

The *apala* dancer herself is no ordinary woman but a symbol of "Black Immanence." The peace that radiates from her face is the "Transcendental stillness of the distanced godhead" (p. 24). Her musical possession is a ritual dance in which she holds a private communion with nature. It is Egbo, the mystic poet, who is most affected by her movement:

> Egbo no longer heard. Seeking to see through the dancer's eyelids which closed slowly until she saw nothing of the leaking armpits of the umbrella centrepiece, and the water ran through her indulgent as hidden hills, sacred. She should have, Egbo decided, *iyun* around her ankles, antimony rings on her breasts and light tooth marks, a full circle of flat volleys sunk in antimony. (p. 23)

The lone dancer will reappear in *Season of Anomy* as Iriyise, and she will be decked with similar bangles of honor made of antimony and decorated with chalk and camwood.

Egbo's sexual excitement finds an outlet in incantatory utterances:

> I am that filled bag in a stiff breeze riding high grass on Warri airfield. (p. 60)

> And a lone pod strode the baobab on the tapering thigh, leaf-shorn, and high mists swirl him, haze-splitting storms, but the stalk stayed him. . . . (p. 60)

Later, he celebrates the "freeing of the man" in company of the gods. His loss and gain attain epic proportions. With his energies sapped by his physical exertions on the night of initiation, Egbo is

> like the quarry at Abeokuta when all granite had been blown apart and nothing but mud-waters of the rain fill the huge caverns underground. (p. 125)

And when he has been born again after his immersion into the womb of darkness, he sees himself as a traveller who has bearded the gods in their den and must depart with a divine boon (p. 127). Because Simi is unbroken and is perhaps unbreakable, her personality is merged with the landscape of the scene of celebration: "the light filled waters in rock-pools were the weave of Simi's eyes" (p. 126), and Egbo thinks it is proper that he should bathe in "Simi's tears."

On the eve of his loss of innocence Egbo felt a terror that rocked the foundations of the universe:

> his body was in that instant gelled to the earth and heavens, and the pull of life within his sensuousness he felt as the rending of heavenly vaults and upheaval in earth's core;

and we are told that

no single man had the right to feel what he felt, to
command rebellions of the ordered cosmos in the with-
ering of his boastful rise amidst talcumed brambles.
(p. 123)

Natural phenomena fulfil themselves through heroic actions. Part Two opens with a powerful description of a
tropical downpour:

The rains of May become in July slit arteries of the
sacrificial bull, a million bleeding punctures of the
sky-bull hidden in convulsive cloud humps, black,
overfed for this one event, nourished on horizon tops
of endless choice of grazing, distant beyond giraffe
reach. (p. 155)

Soyinka's epic imagination is out of gear in this overwrit-
ten passage. "Bull" as an image for rain clouds is a metaphysical conceit, more ingenious than appropriate. It falls
short, even if one is thinking of a cosmic bull, of the
enormous mass and size of atmospheric cloud formations
in the rainy season; "giraffe reach" does not quite convey
the sense of cosmic distance intended, and the information
about the sky-bull's grazing grounds is superfluous rhetoric.

The passage is replete with Soyinka's favorite ritual images: "bull," and the traumatic palpitations of its "convulsive cloud-humps." Later in the novel, the severed throat of
the sacrificial black ram slaughtered by Egbo to mark the
completion of Kola's canvas rocks itself in tremulous death
throes:

and they all stood, horrified, round the reek of blood
and the convulsive vessel of the severed throat. (p. 243)

In *Season of Anomy* one is confronted with the image of
an enormous sacrificial bull "proud-horned" and "rich-
humped";[30] and at the work site at Shage in the same novel,
Ofeyi

> looked upwards at the shifting cloud-humps at the sky
> as yet undarkened by a hint of rain and muttered—
> when again? (p. 176)

The epithets are deliberately invested with an epic
energy. Soyinka, the poet who celebrates the deeds of heroic
gods, frames his epithets on a double-montage in the urge
to situate them in the context of action. Ogun is the
"blood-spattered fiend," a "gore-blinded thug," or "a
damned blood-thirsty maniac" (p. 233), and Sango is "the
snake-tongued lightning" (p. 225).

The image-making process sometimes overrides all other
considerations, including those of clarity. Occasionally
Soyinka overworks his images by compelling them to strike
a forced analogy. For example, Kola, grieved by Lasunwon's irreverent remarks on the late Sekoni, is a "rain-
drop" suspended on "the roof-edge":

> Kola risen, a quivering rain-drop on the roof-edge,
> and then, collapsed into his seat, his face buried in his
> hands. (p. 164)

Kola is deeply moved by Lasunwon's unkind allusions to
Sekoni, but to abstract Kola's whole personality into a rain-
drop strikes one as overlabored comparison. Similarly,
the comparison of Usaye to a moth is improbable:

> A warm yellow moth brushed him on the cheek and
> wedged itself between him and the low table. It peered
> short-sightedly into the glass in his hand, drank from
> it, screwed its face at the bitter taste. Then it pressed its
> face almost against Kola's relaxed fingers from which
> the nuts had nearly begun to drop. With her back
> against him, nuzzling his face with short plaited yel-
> low hair stood an albino girl. (p. 48)

Despite its rhetoric, the passage is unable to force a suspension of disbelief which would have made the analogy between a yellow-haired albino girl and a fluttering yellow
moth credible.

The claim that the novel is charged with high poetic moments needs to be substantiated. One clear example is the sheer lyricism of Egbo's intuitions when he is at his most poetic, such as when he is reacting to a different kind of possession, the religious.

> Egbo longed for the other possession, the triumph of serene joys and sublimated passions. The young maid of *Ela*. The transfigured wrinkles of *Orisa-nla*. Inertly rendered bodies and unearthly exultations in the eyes, and on the skin. Deft whispers of the godhead, numinous presence, flooding the medium's sympathy; in such communion he would partake, not in the woman's violation of the body. (p. 176)

Enhancing the poetic atmosphere is Soyinka's exploitation of the resonance and rhythms of words for their own sake: "apoplexies of turgid disciplinarian" (p. 204), and "optimist delusion of continuity" (p. 233). Sometimes sentences move gracefully like lines of verse to their close:

> midnight visitations of aunts and mothers bearing love, and transparent intentions, and manufactured anxieties, and quite simply, blood cruelty. (p. 39)

The prose style is light-hearted in Sagoe's "voidancy" essays (p. 71), cabalistic in the passage on Sekoni's homeward voyage from Europe (p. 26), and surrealistic in Egbo's recollection of childhood memories toward the end of the novel. In Egbo's daydreams "the movement of words is the very passage of music and the dance of images"; words and phrases collide into one another, unseparated, most of the time, by punctuation. For example,

> There were black rains from dwarf skies, and clean quicksands beneath his feet were drenched in this one dye of his choice. Joe Golder pressed his foot anywhere and springs uprushed of dye and old women's long straddled piss, straddled across the rims of their own dye-pots, and black pap frothing through black

> bubbles from cornices from black lava deep in the
> bowels of seasoned pots deep in rim levels with the
> ground, oh I've played among them Egbo said where
> old women dye their shrouds and grief is such women,
> old as the curse from snuff-lined throats. Joe Golder
> uprushing dye from quicksands stepped through the
> torn mouth of sunken cauldrons and wet shrouds
> swirling heavy in the wind, frothing indigo lather.
> They wrapped his feet and bore him round and round
> and down and down and the black bubbles were huge
> as Olokun's angered eyes bubbling, Egbo-lo, epulu-
> pulu, E-gbo-lo, e-pulu-pulu, E-gbo-lo. . . . (p. 246)

The prose is occasionally punctuated with the rhythms of
impressionistic statements, such as the haunting music of
the elliptical renderings of Egbo's impressions and intro-
spections around the Osa neighbourhood.

> Mud-dark stilts, and above them, whites and greys on
> smooth walls, and over these a hundred nests of thatch
> roofing. Dry-docked canoes in bright contrasts be-
> neath plank flooring, relics of the days when fishes
> over whom hunting rights were fought fed on the
> disputants. (p. 10)

and

> A shade of anger over his face, resentment at his fail-
> ure to bury the abortive quest finally, especially the
> promise it still held for him like a salvation. (pp. 14, 15)

Music, that is, ritualized utterance, is the main inspiration
for Soyinka's language. His sensitive ear is ever reaching
out for those words that are invested with specific musical
intonations. The obsession with music is Soyinka's inheritance from his ethnic culture. His language is affected by
the nature of his creative imagination. As a poet given to
the search for mystery in things and whose imagination
reaches out into the realm of the epical and the cosmic,
Soyinka's language is bound to be difficult. His personal
idiosyncracies as well as his neo-modernist temperament

have compelled him to rely increasingly on suggestive and allusive strategies rather than on narrative statements. His more obscure passages should be regarded as symbolist poems in which an atmosphere is more important than the literal meaning of the words.

Notes

1. Alan Friedman, "The Novel," in C. B. Cox and A. E. Dyson, eds., *The Twentieth Century Mind*, Vol. 1 (London: Oxford University Press, 1972), pp. 414 and 415.

2. Eustace Palmer, *An Introduction to African Novel* (London: Heinemann, 1972), p. xiv.

3. Juliet I. Okonkwo, "The Essential Unity of Soyinka's *The Interpreters* and *Season of Anomy*," *Ufahamu*, Vol. IX, No. 3 (1979–1980).

4. He insists that there is no "logic and inevitability" in Soyinka's use of flashbacks. See his recent book, *The Growth of the African Novel* (London: Heinemann, 1979), p. 242.

5. See the essay, "The Fourth Stage," in Wole Soyinka, *Myth, Literature and the African World* (Cambridge: Cambridge University Press, 1976), pp. 143–144. This work will hereafter be cited as *Myth and Literature*.

6. Wole Soyinka, *The Interpreters* (London: Heinemann, 1979), p. 11. Subsequent references are to this edition.

7. The non-event is a distinctive feature of modernist writing. See Michael Hollington, "Svevo, Joyce and Modernist Time," in Malcolm Bradbury and James McFarlane, eds., *Modernism* (Harmondsworth: Penguin, 1976), p. 430.

8. There is a brief reference to the theme of power in chapter 9, p. 120.

9. Marxist critics of African literature have castigated Soyinka for presenting in his works elitist effeminate heroes who pay lip service to social change. In *Season of Anomy* Soyinka endeavors to accommodate the views of

this school of thought by offering us two characters, Ofeyi and the Dentist, who believe in revolutionary action as a means of effecting changes in society (though they differ in their methods).

10. See Eustace Palmer, *The Growth of the African Novel*, pp. 245 and 248.

11. "The Fourth Stage," in *Myth and Literature*, p. 145.

12. Wole Soyinka, "Drama and the African World-View," in *Myth and Literature*, p. 41.

13. "The Fourth Stage," in *Myth and Literature*, p. 149.

14. E. Bolaji Idowu, *Olodumare: God in Yoruba Belief* (London: Longmans, 1977), p. 19. I am indebted to Idowu for much of the information given in this section on the Yorubu creation myth.

15. Idowu, pp. 99–100.

16. "The Fourth Stage," p. 153.

17. Wole Soyinka, *Idanre and Other Poems* (London: Methuen, 1967), p. 69.

18. See Wande Abimbola, *Ifa: An Exposition of Ife Literary Corpus* (Ibadan: Oxford University Press, 1976), p. 115.

19. The pictures in the appendices are reproduced from Wande Abimbola, *Ifa*, plates 2, 3, 4, and 10.

20. Abimbola, *Ifa*, p. 12.

21. "The Fourth Stage," p. 143.

22. R. C. Abraham, *Dictionary of Modern Yoruba* (London: Hodder and Stoughton, 1958), p. 164.

23. See *Idanre and Other Poems*, p. 37. In the long poem *Idanre*, the two gods are regarded as two separate deities, see *Idanre*, p. 70.

24. Abimbola, p. 3.

25. Idanre, p. 78.

26. Idowu, p. 103.

27. *Ibid.*, p. 106.

28. Eldred Jones, "Notes to *The Interpreters,* p. 253.

29. "The Fourth Stage," p. 147.

30. Wole Soyinka, *Season of Anomy* (London: Rex Collings, 1974). p. 14. Subsequent page references are to this edition.

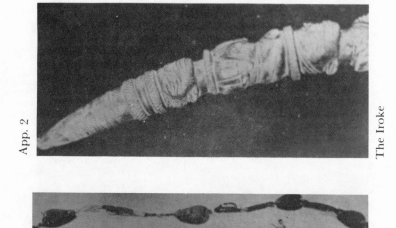

App. 2

The Iroke

App. 1

The Opde

App. 4

Esu

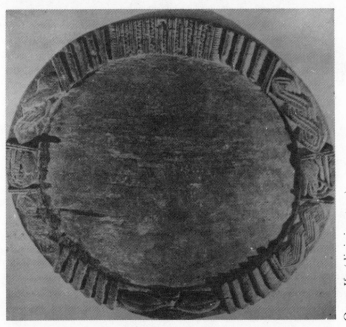

App. 3

Opon Ifa (divining tray)

5

———————— △ △ ————————

OFEYI: SOCIAL REFORMER
AND MYTHIC VOYAGER

BACKGROUND TO THE NOVEL

In writing his second novel *Season of Anomy* (1973), Soyinka has drawn upon social, ideological, religious, and mythic sources. The novel is Soyinka's reaction to the massacre of Ibos in Northern Nigeria during the 1966 pogroms. Following the military coup of January 1966, Northerners were disillusioned with the concept of Nigerian unity and went, in consequence, on a rampage against the Ibos that claimed thirty thousand lives and caused inestimable property damage. Soyinka deplored the killings and went North in the following May to ascertain the extent of the anarchy for himself.[1] He berated the Nigerian intellectuals and students for their indifference to the suffering of the Ibos. The massacres and the absolute disregard of law and order during the pogroms are what Soyinka means by the term "anomy," (anomie). The word appears twice in Soyinka's prison memoir *The Man Died* (1972).[2]

Soyinka responded to the 1966 catastrophe in the October poems of his first book of verse, *Idanre and Other Poems*, (1967) and in the poem, "Conversation at Night with a Cockroach," which is included in his second collection *A Shuttle in the Crypt* (1972). However, it is only in his second novel that the anomy theme engages his attention on a comprehensive scale.

The North (the scene of the massacres) is designated in the novel as Cross-river (not to be confused with Cross River State in former Eastern Nigeria). The Cross-river

113

head of the Cartel, Zaki Amuri, has many of the attitudes of
the Mafia-feudalist reactionary in the Nigerian politics of
the 1960s. The story of the Indian hospital orderly hired by
Zaki is foreshadowed in the account in *The Man Died* of
the Indo-Pakistan incursion into the Nigerian civil service.[3]

Soyinka's prison experience is related to the genocide.
Fictionalized versions of people and places Soyinka encountered during this prison days are integrated into the
narrative. The Kaduna prison where he was held for
twenty-six months becomes "Temoko." The threatening
message transmitted to his psyche by the Kaduna environment, "Abandon hope all who enter here," recurs at Temoko;[4] and Polyphemus, the "cicatriced tower of menace"[5]
at the Kaduna prisons is Temoko's watchdog, "Suberu."

The social ideology propounded in the novel is that of
the Third Force, a neutral, independent body of revolutionary socialist idealists. The Third Force attempted to re-
group during the civil war in order to return the country to
the socialist goals of the five majors of the first army coup.
The Third Force was opposed to the Mafia-feudalist control of the war machine and to the Biafran secession; it was
strongly in favor of a united Nigeria run by men of proven
ability and integrity. The social anomy of the war years
seemed to justify the Third Force's attempt to seize power
and establish a socialist regime in the country.[6]

Both Ofeyi and the Dentist embrace the socialist objectives of the Third Force, that is (as Ofeyi puts it), the
"recovery of whatever has been seized from society by a
handful, re-moulding society itself" (p. 117), but they differ
as to the means by which these objectives are to be attained.
Ofeyi prefers the process of education, which he counter-
poses to the Dentist's espousal of cold-blooded violence.
The ideal society in the novel is clearly articulated by
Soyinka in an interview with the Nigerian critic, Biodun
Jeyifous.

> I happen to believe and accept implicitly what goes
> under the broad umbrella of socialist ideology, a secu-
> lar socialist ideology, believing this to be the logical
> principle of communal organisation and true human

equality. What this means for me is varied. . . : the
eradication of the very policy of wealth accumulation
at the expense of any sector of society; eradication of
the mere possibility of tyranisation by one class of
society over another; the eradication of class distinction within society where class implies a category of
privilege or superiority or advantage. The other logical processes can be assumed; state ownership of all
land and production means; equal education opportu-
nities, etc.[7]

A crude form of this ideology exists in Aiyero. Ofeyi would
improve upon the Aiyero model if he had the opportunity,
but the selfless form of social organization which he finds
there appeals to him.

Aiyero's social philosophy is based on historical reality:
it is modelled on the socialist principles that regulate the
rhythms of life in Ayetoro, a village commune located in
the lagoon district of Okitipupa in the Ondo State of Western Nigeria. Ayetoro is sometimes called the "happy city."
The commune was established in 1947 as an independent
religious organization, which, in turn, developed into a
republic with communalistic ethos. The principles of so-
cialism that govern the commune include common ownership of land, of wealth, and of the means of production;
some allege that even women were commonly owned during the early days of the community. In the novel, Soyinka
has attempted to replace Ayetoro's orthodox Christianity
with a neo-paganism called "the religion of the Grain,"
which, in effect, means the worship of nature, the constant
observance of the rituals of renewal. In working out the
details of this religion, Soyinka might have been indebted
to such cultural anthropologists as James Frazer (*The
Golden Bough*), for the religion of the Grain derives its
liturgy from nature myth and fertility rituals. The earthly
representative of the earth-mother, cocoa maiden, and goddess of love, Iriyise, recalls Demeter and Persephone in
their respective roles as earth-mother and corn maiden. The
dying custodian of the Grain who combines the offices of
King and priest might have been derived from the Frazerian
concept of the dying god.[8] The ceremonies of dawn that

attend his demise smooth his path to the ancestors, but they are also intended to guarantee for the living the continuing operation of his divine essence.

Aiyero is the subject of the first two chapters of the novel, and the Aiyero image continues to lurk in the background as the story unfolds. The chapter headings refer to aspects of the religion of the Grain. In addition, the chapter headings convey the theme of growth, of society as a healthy organism that can blossom fully in a harmonious environment. "The meaning of Grain," says Ahime, "is not merely food but germination" (p. 6). In the larger world beyond Aiyero, the bullet is offered to humanity instead of grain. That larger world is an inverted mirror image of Aiyero's social order; and Ofeyi's humane conscience muses constantly on the contrast between the two worlds.

A further aspect of the novel that requires comment is the mythic background. Early reviewers have commented on the parallel between the story of Ofeyi and Iriyise and the legend of Orpheus and Eurydice.[9] Soyinka surely relied on similarity of nomenclature to draw the reader's attention to the parallel.

Orpheus was a native of Thrace, the son of a local king named Oiagros. His mother was Calliope, the muse of epic poetry. He won great fame with the lyre and could charm both man and beast (and even the inanimate world) with his music. Apart from his fame as a musician, not much is known of Orpheus life prior to his marriage to Eurydice. He was, however, supposed to have been one of the heroes who accompanied the Argonauts to Colichis in their quest for the golden fleece. Orpheus married the dryad Eurydice and lost her soon after his marriage when the god Aristaeus pursued Eurydice and, in her haste to escape his clutches, Eurydice was fatally bitten by a poisonous snake. Orpheus set out to rescue her from the underworld and succeeded in charming Pluto and Persephone by the power of his song. He was allowed to return to the land of the living with his beloved on the condition that he restrain himself from looking back at her until they had both passed out of the world of darkness into the light of day. But shortly before they emerged into the realms of light, Orpheus looked back at his bride. In an instant Eurydice vanished, lost forever, leaving Orpheus stunned and inconsolable at the double loss of his wife. Orpheus shunned the company of women after this tragedy and gave his love only to young men in the first bloom of youth, but in doing so he incurred the anger of the Maenads (the female followers of Dionysus), who set upon him and tore him limb from limb, flinging his head and lyre into river Hebros. Both head and lyre, still singing, were carried by the stream into the sea until they reached the island of Lesbos where they were picked up by Apollo, the god of poetry.

There are three major moments in the Orpheus myth, according to the German scholar, Walter Strauss: the first is Orpheus the singer–prophet, capable of establishing harmony in the cosmos; the second is the descent into Hades; and the third is the dismemberment.

Soyinka has not followed the Orpheus myth closely; he only abstracted from the general outline of the story elements that suit his present purpose—Orpheus as a musician, the love theme, and Orpheus' quest for his beloved Eurydice in the underworld. Soyinka has used the myth as a poetic metaphor only, that is to say, his characters' actions and motivations remind us of the personages connected with the Orpheus myth. Thus, Chief Batoki, who abducted Iriyise and carried her to an unknown destination, is a Pluto figure. Temoko prison where Iriyise was held is Hades. Ofeyi, the revolutionary reformer, is Dionysus. Iriyise is more than Eurydice. She is a combination of earth mother, cocoa maiden, film star, beauty queen, queenbee (like Simi), prostitute, revolutionary agitator, and muse. But the Orpheus myth has provided Soyinka with the motif of an artist protagonist, with the attendant theme of alienation as it has been incorporated, for instance, into the poetry of the Nigerian poet Christopher Okigbo.[10]

THE CARTEL

"Cartel" is essentially a commercial term. *The Oxford English Dictionary* defines it as "an agreement or association between two or more business houses for the purpose of regulating output and fixing prices for a given commodity." In Soyinka's novel the Cartel is both a political power and an economic force; it manages the nation's wealth and controls the production and disposal of those natural resources from which that wealth is derived. Cocoa is mentioned in recognition of its former status as the nation's most important economic product. Soyinka makes the vital point that in post-independence Africa, politics is just another business, a profit-making concern. People go into politics not to serve the nation but to swell their purses by cheating and exploiting the masses. Cocoa becomes a metaphor for the human commodities who are also "sold" and exploited by the ruling oligarchy. Soyinka sees the new business arrangement as a trade in human flesh, and the phenomenon cuts across national boundaries. The Dentist sees the arrangement as

> A conspiracy of power-besotted exploiters across national boundaries, bargaining with outsiders against *us*! Lip-service to revolutionary movements to drown the cries of internal repression. Tell me . . . what are they selling? All this haggling and under-the-counter deals, what is the commodity? *Us*! (p. 104)

The Cartel represents what Soyinka calls the "alliance of a corrupt militarism and a rapacious mafia."[11] This new brand of men has usurped political power in post-independence Africa. They came into power with the rise of military dictatorship in Africa, abolished democratic principles, and ruled by decree alone. Their political philosophy is that of As. Dr. Bero of Soyinka's war play, *Madmen and Specialists* (1971), is a typical example of the military arm of this alliance. In Nigeria, particularly, the marriage between the military and the old political mafiadom was the logical outcome of a civil war that lacked any ideological inspiration:

> Militarist entrepreneurs and multiple dictatorships: this is bound to be the legacy of a war which is conducted on the present terms. The vacuum in the ethical base . . . will be filled by a new military ethic—coercion.[12]

The Cartel is headed by Zaki Amuri, the all-powerful tyrant of Cross-river. His second-in-command is Chief Batoki, the Western arm of the alliance. Then follows Chief Biga, the Cartel's hatchet man. The military is represented by the anonymous Commandant-in-Chief. The Cartel is not observed at close range; they operate mainly behind the scene. They are best characterized by the bloody trail they leave behind. The animal images with which they are constantly associated indicate the extent to which their humanity has been eroded by a cannibalistic blood-lust. A typical descriptive phrase is the "ardent bloodhounds of the Cartel" (p. 20) or the "hulldogs of the Cartel" (p. 21) or the "Cartel's superstructure of robbery, indignities and murder" (p. 27). The evil genius behind the power syndicate, Chief Batoki, sows bullets instead of grain:

> And Batoki sowed a forest of bayonets in the sun,
> laughed through the curses of the people and mocked
> their tears of frustration. He was endowed with the
> patience of a lizard and he bridged time with mounds
> of the dead and the living. (p. 139)

The members of the Cartel are caricatures, buffoons, or villains. Chief Biga, the first Pluto to abduct Iriyise, gives her the option of either payment or a scarred face: "Here it is. Two hundred cash [or a] scarred face for life" (p. 64). The Cartel are real cartoons at the garden party given by the Chairman of the Cocoa Corporation. We encounter here "four familiar faces, puppet-form, suspended . . . from balloons" (p. 46).

The Cartel and their subagents are truly creatures of a cartoon mentality. As humans, they lack all individuating qualities; what survives in them are only their bloody attributes and their official designations. The military agent (Commandant-in-Chief) in the Cartel is nameless, and the Chief of prisons at Temoko is nicknamed Club-foot. Chief Batoki is briefly observed at close quarters in the domestic scenes between him and his wife. The reader sees that the chief is not worth killing after all. He might be a boisterous single-minded murderer in the Cartel's conference rooms,

but at home he is a pathetic lonely man harrassed to death
by hs amorphous harridan:

> Batoki, shrunk to half his size appeared to shrink
> further into a deep arm-chair in a huge living-room
> festooned in gold framed photos of dead family fore-
> bearers, smiling reception scenes and parades. An enor-
> mous figure of a woman loomed over him, her lips
> vibrating in an incessant sizzle over the unfortunate
> chief. (p. 181)

The cartoon figures enhance the author's satirical purpose,
but the farce undermines characterization. There is a great
deal of action in *Season of Anomy*, but the engineers of the
actions are hardly seen.

The military, in general, is suspect in Soyinka's work.
His contemptuous attitude towards that profession is un-
disguised in the poem, "Civilian and Soldier,"[13] in which
soldiers are seen as natural dealers in death. Still, Soyinka
holds in high regard the advocates of justice and fair-play
in the military such as, in the present novel (p. 207), Captain Magari and Lieutenant Sayi. It is the callous abuse of
the power of arms that earns his anger.

The implications of the Cartel mafiadom go beyond the
present era of military dictatorship in Africa. That "monster child" as the Dentist calls it (p. 134), is Soyinka's term
for all dictatorships, whether military or civilian. This
pattern of awareness began in *A Dance of the Forests* (1963)
and runs through *Kongi's Harvest* (1967) to *Madmen and
Specialists*.

THE IDEOLOGICAL MOTIF

Season of Anomy is the closest Soyinka has come to
revolutionary art. As such, the novel anticipates the emergence of a new form of fiction currently gaining ground
in African literature—socialist realism.[14] Writers of this
school aim to create literature that reflects the interests of
the masses in their struggle for a just society. The Kenyan
novelist Ngugi wa Thiong'o sounded the clarion call when
he urged African writers in the 1960s to liberate their imag-

ination from the past or, at least, to modify their visions of that past so as to incorporate present realities. He wrote, "it is only in a socialist context that a look at yesterday can be meaningful in illuminating today and tomorrow."[15] Ngugi's own *Petals of Blood* (1970) and Sembene Ousmane's *God's Bits of Wood* (1970) and Ayi Kwei Armah's *Two Thousand Seasons* (1973)) are often cited as examples of socialist realism in African fiction.

Soyinka's approach differs from Ngugi's and Ousmane's, for his socialist vision is crystallized through the consciousness of an elitist sympathizer. Soyinka's philosophy is not properly embodied (as in Ngugi and Ousmane) in the revolutionary intransigence of a collective proletarian leadership. The masses are almost non-existent in Soyinka's novel. The working class community that attempted the project at Shage was anonymous.

Nevertheless, the leading characters in the novel, Ofeyi and the Dentist, entertain socialist views and are presented in contrast to the social apostates in Soyinka's first novel, *The Interpreters*; They might have been offered deliberately to Soyinka's Marxist critics as evidence of his ideological conversion. And yet some irony, even mockery, colors the portrait of the leading ideologue in the novel, the Dentist. Is the Dentist one of what Soyinka has called "the parrots of ideology"?[16] The answer to this question requires a brief discussion of certain events in Soyinka's personal life.

In the essay "Who Is Afraid of Elesin Oba?" Soyinka sketched the genesis of his interest in Marxist thought. His interest began at Leeds in the 1950s when he encountered the Marxist scholar, Arnold Kettle. When Soyinka returned to Nigeria in 1960, he saw only vulgarized versions of Marxism and became disillusioned with this ideology as it was understood and disseminated in Nigeria at the time. His account of that disillusionment runs as follows:

> Back to Nigeria [in 1960], to be confronted by the Marxist jargonizing of corrupt trade union leaders who sold out their followers at every opportunity. I recall only two dedicated Marxist theorists during this time—Bankole Akpata and Eskor Toyo. Gogo Nzeribe

was marginal. He knew his Marx but was no Marxist. I recall losing my temper with Eskor Toyo during the Morgan Commission strike (1964). I felt certain that all the forces were right for the overthrow of the civilian government by a workers' revolution. He thought differently. My assessment at the time was that he was text-bound, incapable of making the "quantitative leap" across the missing condition for a text-book revolution. I cannot be certain today [1977] that I was right.[17]

Following this disillusionment, Soyinka has made it a point of duty to consistently dissociate himself from the Nigerian brand of Marxism in the early 1960s:

I would rather not be bracketted with those pseudo-Stalinists-Leninists and Maoists who are totally unproductive and merely protect themselves behind a whole barrage of terminologies which bear no relation to the immediate needs of society.[18]

and again:

I am not a Marxist, I do not spout Marxist rhetoric. And when I say I am not a Marxist I mean that I dispute any form of thinking which insists on conceptualizing the entirety of experience through a Marxist framework.[19]

Soyinka's discontentment with vulgar Marxism has conditioned his attitude to Nigerian intellectuals with socialist leanings. His relationship with these men has operated in an atmosphere of ideological cold war. He has of late, however, reconsidered his stand toward them:

It is only in recent years indeed that it has become possible to hold, in this country, an intelligent dialogue with self-declared Marxists—I would say, only within the last seven years to a decade—at the most.[20]

Soyinka's warnings against the simplistic mouthing of ideologies concentrate on the character of the Dentist. He is

caught in attitudinizing postures in the early sections of the
novel. As an old-fashioned, self-styled revolutionary, he is
indifferent to drink and women and distrusts works of
fiction. He sees himself as hero of liberation movements,
having been trained as a freedom-fighter for the trouble
spots on the African continent such as Mozambique and
Guinea Bissau. His rhetoric of violence is shown to have
been inspired partly by conviction and partly by the ideal-
ism of youth—it has yet to be mellowed by the wisdom that
comes with age. The Dentist recalls, in a way, the radical,
self-dramatizing Soyinka who thought in 1964 that the
time had come for the worker's revolution and, thus, had
the courage to hold up a radio station during the crisis in
the former Western Nigeria the following year.

The Dentist enables Soyinka to reassess the philosophy
of "elimination," that is, the idea that violence can provide
a solution to society's problems. Soyinka questions the use
of violence in military coups and in war. In *The Man Died*
Soyinka claims that the Nigerian Civil War was prosecuted
without "a simultaneous programme of reform and redefi-
nition of social purpose."[21] The war, he notes, was a war of
solidity and not of unity. The reevaluation process in the
novel should not be taken to mean that Soyinka is opposed
to violence as a means of effecting change, he merely insists
on a distinction between purposeful violence and uncon-
trolled, manic violence. For the Dentist, violence is part of
an ideology borrowed from a Fanon or a Cabral, which can
be applied indiscriminately to every situation that calls for
change. The Dentist has no alternative program of reform
to replace the social order he wishes to destroy:

> I am trained in the art of killing. I utilize this acquisi-
> tion on behalf of my society. . . . Beyond the elimina-
> tion of men I know to be destructively evil, I envisage
> nothing. What happens after is up to people like you
> [Ofeyi]. (pp. 111–112)

Soyinka's appraisal of the role of violence in Armah's
Two Thousand Seasons throws some light on his own
attitude. Armah's revolutionary heroes, says Soyinka, have
not sacrificed their humanity to the fascinations of brute
force:

Most remarkable of all in a book which is hardly
squeamish in its depiction of violence is Armah's insistence on a revolutionary integrity, a refusal to be
trapped into promoting the increasingly fashionable
rhetoric of violence for its own sake.[22]

Soyinka's criticism of violence for its own sake applies to
the actions of the masses themselves, for whom the revolution is made. They, too, are guilty of misapplied violence.
The rage for "operation," Soyinka's euphemism for senseless killing, took in its wake the life of a seven-year-old son
of an unpopular returning officer whose car was set ablaze
in an "operational" rampage. The child was "guilty by
association" and was doomed to share the destiny of the ill-
fated car. One recalls the blood-lust of a murderous crowd
in *The Interpreters*. A further inditement of violence is
contained in Ofeyi's remark as he reflects on what violence
has made of the Dentist: Too much reliance on violence, he
thought, erodes youth:

> Youthful as he looked, a lonely concentration of the
> will to action within his own person rendered him
> grave and aged. (p. 108)

Ofeyi might carry much of the author's position in the
ideological debate, but his ideas are not practical. He
stands for a rational intellectual appraisal of the merits and
demerits of all revolutionary alternatives. He is opposed to
a violent confrontation with the Cartel's superior fire
power and favors, instead, a strategy that operates through
the education of the masses or, where that fails, through
cautious resistance. Ofeyi is best understood in the light of
Soyinka's contention that, to be meaningful, ideology must
be tempered by humanistic ends:

> Ideology, once it departs from humanistic ends, is no
> longer worthy of the name. The ultimate purpose of
> human striving is humanity.[23]

Ideologies, including those of violence, must be mellowed
by a humanizing influence. Ofeyi insists, characteristically,
therefore, that he cannot "foul up the remnants of my

humanity as others do by different means" (p. 135). Events
prove Ofeyi's line of thought to be impractical, and, when
the hopelessness of his position dawns on him, he retreats
into Aiyero's groves and sanctuaries to reminisce and meditate. Wars of liberation, one notes, are not won through
introspection but by confrontation. In spite of his reformist
zeal, therefore, Ofeyi appears to be no more than an improved version of the social apostates in *The Interpreters.*

And this leads us to another dimension of the Dentist's
personality. In spite of Soyinka's irony, the Dentist is much
more than a vehicle for satire. Soyinka means him to be
taken seriously. From chapter VII where he emerges as a
self-confessed assassin, Soyinka begins to modify his attitude toward the Dentist. Prior to this point, he was presented as an ideological maverick, but from chapter VII
onward, he becomes the spokesman for the philosophy of
violence, a role he fulfills with unassailable logic. His
observation, for instance, that in warfare "hesitation means
consolidation by the opposition" (p. 135) is practical common sense. It is a measure of the Dentist's success as a
logician that he occasionally succeeds in making Ofeyi
question the merit of his rational, humane approach to
social issues. The Dentist's practical rhetoric undermines
Ofeyi's rationalistic conscience, but the novel maintains
that conscience is the better option.

The Dentist is not fully integrated into the novel's narrative structure. His function is to defend a possible option in
a revolutionary struggle, and, once he has fulfilled that
role, the Dentist makes his exit. His later appearance in the
novel (p. 216, chapter XI, and at the very end) is an after-
thought; it adds little to the novel's artistic design. It is as if
Soyinka had suddenly remembered the character as he knot-
ted up the strands of the plot. This criticism is also true of
the *deus ex machina* toward the middle of the story in
regard to the Dentist's links with Aiyero.

THE THEME OF QUEST

Season of Anomy is an intensely religious book, both in
its preoccupation with moral issues and the strong impact
of its ritual undertone. Soyinka's imagination is nurtured
by the same moral outrage that occasioned the October

poems of *Idanre* and most of the elegies in *A Shuttle in the Crypt.*

One does not have to venture far into *Season of Anomy* to encounter passages of pathos and moral indignation similar to those in these two verse collections.[24] Soyinka's moral imagination became even more sensitive, more outraged after his experience in prison. The declaration in *The Man Died* that "For me, justice is the first condition of humanity"[25] sounds like an ethical manifesto.

One of the consequences of his increasing dedication to the cause of justice is that his postwar imaginative writings are frequently dominated by visionaries. We first encounter these pilgrims in the poems of *A Shuttle in the Crypt.*

The insistent quest motif in *A Shuttle* attains a climatic dimension in *Season of Anomy*. There are, of course, earlier reminders of the image of the seeker in Soyinka's own works, for example, Sekoni and his obsessions with the universal dome of existence in *The Interpreters* and the Professor's quasi-mystical and quasi-magical groping for the word in *The Road* (1965). But neither in *The Interpreters* nor in *The Road* is the quest theme developed on as grand a scale or explored with so complex an interplay of allegory and myth as in *Season of Anomy*.

The quest theme in the later work runs on two levels— the social and the personal. The two dimensions are interrelated for each reinforces the other. Ofeyi the social reformer is also the archetype of eternal voyagers and lone seekers. If allegory is the language of the social dimension of the quest, myth has provided Soyinka with metaphors for the enactment of its personal dimension.

On the social level, the quest is for a moral alternative in a nation in a state of anomy. It is suggested in *The Man Died*[26] that Nigeria of the era of civil war might have been spared much bitterness and much suffering if it had submitted to the mediation of an ethical revolutionary movement. The ethical qualification is crucial, for it is on such a moral absolute, Soyinka implies, that a new national solidarity transcending ethnic and religious loyalties could be founded. Victor Banjo was for Soyinka the hero of such a movement. He is remembered in *A Shuttle* in the poem entitled "And What of It If Thus He Died?"

Victor Banjo's Third Force was short lived, but the idea behind the movement persists in Soyinka writing and in his character, Ofeyi. Explaining the Shage project to Zaccheus, who is possessed of beauty of soul even though he is utterly lacking in heroic aspirations, Ofeyi says:

> New projects like the Shage Dam meant that we could start with newly created working communities. New affinities, working-class kinships as opposed to the tribal. We killed the atavistic instinct once for all in new ventures like Shage. (p. 170)

The method advocated in *Season of Anomy* for the transformation of society differs from what Victor Banjo had contemplated. Banjo would have relied on such military operations as he felt were required by the emergency in Nigeria when he emerged on the national scene. Ofeyi, on the other hand, desires to carry out a quiet revolution, relying essentially on the "trick of conversion," on a subtle incursion into the territories of the human heart.

The agricultural community of Aiyero appealed to Ofeyi as representing social solidarity founded upon humane and spiritual values. In Aiyero, rituals still function as symbolic affirmations of man's indebtedness to nature; ceremonies of renewal are frequently enacted; familiar images of rebirth in Soyinka's iconography such as camwood, chalk, and oil feature in the invocations to the dead; and dawn remains the hour of communion with the divine. Aiyero represents the moral order that Ofeyi seeks, but he has first to master its heartbeat, to thoroughly understand its essence before he may transmit its values to his own society. One way to do this is to come to terms with those nonsexual values which Iriyise embodies, for Iriyise is earth, the mother earth that was symbolized by Oya in *Idanre*. In one moment of insight, Ofeyi recognizes Iriyise's identity with the soil of Aiyero. "She took to Aiyero," he notices, "as a new organism in search of its true element" (p. 3). Iriyise's embodiment of the creative potency of earth is not lost on the people of Aiyero. The women readily identify her personality with the forces that encourage growth and vegetation. "Her fingers spliced wounded sap-

lings with the ease of a natural healer. Her presence . . .
inspired the rains" (p. 20).

Iriyise is linked, then, with the agricultural world of
Aiyero and, by extension, with the spiritual values of that
world. For there is a strong bond between the land and the
moral priorities of the people that inhabit it. Even in Ilesa
where Iriyise is a metaphorical seedpod, the exploitation of
the resources of the land by the Cartel is spoken as the
"outrage of the Pod" (p. 48; my italics). But Iriyise's role as
the personification of the spirit of revolutionary daring is
probably more important. She embodies energy and motion as well as the positive forces of social change. The
Dentist's appraisal of her in this regard is significant. He
sees her as a "torch and standard-bearer, super-mistress of
universal insurgence. To abandon such political weapon
in any struggle is to admit to lack of foresight. Or imagination" (p. 219).

The Dentist himself also advocates change, but his ethic
of indiscriminate assassination is rejected on moral
grounds. His obsession with sheer violence links him with
Chief Batoki or Zaki Amuri, whereas Soyinka wishes to
distinguish Ofeyi's humane, almost religious, approach.
toward social problems from the brutal means by which the
Cartel oligarchy imposes the dictatorship of the privileged
few on an unwilling many. "When you eliminate, you
have in mind something to follow," Ofeyi tells the Dentist,
"something to replace what you eliminate. Otherwise your
action is negative and futile" (p. 111).

Iriyise is a more acceptable agent, not only because her
revolutionary impulse is under Ofeyi's control but also
because she operates by a strategy of disguise (for example,
her performance in the melodramatic Pandora's Box episode or the more subtle dance at Shage). Furthermore, her
spiritual affinities with Aiyero allow her to effect changes
within Aiyero itself. Ofeyi is critical of Aiyero as an esoteric
hinterland: Aiyero's values must replace the ethos of a
materialistic society. The Asian girl, Taiila, is ultimately
rejected as Ofeyi's companion in the quest because Taiila is
the personification of the placid will, the serene spirit of
conformity. She is an "insulated oasis of peace," a "still
centre" that shies away from tragic encounter with "outer

chaos" (pp. 238–40). She lacks the "caged tigress" in Iriyise. She is Aiyero as Pa Ahime conceives it—her family is described as a microcosm of Aiyero (p. 238). Iriyise, on the other hand, stands for the image of Aiyero that Ofeyi is endeavoring to create—a more assertive, more militant, and evangelical Aiyero whose values extend beyond its boundaries.

Shage is Aiyero's most crucial contact with that outside world represented by the universe of the Cartel. The initial success of Aiyero's operations at Shage is a personal triumph for Iriyise. Her dance of the young shoot reenacts the process of sowing, germination, and budding. The dance becomes a mystical experience, transforming her person into a blossoming shoot: She sprouts "leaves and fresh buds from neck and fingers, shaking her hair free from dead leaves and earth and absorbing light and air through every pore" (p. 41). As a goddess of earth, she is capable of reactivating the recreative energies of earth that lay dormant in Shage. The dance neatly combines the double sense of shoot as seed and idea. The Shage earth is favorable for the growth of the physical seed as well as the ideological seed. But Shage is also the scene of the Cartel's most deadly assault on the forces of renewal in both the human and the natural realms. The success of the Cartel's destruction at Shage plunges Ofeyi into one of his visionary moments. As he contemplates the ruins of Shage, his mind conjures up an immense chasm of nonbeing as a universal grave for desecrated humanity. The underworld has consistently functioned as a mirror image of the actual world inhabited by doomed humanity. Such is the implication of the entombed existence of the church at the Tabernacle of Hope and of the graveyard metaphor of the mortuary episode. At Shage Ofeyi sees "where the rest of mankind had rushed, and now his was the only consciousness observing the dark pulsating chasms of tearing, grasping, clawing, gorging humanity" (p. 176). Ofeyi's role is to heal, to infuse new life in flesh where the "blood . . . had caked."[27] But at Shage he sought in vain to invoke Ahime's scalpel of light and life on the ravines of death and waste, to innundate the chasms of nonbeing with sympathetic bleeding from the bull's elixir. After the Shage debacle, the Aiyero idea returns to its source, but, according to the Dentist, the journey back marks the route for a more definite return.

The social quest extends into the personal quest for Iriyise, the social activist, is also Ofeyi's lover. The same evil agencies that frustrated her social aims held her captive within Temoko prison. Her captors, Zaki Amuri and Chief Batoki, are the Plutos of the Temoko underworld, jealously guarded by the human Cerberus, Suberu. The threatening presence of the watchdog, Suberu, brings Ofeyi's charm to the surface. Ofeyi's verbal assaults on Suberu eventually wins that husk of silence over to his side. The quest for Iriyise terminates within the embryo of universal chaos.

Still, Ofeyi is unassuaged. The quest will go on, he discloses (p. 242), even after Iriyise has been found. Man's eternal restlessness, Soyinka wrote,[28] is always symbolized in a search. At this point, the quest theme embraces more fundamental and more personal issues, such as the artist's quest for self-knowledge, his search for beauty in its relation to art; the search for truth in its ontological context, and, for restless individuals like Ofeyi who are forever plagued by what Taiila called his "eternal discontent" (p. 242), the search for an emotional ballast to steady a mind in turmoil. These other quests are summed up by Ofeyi in one important statement: ". . . every man feels the need to seize for himself the enormity of what is happening, of the time in which it is happening. Perhaps deep down I realise that the search would immerse me in the meaning of the event, lead me to a new understanding of history" (p. 218).

The quest is, in Ofeyi's understanding of it, a tragic undertaking. "Mire and mud, for some these are the paths to beauty and peace" (pp. 97–98), he tells Taiila. Another remark to Taiila is equally revealing: "I also seek beauty, but that kind which has been tested and stressed" (p. 99). Ofeyi, the mythic explorer, must pass through a landscape of grottos and tunnels, of stunted scrublands and hyenas, cats and vultures, all symbolic representations of the ordeals of the questing pilgrim. To overcome these obstacles, Ofeyi relies increasingly on the restorative potency of ritual. He frequently evokes Ahime at moments of spiritual crisis, for he has come to associate Ahime's ceremonial scalpel with restorative essences. Thus, after his first major encounter with the agents of the Cartel (Chapters III–V), Ofeyi retreats to Aiyero's bowered sanctuary for spiritual rehabilitation. Aiyero is a resting-place for all combatants in the battles of the world. Ahime explains: "After all the battles of the world, one needs a resting-place. And often, in between the battles. Aiyero was created for such needs" (p. 28). On this occasion, however, the restorative powers within the sanctuary speak to him of failure. The cleansing rite he performs at Labbe Bridge is more rewarding. Nature herself participates in the ritual of cleansing. The egrets "picked him clean of blood-infesting ticks," and the waters "shut his ears to all cacophony, his nostrils to pollution, transmitting only the rhythm of cropping and quiet germination" (p. 195). The water reeds evoke memories of Ahime's healing hands. They whisper healing "incantations over a child in agony" (p. 195). Their healing vibrations stand in sharp contrast with the death exhalation emitted by the Cartel's machinery of destruction.

Aiyero is always contrasted with the universe inhabited by the agents of the Cartel. The juxtaposition of two worlds with two opposed moral orders tends to resolve the tensions within the novel into an allegorical conflict between good and evil. The voyager Ofeyi advances from the pastoral enclaves of Aiyero to the scenes of conflict represented by Cross-river. But the allegorical demarcation has its own limitations; it imposes on the novelist's imagination certain *a priori* conclusions in regard to his conception of the characters. He cannot expand their human qualities to the full, since their role, and even the face of the landscape, are predetermined by the allegorical logic. Pa Ahime or Chief Batoki is more important as a symbol than as an individual; each is a factor in the novel's two opposed moral orders. But it is the cripple, Aliyu, a native of Cross-river, who is the best illustration of the impact on characterization of the author's allegorical imagination. Aliyu is simply an embodiment of the "metaphysic [sic] condition called evil" (p. 276). His physical distortions reflect the absolute deformity of mind among his Cross-river compatriots, but Aliyu is himself not evil (an ironic twist by Soyinka).

Landscape sustains more successfully the burden imposed on it by the allegorical technique. As noted, the condition of the land reflects the moral character of the people who live on it. Aiyero's ceremony of renewal is replaced in Cross-river by a deadly ritual whose libations paint a testament of damnation on earth (p. 141): The earth is smeared with human brains and embryos. The enormity of the crime is suggested by an allusion to the Apocalypse: ". . . this is the fifth face of the Apocalypse . . . the plague of rabid dogs" (p. 159).

Compared to such a physical and spiritual wasteland, the Aiyero idea maintains a precarious existence, a glimmer of light shining in the darkness. The underground church at the Tabernacle of Hope is a refuge for those who live in fear. The priest's "path-finding form" (p. 271) is truly the Way. Religion is the final hope of salvation for those who live in the darkness of terror. It is at the Tabernacle that Taiila finds herself as a messenger of love and peace. Her humanity is aroused by the dead and the dying, and her place is ultimately with the suffering, not with the revolutionary movement.

Of the two dimensions of the quest already discussed, it is as a depiction of a personal quest for self-knowledge that the novel is likely to have a permanent impact. Amos Tutuola has given us a folkloric version of this form of quest in *The Palm Wine Drinkard* (1952), and Camara Laye has explored its implications in the tradition of Kafka in *The Radiance of the King* (1961); but Soyinka's technique is more sophisticated and more complicated than Tutuola's or Laye's. His seasoned approach represents a major advance in the growth of the African novel.

RELIGION, NATURE AND RITUAL

Earth is a sacred element to Soyinka. His reverence for earth is closely linked to his sacred view of human life; for earth is the source of life. Because of its capacity to generate life, earth is often assigned human attributes. Iriyise in *Season of Anomy* and Oya in *Idanre* are both earth-mothers.

The equation of earth with womanhood is persistent in Soyinka. In an early poem, "Psalm," a woman's pregnant womb is "sealed in earth," and the poet proceeds to draw an analogy between the development of the embryo and the germination of a seed: "sealed in earth your sanctuary/ yields to light" [29] the poet affirms.

Disruptions in human relationships are reflected on the face of the earth. In another early poem, "Bringer of Peace," peace is restored between two contending parties only when an intercessor (a messenger of peace) has come to "soothe/The rent in earth." [30] In some of the poems in *A Shuttle*, social disorder is directly visited upon the earth. In the poem "Conversation at Night with a Cockroach," earth herself recoils from "rites of defilement," and "tears are a watering shed to earth's/unceasing wound." [31] Cosmic disharmony too takes its tolls on the face of the earth. In *Idanre* a cosmic contest is settled when "earth's broken rings were healed" by a sympathetic deluge. [32]

Earth is, then, a symbol of continuity and of social and moral order according to Soyinka's idea of moral justice. Cracks on the earth's surface indicate disruptions in human, social, and cosmic relationships. It is in the light of this religious reverence for earth that Aiyero's religion of the Grain becomes meaningful; its moral implications are relevant to the ethics of another religious organization in the novel, that is, the Christian church. In Aiyero, earth is sacred, and that precisely is what Ahime means by the repeated assertion that food is sacred (pp. 58, 194, 215). Aiyero's destiny is tied to the fortunes of the earth. "We are a farming and fishing community so we acknowledge our debts to earth and to the sea," Ahime tells Ofeyi (p. 11). The reader witnesses in detail the ceremonies of renewal at the beginning of the novel. Soyinka is at his most poetic and Ahime at his most acrobatic in those entranced passages at the beginning of the book in which Ahime acts as the priest of renewal:

> He of the masseur's fingers stooped at each succeeding sluice gate, a fountain-head covered in rime, his arms were supple streams in a knowing course through

ridges bathed in a sun's downwash. He nudged the
ridges' streams awake and they joined their tributaries
to his fountain head. A deep beneficence rested over
the motions of his hands, opening red sluices for the
land's replenishment. (p. 17)

Ahime was a reed of life in the white stillness of a
memorial ground, a flicker of motion among marble
tombstones. An intuitive priest, he knew better than to
disturb the laden altar until his followers had drunk
their fill of it, he let the ponderous mass for the dead
emit vibrations of abundance, potency and renewal,
binding the pulses in his own person, building a force
for life within the pen until he judged the moment
right for the magical release. (p. 16)

The climax is the magical release as fountains of "red
sluices" issuing from the throats of the felled bulls mount
heavenward to a sun-scorched sky, only to descend to earth
in torrents of regenerative floods. One is reminded of the
cosmic deluge in *Idanre,* which fertilized the womb of the
earth so that seeds may swell and roots take hold within her
and men wake naked into harvest-tide. At the induction
ceremonies in Aiyero, the bulls continue to discharge their
rich elixir until "a final shudder of love gave all to a
passive earth" (p. 17). These life-giving rituals stand in
sharp contrast to the death rituals performed in Ilosa by the
members of the Cartel. Whereas Ahime and his aids must
plant the horn to release the reproductive energies of the
earth-bull convenant, Chief Batoki and his collaborators
seek to perpetuate their hold over the people by means of a
ritual which required them to bury a live cow in the dead of
every night. And in contrast to Aiyero's sluices, we have
poisoned pools and polluted streams in Cross-river.

No stream remained unpolluted, no pool existed in
which a man could throw a stone without bursting a
bloated skin of decay. Not even the wells, for in their
mindlessness the hordes of the Cartel had not re-
frained from soiling the needs of the living for pure
sources. (p. 193)

In his journey through the arid landscapes of Cross-river, Ofeyi rejects the pastoral invitations of familiar delightful spots, where serenity seems to reign. Those are only anachronistic deviations from the genral "seepage of pus and bile" that have poisoned "the living streams of earth" (p. 195). Aiyero's reverence for the earth highlights its defacement by the people of Cross-river. The pregnant woman whose heavy womb was ripped open by the mindless hordes of the Cartel is the most outrageous rite of earth's defilement, for the woman is herself earth incarnate. Ofeyi recalls the incident with all its sinister details and horror:

> Conspicuous as a shield, a plea or an accusation for the rest was a frail creature nearly overbalanced by the heavy pregnancy that stuck out of her and seemed ready to weigh her to the ground. Ofeyi held his breadth, unable to tear her eyes from the confrontation. Until that moment when her head jerked suddenly downwards to stare in surprise at the unnatural blossom that her womb had sprouted. (p. 201)

After Aiyero, the most morally conscious community in the novel is the Christian church. Taiila is the link between Aiyero and the Christian church. She is the symbol of the peace that passeth all understanding, although Ofeyi's early assessment of Aiyero as a monastic enclave anticipates the later cooperation between Aiyero and the church. As an ex-nun, Taiila anticipates the role of the church in the novel. Her presence is often signalled by images associated with the Christian church: church bells, steeple, vespers, the infinite, peace, harmony (p. 98). The morals that regulate Taiila's life are based on the teachings of the church. Her family as has been noted, is a miniature image of Aiyero. Taiila's mother radiates in her person the same peaceful halo and serenity we associate with Taiila herself and with Aiyero: "Hands, brow and eyes of radiating calm and paradoxical alertness" (p. 237). The first encounter with Taiila introduces the theme of healing that is associated with Ahime and Aiyero. "The true doctors," she tells Ofeyi, "are the real healers and healers radiate beauty. That

is what heals you know. The beauty they radiate from their
own persons" (p. 99). She thinks of herself too as a healer:
"A nun too is a form of healer, and healing is beauty"
(p. 99).

In Cross-river, the fortunes of the church are linked with
those of Aiyero by a common bond of suffering and healing. The Christian images and symbols at the underground
church at the Tabernacle of Hope—the baptismal font, the
altar, the cross, the cherubs and angels, the vestry—are the
Christian counterparts of the native ritual elements in Aiyero's ceremony of renewal—blood, oil, colanuts, camwood,
and chalk. At the Tabernacle of Hope, the entombed congregation derives spiritual succor by contemplating these
Christian images and symbols. The quiet rituals of the
church represent a subdued version of the magnificent rites
performed on Aiyero's sacred grounds. In spite of the
general gloom and the universal suffering, the church is
alive with quiet activities. There is fear in each eye-flare in
the dark, but there is also hope and defiance. The aged
among the refugees break into hymns, singing "the Lord is
my shepherd, I shall not want" (p. 269).

In spite of the might of the Cartel, the presence of Aiyero
and of the church is firmly entrenched in the background,
and this presence gives the novel its structure. The novel's
section headings take their titles from nature myth except
for the section entitled "Tentacles," in which the Cartel
spreads its poisonous tentacles throughout the land. The
ironic section headings point to the contrast between what
is expected of the human heart and what it actually gives.
Instead of the harvest suggested by the title of section four,
we have murder and carnage. "Buds" tells the story of how
the Cartel had nipped in the bud the shoot that had been
transplanted into its borders from Aiyero. Iriyise's dance of
the young shoot at the Shage Dam represents the budding
of the subversive Aiyero idea sowed in the soil of Cross-
river.

> Iriyise lay within the giant shell in darkness, for ever
> and for ever as it seemed to her. No speck of light
> filtered through the airholes, no sensation except of
> being buried alive. But peacefully, without panic. Tin-

gling for the moment of light and life. Then the moment of rising through the soil, light coming at last through the air-holes, little dancing pepper-mints. The pod lifted slowly, guided by unseen forces and emerged prow first, splitting lengthwise along its ridges into thin orange wedges. (p. 40)

But "Buds" also suggests the emergence of the military dictatorship as well as the gradual assemblage of the Cartel's arsenal of vengeance and destruction. In the final section, "Spores," we encounter not the spores of a living organism but the convoluted bowels of Temoko prison where Iriyise is hidden. We are conducted on a walking tour through the Leper's Yard, past the Yard of the condemned to an outhouse close to the Yard of Lunatics where Iriyise lies in a coma. Only in "Seminal," the first section, is the narrative related to the theme of the healthy growth of the ideological seeds of Aiyero and the prospect of disseminating those seeds outside Aiyero's boundaries. Ofeyi envisions "the parallel progress of the new idea, the birth of the new man from the same germ as the cocoa seed, the Aiyero ideal disseminated with the same powerful propaganda machine of the Cartel throughout the land, taking hold of undirected youth and filling the vacuum of their transitional heritage with virile shoot" (p. 19).

LANGUAGE AND NARRATIVE TECHNIQUE

The narrator at the beginning of *Season* appears to be eager to supply all the information at his disposal but his observations are obscured by a penchant for poetic language. By poetic, one means the narrator's preference for a compact, elliptical and symbolic idiom. Most readers of Soyinka's fiction find this language very difficult at first. Soyinka brings to his prose works the same linguistic complexity that characterizes his poetry.

The first paragraph of *Season* is verbally overloaded. The first sentence runs to nearly eight lines with seven punctuational interruptions within it. There are rapid shifts in the first paragraph from one aspect of Aiyero's background and history to another. We move rapidly from

Aiyero's economic policy to its relaxed relationship with the capital, Ilosa to the new attraction the commune became for tourists and sociologists to Aiyero's present predicament as an object of sinister curiosity by the "radical centres of debate." The vocabulary is difficult and informal from the start: "a quaint anomaly," "pith-helmeted assessor," "anachronism," "definite guffaw," "erudite irrelevances," etc. (p. 2).

Throughout the first section, "Seminal," the reader is not quite sure of what the story is all about although the difficulty of the opening paragraphs is not sustained in the rest of the section. The reader must still make strenuous imaginative efforts during Ofeyi's dialogues with Ahime. Ahime's language is steeped in agricultural metaphors and vegetation rituals. At the induction ceremony, language has grown tense and expectant, even mystical, although it is frequently mellowed by the ritualistic overtones of the diction. One would rather prefer the simplicity of such expressions as "the climax of bright red sluices" to the turgic syntax of the opening paragraph. "Seminal" is about Aiyero's origins, background, customs, occupations, and ceremonies as communicated in a compact and strained manner.

In "Buds" the narrative begins to assume a more leisured pace. Here is the true beginning of the story. The opening lyric passage illustrates this fact ironically: "In the beginning, there was nectar and ambrosia/A golden pod contained them . . ." (p. 32). Ofeyi's language is solemn and reverential when speaking of Aiyero or the church, but he is sarcastic, humorous, and ironical in his portrait of the agents of the Cartel. The first victim of the narrator's sardonic humor is the incompetent Corporation Chairman who relies on the Corporation's I.Q. (the Intellectual Quota on the Director's Board) for the text of his public speeches. In presenting the Chairman, Soyinka relies on his dramatic technique. The Chairman reveals himself by what he does and says; his crude, unrefined utterance betrays his character: "It is not me who has to be unveiled; my better half standing over there did that a very long time ago" (p. 43). As for his intellectual abilities, look at his strenuous mental effort to distinguish the pips of a lieuten-

ant from those of a captain: "One pip make one captain,
two pips make one major, three pips make . . . oh dear, got
it all wrong . . . one pip, one lieutenant, two pips make one
captain" (p. 36).

With the Cross-river lords of the Cartel on the other
hand, Soyinka achieves his satirical effects by highlighting
each bodily deformity. Most of his victims are either in-
flated hulks of flesh or diminutive skeletons. Satire
through exaggerated deflation or inflation of the human
body was a technique perfected by the English Neo-classical satirists. Soyinka utilizes this technique to advantage in
his presentation of the Cross-river citizens. Zaki Amuri is a
mass of such boredom and inertia that he is presented as a
lifeless form rather than a living person: "Impassive and
expressionless, permanent slits of boredom and disdain
served for a pair of eyes. His figure filled a huge ornate
chair" (p. 119); in another instance his enormous flesh is as
immobile and as lifeless as the statue of a Buddha: "a faint
indulgent smile issued from the immobile Buddha form"
(p. 120). We notice the same concentration on physical
deformity in our first view of the governor of Temoko
prison:

> In vain he tried to keep his mind on the object of his
> search. So he turned it on the club-foot of the grinning
> governor of Temoko before him, most of whom was
> swallowed by the wide polished desk and terraces of
> files. Dwarf? He reminded him of a rounded egg on
> the back of an ant; that timber neck thrust over folded
> arms gave his back a strong suspicion of a hunch.
> (p. 282)

The deformity of the body reflects the deformity of the
mind, and enlarged parts of the human body mirror the
mass of cruelty in the soul.

The Cartel's peasant collaborators are primitive cannibals. Predatory images serve to emphasize their hunting
frenzy. Soyinka has consistently characterized their lust
for human flesh and blood with animal imagery. They
are "slaving bare-fanged creatures" whose "spear-point
snouts" are aimed at human breasts (p. 159).

The story reeks with the odor of decaying human flesh in the Labbe Bridge and the mortuary episodes (chapters XI and XII), but in the passage dealing with the wreckage of the hydroelectric dam which the men of Aiyero were building at Shage, Soyinka's language is poetic. The prose moves with a measured cadence, enlisting familiar poetic devices such as alliteration, assonance, consonance, internal rhyme, onomatopoeia. Short sentences interact with long ones, which build gradually to a climax.

> Brown claws, dead weights, slack iron jaws of monsters, caterpillar treads had churned and buckled through slag and swamp, angry rhinoceroses charging at prides of the forest, bringing them crashing down one after the other. Always they left the earth a little more naked, a little more exposed than before. The hope was that something took their place, and he meant something beyond the concrete structures. The silence erupted in his ears with the sounds of those iron mastodons in motion, and the army of rubber boots trampling earth into submission, the clangs of picks and shovels, blackskin, whiteskin, red and sweatskin, of levers, bolts and strains, luscious mudbath for the flesh and metal bestiary to tear up earth and throw it back in stronger, fructifying forms. Underneath his feet sank the inchoate gurgle of electric power. (p. 174)

This passage consists of two long sentences and three short ones. The poetic effect is concentrated on the long ones, the first and the fourth. Notice, in the first sentence, the musical cadence of the paired units: "brown claws" and "dead weights"; the assonantal echoes of "dead weights" and in "churned" and "buckled"; the internal rhymes "claws" and "jaws"; and the alliterated consonants in "slag and swamp". In the fourth sentence, Soyinka provides the onomatopoetic effect of "clangs of picks and shovels," and the triple rhymes, "blackskin," "whiteskin," and "sweatskin." Each unit of the fourth sentence is a line of verse, and the two leading sentences are erected as a montage. In the first sentence, for instance, the apocalyptic monsters begin their civilizing assault on the heart of darkness quietly but soon escalate into a frenzied crescendo of action.

The language is as heroic as the heroic aspirations of the architects of the hydroelectric dam. This epic action involves cosmic giants—the iron monsters with caterpillar treads, the angry rhinoceroses, the iron mastodons, and the army of rubber boots trampling earth into submission. The language is densely textured and evocative; the images are powerfully visual. One is reminded, from the epic intensity of the passage, of the opening lines of *Idanre*, which etch the actions of the "skymen of Voids' regenerate Waste."

If the Shage passage is tense with heroic action, the Labbe Bridge episode vibrates with putrefaction. The Labbe Bridge incident is the bathetic converse of the heroic activities at Shage:

> . . . after this bridge it was even more certain that no stream remained unpolluted, no pool existed in which a man could throw a stone without bursting a bloated skin of decay. Not even the wells, for in their mindlessness the Lords of the Cartel had not refrained from soiling the needs of the living for pure sources. (p. 193)

Language is impassioned and rhetorical, informed by a sense of moral indignation similar to that found in *The Man Died*. Here, for example, is the narrator's disquisition on the rage for destruction which he calls "operation":

> Operation! Usually the word came from the more hardened thugs, the crude strong-armed gangs who roamed the cities creating mayhem in strongholds of opposition. But he [the Dentist] made it sound far more diagnostic, an inevitable course for a patient who had gone beyond the stage of simple medications. Nothing would serve, now but the operating table, a clean, drastic surgery. Even the venerable vendors of compromise, miscalled peace, had come to recognize the failure of their surrogates. One after another they withdrew into silence, admitting the impotence of their solution. (pp. 108–109)

Compare this passage with the rhetorical intensity of this example from *The Man Died*:

> A private quest? Stuff for the tragic stage and ritual
> rounds of passion? A brave quest that diverges from,
> with never a backward glance at history's tramp of feet
> along the communal road? Is this then the long-threat-
> ened moment for jettisoning, for instance, notions of
> individual responsibility and the struggle it im-
> poses?[33]

In *Season*, as in *The Man Died*, there is a rage and an
urgency in the language which is the direct consequence of
Soyinka's own circumstances at the time both works were
conceived. *Season* is inspired, in parts, by Soyinka's prison
experience and *The Man Died* is a direct account of that
ordeal.

This novel, like many of Soyinka's works, has not escaped the influence of his traditional culture. Near the end
where Ofeyi exercises his mythic abilities as a magician, he
assails Suberu with a barrage of aphorisms culled from
traditional lore. Like his mythic ancestor, Ofeyi succeeds in
winning Suberu to his side through the power of words:

> The milk rots in the coconut if left too long. The child
> rots in the womb if it exceeds nine months. . . . The
> life-yolk rots in the shell if it is not opened in time. . . .
> Haven't you seen the butterfly struggle like mad out of
> the cocoon, Suberu? What happens if your talisman is
> buried in rubble by your enemy. . . . Don't you know
> that even the kernel in the palm turns rancid sooner or
> later, disease finds the weak eye in its hard shell and
> rots the inner flesh! (pp. 315–316)

The appeal to traditional wisdom in this passage is to be
contrasted with the abuse of that wisdom in an episode in
The Interpreters in which Chief Winsala, caught red-
handed as he takes a bribe, tries to hide his shame under a
cloak of proverbs:

> . . . it is no matter for rejoicing when a child sees
> his father naked. . . . The wise eunuch keeps from
> women; the hungry clerk dons coat/over his narrow
> belt and who will say his belly is flat? But when
> *egungun* is unmasked in the market can he then ask
> *egbe* to snatch him into the safety of *igbale*? Won't
> they tell him the grave is meant only for the keepers of
> mystery? When the Bale borrows a horse-tail, he sends
> a menial so when the servant comes back empty-
> handed he can say, Did I send you? The adulterer who
> makes assignations in a room with one exit, is he not
> asking to feed his scrotum to the fishes of Ogun?[34]

Such symbolism is readily available to Soyinka. The
most obvious example is the symbolism of St. George and
the dragon, which receives a satirical treatment. "St.
George seated on that horse," says the unabashed Corporation Chairman, "is representative of the new order which is
battling the dragon which represents the forces of our greatest national enemy—corruption" (p. 44). The real St.
George is not the Chairman but Ofeyi and the revolutionary vanguard of the new order from Aiyero. Another obvious symbol is the lone baobab tree straining to survive on
the arid landscape of the Cross-river desert. Soyinka is less
esoteric in his deployment of symbols in this novel. They
are shorn, unlike those in his poetry, of their esoteric ab-
stractness. He works and reworks such symbols as the baobab tree and the cripple Aliyu, until their import can
hardly escape the most casual reader. The baobab tree is the
natural counterpart to Aliyu. Both characters are metaphors for the Cross-river mind, the visual representation of
the disease of the soul. As befits the land of death, the
Cross-river environment thwarts growth, and Soyinka
could hardly have improved upon his use of the monstrous
baobab and the apparition called Aliyu as metaphors for
this idea. The baobab tree, which, under normal circumstances, is a tree of life is here a tree of death (the reader
might recall that in *Two Thousand Seasons* Armah also
perceived the baobab as a tree of death).[35] In *Season*, both
characters (the baobab and Aliyu) are delineated with a
special emphasis on physiognomy:

Against the landscape rose a single baobab, dry and stunted. Its trunk was broad and even up to a few feet, then it was overtaken by an abnormality or retardation that seemed, from the lumps, swellings and contortions, a blight of human infection—rickets, beri-beri, kwashiokor, and a variety of goitres. A distended belly in the middle of the trunk thrust its wrinkled navel at the black horizon. From malformed shoulders balanced on a flat chest writhed an abortion of limbs. Where the head might have been thinner branches hissed skywards, daring forked tongues in a venomous protection of whatever mystery hoard lay within the so-called tree of life. (p. 212)

And here is Aliyu:

Now they saw a wasted limb twine itself creeper-like around the staff; the other, hardly more fleshed or disoriented, but with more apparent pith stabbed the ground at an incongruous angle. Only the arms were strong, the entire locomotion of this strange human contraption appeared to depend on the propelling force of the arms. Above those arms and powerful shoulders a head was stuck with the barest suggestion of a neck. It was an elongated head with a distinctly horizontal axis, ravaged by smallpox marks and with one eye permanently closed. (p. 275)

Egrets, on the other hand, are symbols of purity; the egrets remind Ofeyi of that other strifeless, peaceful world which he envisions, the pastoral world of order and loveliness represented by Aiyero, where serenity still reigns on the face of nature (pp. 148 and 195).

The story moves on two planes, the external and the internal. The external narrative is the account of the Cartel's activities in Cross-river and Ilosa—the killings, the maimings, the burnings, and other external details of the plot. The internal narrative concerns itself with Ofeyi's visions, his soliloquies, his daydreams, his nightmarish perceptions of monsters. His visions are the direct legacy of Soyinka's prolonged deprivation of external contacts dur-

ing his prison days. As a result of his mind's extended
acquaintance-ship with dark interiors, an increasingly introspective tone has crept into much of Soyinka's post-war
writings, especially his poetry and fiction. His imprisonment might be responsible for the frequent evocation of
enclosed spaces in the novel. The catacombs of the mortuary episodes, the entombed congregation in the Tabernacle
of Hope, the underground refugee camps in Cross-river,
the convoluted bowels of Temoko prison, Aiyero's bowered
sanctuaries—these are the manifestations of an imagination that is increasingly Orphic. These underworld settings
owe their persistence to the novel's mythic background, but
they cannot be dissociated from Soyinka's long familiarity
with dark spaces during his prison days.

Memories of his gropings in the dark, of the urge to
extend his consciousness into outer space, impinge themselves on his imagination as the story progresses. Ofeyi
frequently lapses into visionary states, in which distinctions in time and space are annulled and monsters become
actors in the narrative. He manifests early in the novel this
tendency to slip without warning into animystic landscapes. As he watched the body of the dead Custodian lying
in state, Ofeyi transformed himself suddenly into a floating
corpse:

> Submitting to a sensation of floating Ofeyi watched
> the body levitate towards the four golden ostrich eggs
> which crowned the bedposts. He took the place of the
> dead man, sinking deep in the feather-bed. (p. 13)

Ofeyi's vision of the monsters of the underworld at the
wrecked worksite at Shage is the most frightening of his
hallucinations. The gigantic cranes, the "mud-poulticed
caterpillar wheels" and the "concrete mixer cauldrons"
earlier been described as "iron mastodons in motion" transform Shage into a chasm of nonbeing, peopled by the
Anubis-headed multitudes of Ofeyi's dreams.

Earlier in the novel, when Ofeyi retreats to Aiyero's
bowered sanctuary after his first unsuccessful encounter
with the agents of the Cartel, he is lulled into somnolence
by the unearthly calm that pervades the bough-vaulted

pool and his mind sinks back to the silt-beds of history,
conjuring up all the historical associations known to the
pool. On this occasion, his daydream is fed by his immediate experiences in Cross-river of violence and exploitation. The pool had witnessed several centuries of exploitation on the African continent. To the slave-raiders, the
pool had served as an escape-route; to the colonial invaders,
it was a port of anchor; and in a recent past, the pool was a
base for gold and oil prospecting companies. We have here
an interplay of violence and exploitation affecting three
phases in Africa's history—pre-colonial, colonial, and
post-colonial. Ofeyi's mind invokes the ghosts of the historical personages who are associated with those periods in
Africa's history:

> He felt borne on a vintage fluid and potency of the
> past, as if invisible denizens of that space had laid
> their hands on him. What answers shall I make you
> then you restless questioners rising from dark silt-
> beds? How change your whitened bones into some-
> thing rich and strange? (p. 90)

But the eras of plunder are repeating themselves in the
present-day exploitation by the Cartel. To the ever-increas-
ing hordes of imaginary accusers conjured up by Ofeyi's
restless mind, he has this answer to make:

> Embarrass me no more with your accusations. . . . Ask
> your questions of the Cartel who will drain the oil as
> they have the milk of the cocoa. (p. 91)

Soyinka uses here a sophisticated form of flashback
which operates, as in certain episodes in *The Interpreters*,
by means of associational logic. We shall encounter more
examples of this form of flashback later in the novel. Meanwhile, there is yet another apparition at the pool, the figure
of the "mystery virgin at transit lounge," Taiila. This
figure appears first as Iriyise and transforms itself later into
Taiila. We are reminded of the mysterious airport encounter between Ofeyi and both the Dentist and Taiila.

This story was first hinted at in Chapter II (p. 25). It has resurfaced here (Chapter VI) with clearer outlines in Ofeyi's hallucinatory visions.

Associational linkage of events recurs at the Tabernacle of Hope where the condition of the entombed congregation reminds Ofeyi of previous religious persecutions, especially the Spanish Inquisition. In one instant the underground church is transformed into an archaeological catacomb in which archaeologists are digging out the remains of religious martyrs of history. What follows is an imaginary dialogue among the excavators:

> This sector . . . I suggest we dig here, this sector . . . poke poke poke . . . there, a rare piece of luck! A child skeleton entire. A bit of the skull is gone, could have been done with an axe . . . now, we had better scrape away carefully here . . . what did I tell you? A most remarkable story. Unique graphic details. Mother obviously trying to shield infant . . . most touching. (p. 272)

The appeal to history through a retrospective reconnection of events of similar background (a form of fictional objective correlative, if one wishes) reaffirms Soyinka's awareness of the eternal recurrence of evil and man's natural disposition toward it. It is a truth asserted in *A Dance of the Forests* (1963) and reaffirmed in *Madman and Specialists* through the philosophy of As. Apart from the visionary interruptions in the narrative, *Season* advances on a more linear progression than *The Interpreters*.

POSTSCRIPT ON CHARACTERIZATION

Season of Anomy is not a novel of character but one of ideas, something close to the *roman a these*, a typical example of which is Hamidon Kane's *Ambiguous Adventure* (1963). For a work of its size, *Season* is sparsely populated. Soyinka's primary intention is not to plumb characters to the depth or develop their psychology in full but rather to project his obsessive ideas through them. Characters are merely vehicles for the author's thesis that justice is the first condition of humanity. Only Ofeyi is seen whole. The other characters must take their cue from elements of an already predetermined schema: they are either good or bad. Soyinka betrays early in the novel his intention to view his characters from a two-dimensional perspective as soon as he resorts to biblical allegory. In chapter II (p. 25), Ofeyi speaks of the Faustian tussle for his soul between two opposing forces represented, on the one hand, by the good angel Taiila, who would pilot him to safety along the road of salvation, and on the other, by the bad angel, the Dentist, whose road leads to damnation. The Dentist is not truely evil, only an advocate for social change through shock. The Dentist's road actually leads to salvation through damnation. In an unguarded moment when the mask of fiction is lifted, Soyinka speaks like the Dentist:

> A war with its attendant human suffering, must, when that evil is unavoidable be made to fragment more than buildings: it must shatter the foundations of thought and re-create. Only in this way does every individual share in the cataclysm and understand the purpose of the sacrifice.[36]

However, the allegorical distinctions between good and evil are deeply entrenched, and they tally with the novel's two diversely opposed moral orders: the world of Aiyero and the world of the Cartel. Characterization is influenced by the allegorical dialectics, for it compels a choice between one or the other of the two angels. Ranged alongside Aiyero, the good angel, are Ahime; Ofeyi, his mistress Iriyise and his aide Zaccheus, who is addicted to trees like his biblical namesake; Taiila herself, her brother Dr. Chalil and her mother, Mrs. Ramath. The Christian refugees at the Tabernacle of Hope belong to this camp. On the side of evil we have the Cartel quadruplets—Zaki Amuri, Chief Batoki, Chief Biga, and the military spokesman, the Commandant-in-Chief—and their sub-agents: the journalist named Spyhole and the governor of Temoko nicknamed Club-foot, and Suberu who later came over to

Aiyero's side. On this side must also be included Batoki's family—Mama Biye, his wife and Biye his daughter.

The animosity shown toward the Indo-Pakistanis in *The Man Died* is tempered by the sympathetic portrait of Taiila and her family. Soyinka considers the Orient as a symbol of religious mysticism. Hence, in *The Man Died*[37] he ridicules the Asian doctor who prostitutes his conscience in the service of a corrupt establishment. He holds in high esteem such Asians as Taiila, her brother, and her mother who stand for the mysticism that is India and the humanity which might reasonably be expected to go with mystical life.

In a lesser hand the schematized characterization might have been detrimental to the overall aesthetic intent; in this instance, it has not seriously undermined the novel's artistic appeal. *Season of Anomy* is unquestionably a powerful novel. Its impact on the reader's imagination is considerable in spite of the unevenness in character development.

Notes

1. The key to an understanding of Soyinka's novel is his prison memoir, *The Man Died*. Much of the background material in this chapter is taken from that book. For more information on Soyinka's journey to the North, see *The Man Died* (London: Rex Collings, 1972), pp. 164–169.

2. *The Man Died*, pp. 92 and 119.

3. *Ibid.*, p. 192.

4. This threatening injunction appears in *The Man Died*, p. 129 and in *Season of Anomy* (London: Rex Collings, 1973), p. 282. Subsequent references are to this edition.

5. *The Man Died*, p. 125.

6. Chapter XII, p. 94 of *The Man Died* and the whole of Chapter XXXIII speak of the Third Force.

7. Wole Soyinka, "An interview by Biodun Jeyifous," *Transition* 42 (1973), p. 62. See also John Agetua, *When*

the Man Died (Benin: Bendel Newspapers Corporation, 1975), p. 41.

8. For the myth of the dying god, see *The Golden Bough*, one-volume edition (London: Macmillan, 1963), pp. 348-355.

9. For the outline of the Orpheus myth provided in this chapter, I am indebted to the study of the myth done by the classical scholars, Walter A. Strauss, *Descent and Return: The Orphic Theme in Modern Literature* (Cambridge: Harvard University Press, 1971), pp. 5-6; and Philip Mayerson, *Classical Mythology in Literature, Art and Music* (Lexington Xerox College Publishing, 1971), pp. 270-274.

10. The protagonist in Okigbo's *Labyrinths* (London: Heinemann, 1971) is an Orpheus figure.

11. *The Man Died*, p. 182.

12. *Ibid.*, p. 182.

13. Wole Soyinka, *Idanre and Other Poems* (London: Methuen, 1967), p. 53.

14. The term "socialist realism" is borrowed from the illuminating essay by Omafume F. Onoge; "The Crisis of Consciousness in Modern African Literature: A Survey," *Canadian Journal of African Studies*, Vol. VIII, No. 2 (1974), pp. 385-410.

15. Ngugi wa Thiong'o, *Homecoming* (London: Heinemann, 1972), p. 46.

16. Agetua, *When the Man Died*, p. 41.

17. Wole Soyinka, "Who's Afraid of Elesin Oba?" Paper presented at the Radical Perspectives of African Literature Conference, Ibadan, 1977 (mimeographed), p. 4.

18. Agetua, *When the Man Died*, p. 41.

19. "Who's Afraid of Elesin Oba?," p. 5.

20. *Ibid.*, p. 6.

21. *The Man Died*, p. 181.

22. Wole Soyinka, *Myth, Literature and the African World* (Cambridge: Cambridge University Press, 1960), p. 114.

23. Wole Soyinka, "An interview by Biodun Jeyifous," *Transition* 42 (1973), p. 62.

24. See the poems "Massacre, October '66" in *Idanre and Other Poems*, pp. 51-52, and "Conversations at Night with a Cockroach" in *A Shuttle in the Crypt* (New York: Hill and Wang, 1972), pp. 5-13.

25. *The Man Died*, p. 95.

26. See Chapters Two, Twelve, and Thirty-three.

27. *A Shuttle*, p. 9.

28. Wole Soyinka "From a Common Black Cloth: A Reassessment of the African Literary Image," *The American Scholar* 32 (1963), p. 392.

29. *Idanre and Other Poems*, p. 34.

30. *Ibid.*, p. 37.

31. *A Shuttle*, p. 13.

32. *Idanre*, p. 68.

33. *The Man Died*, p. 87.

34. *The Interpreters* (London: Heinemann, 1965), pp. 91-92.

35. Ayi Kwei Armah, *Two Thousand Seasons* (London: Heinemann, 1973), p. 47.

36. *The Man Died*, p. 183.

37. *Ibid.*, pp. 191-192.

6

――――――――――――― △ △ ―――――――――――――

AUTOBIOGRAPHY AS LITERATURE:
AKE AND *THE MAN DIED*

S oyinka has published, to date, two books that belong to
the genre of autobiography. The first is, of course, the
controversial prison memoir, *The Man Died* (1972), which
created a good deal of controversy on its first appearance.
The popular view is that it is a political autobiography not
completely distanced from the actual events. Many years
have passed since its publication, so it is perhaps time to
take another, more dispassionate look at this book. Were
the judgments of early commentators hasty? This chapter
examines the relative merits of *The Man Died* and *Ake*
(1981), his memoir of childhood.

Ake covers Soyinka's life up to his tenth year or there-
abouts. Those years were uneventful according to personal
records, although Soyinka nearly lost his life in two accidents and an eye in a third. *Ake* is, however, an important
document for students of Soyinka. The book affords a
clearer insight into Soyinka's family background and confirms our present view of the man as a nonconformist.
Because his character was formed early in his life, the
memoir provides, in addition, some insights into his early
works and underscores the mystical, the inexplicable, and
the irrational as permanent features of the African worldview.

Soyinka was born into an educated family, the son of the
Headmaster of St. Peter's Primary School, located in the
Ake neighbourhood of Abeokuta. His mother, who was
moderately well educated, managed a provisions store close
to the Oba's Palace. The family was deeply religious. Soyin-

ka's parents were among the second generation of converts to the Christian fold as a result of the Christianizing efforts of the indefatigable Rev. J. J. Ransome-Kuti. Soyinka's mother, humorously nicknamed the "Wild Christian" because of her impatience with infidels, endeavored to create a Christian home. Lying, stealing, stubbornness, sulkiness, etc., were attributed to the influence of *emi esu*, the evil one, and were discouraged. The rod was liberally applied for the slightest infraction of the domestic code of conduct. Soyinka's father, nicknamed "Essay," enforced these codes in the classroom with an even greater rigidity.

The family lived at Ake Parsonage, a sprawling establishment rapidly losing much of the luxury and the grandeur that its grounds possessed when the bishops lived there. The deterioration in physical condition was thought in some quarters to reflect the gradual lapse in faith among later-day Christians. However, Essay and Wild Christian endeavoured to transform their Ake residence into a model Christian home. That home succored numerous waifs and strays and other hangers-on who found their way there. Those among them who had not yet heard the Word of God were quickly Christianized and baptized. Soyinka reveals the beauty as well as the severity of that homestead; it had order but also discipline, which Soyinka rebelled against. The bugs hiding in cushion crevices have not been forgotten nor have the bags of rice and black-eye beans jostling with the children for sleeping space on the floor in his mother's bedroom. Soyinka has more sympathy for his father, Essay, who was sparing of food, while his mother, because she had an eye on the family budget, resented the presence of uninvited guests during mealtime.

The young Wole who emerged from this household was an "enfant terrible," bold, stubborn, self-confident, argumentative, proud of his precocious abilities and prone, like every other child, to childish wiles and guiles. His rebellious temperament might have been natural to him, but his rebellion appeared often to be no more than a means of sheltering himself from the too-rigid regimentations of his home. The whole effort of his parents toward discipline produced, in Wole's own case, the opposite effect; It led him to distrust the world of grown-ups, which he equated with injustice and cruelty: "There was neither justice nor logic in the world of grown-ups";[1] it was a world of beatings, standing in the corner, or resting one finger on the ground while bent over as a form of punishment. His concern for justice remained with him in adult life. He ridicules his mother's faith in prayer and religious passion, but this attitude might have been conditioned by his present religious scepticism. That is, he may now feel differently toward his mother's faith than he actually felt when he was a child.

Young Wole was a sad, lonely boy who loved groves and secluded places where he could commune with nature and meditate. This quest for isolated spots might have become a habit as a result of his consciousness of that hostile adult world. One of the places he loved to retreat to at Ake was a rock named Jonah:

> On the other side of the school building, hidden from us was a rock that was smoothed by our feet. It appeared to cover the earth. . . . This rock is called Jonah. That was my rock. My own very private rock. Jonah was my own very secret habitat. (pp. 63–64)

One will recall Egbo in *The Interpreters* and his love for isolated places, especially secluded rocks. *Ake* teems with such insights into Soyinka's early works. The episode of Egbo, the lover of rocks, who would not prostrate himself to grown-ups because he does not prostrate himself to God are infiltrated into the world of fiction from Soyinka's childhood experiences. At Isara, his father's native home, young Wole replied tartly to a village chief who insisted that he should prostrate himself before him:

> If I couldn't prostrate myself to God, why should I prostrate to you? You are just a man like my father aren't you? (p. 128)

T. S. Eliot said that materials from life have a way of infiltrating themselves subconsciously into the world of art. Childhood images, Eliot believed, tend ultimately to embed themselves permanently on the writer's imagination: "only a part of an author's imagery comes from his reading. It comes from the whole of his sensitive life since early childhood."[2] The two episodes—of Egbo the lover of rocks and the stalwart champion of human rights—are directly lifted from Soyinka's own childhood experiences. There are other episodes in *The Interpreters* that bear some subconscious relationships to those experiences. Isara, Soyinka writes, is characterized by laterite mud houses, floors of dung plaster, and indigo dye on old women's hands, and he adds: "I hated the touch of hands transformed by the indigo gloss. And it was in Isara also that we saw so much indigo-green tattoo on the arms and bodies of women" (p. 67). Is this aversion for indigo not subconsciously recalled in the surrealistic passage in *The Interpreters* in which Joe Golder imagined himself to have been drowned in enormous pots of indigo?[3]

At the Oba's palace at Abeokuta the images of deities engraved on the palace walls made a deep impression on young Wole. Kola's "Pantheon" in *The Interpreters* might have been inspired by Soyinka's memories of the gods carved at the Alake's palace walls. The images include the following representations:

> the eyes of Ifa, Sango, divination priests, Ogun, Obatala, Erinle, Osanyin, iron staffs with their rings of mounted divination birds . . . even the Ogboni in procession, frozen in motion. (p. 204)

The *Ogboni* is a strong motif in *Ake*. It is one of the images of childhood that is deeply engraved on Soyinka's memories. The *Ogboni* instill fear into all who are not members of the cult. To young Wole, the *Ogboni* was a symbol of terror and of supernatural power. I quote the passage on Ogboni at length to show the cultic functions of this secret society and the impressions that registered on the imagination of young Wole:

> From the shop we saw them pass at all hours of the day on their way to attend a meeting of chiefs at the Aafin or their own periodic sessions within the Ogboni compound. Age appeared to be the condition for

this numinous society, yet a number of them also strode by in crude, vigorous health, called out their greetings in robust voices, looking more like warriors than participants at sessions of cunning, experience and wisdom. . . . The Ogboni slid through Ake like ancient wraiths, silent, dark and wise, a tanned pouch of Egba history, of its mysterious insights, or thudded through on warrior's feet, defiant and raucous, broad and compact with unspoken violence. We were afraid of them. Among other furtive hints and whispers we heard that they sent out child kidnappers whose haul was essential to some of their rites and ceremonies. . . . Their weird chants drifted many evenings into the parsonage, punctuated by concerted thuds which, we learnt, was the sound of their staffs striking the clay floor as they circled round in their secret enclave. In Ogboni reposed the real power of the King and land, not that power which seemed to be manifested in the prostrations of men and women at the feet of the king, but the *real* power, both supernatural and caballistic, the intriguing midnight power. (pp. 203-204)

The *Ogboni* theme is one of the memories included in the passage dealing with reveries of childhood in the long poem *Idanre* (1967). The apocalyptic vision here reveals a "gaunt *ogboni*" scuttling for shelter on a zebra's back:

Later, diminutive zebras raced on track edges
Round the bed, dwarfs blew on royal bugles
A gaunt *ogboni* raised his staff and vaulted on
A zebra's back, galloped up a quivering nose
A battle with the suffocating shrouds.[4]

The insights into *Ogboni* in *Ake* will illuminate the *Ogboni* imagery in the above poem; thus, in some cases, specific childhood experiences are directly commented upon in later works. Such is the case with the death of Soyinka's sister Folasade (pp. 95-98), who was an *abiku* and died when she was exactly one year old. This episode is recalled in an early poem, "A First Deathday," published in *Idanre and Other Poems* (p. 26).

The world revealed in *Ake* is a world of incomprehensible occurrences, a world of the inexplicable, of mysteries and supernatural happenings. The *Ogboni* is only one of the dark, mysterious forces that inhabit the world. Their midnight rituals, the sounds of which drifted to the parsonage from their enclave at the palace, have become part of the images of night in the imagination of Soyinka. The cult itself is synonymous with the *essence* of dark mysterious power. The nocturnal mumblings of Sorowanke, the mad woman who muttered to herself, recall it. And because the itinerant women traders from Isara arrive at the parsonage by night and depart at dawn and because their body and arms are painted with indigo dyes, they, too, form part of the images of night. Their low-voiced mumblings on the parsonage premises became "a weird cultic dirge not dissimilar from the chanting of the Ogboni which sometimes reached our house from their meeting-house at the Aafin" (p. 129).

The mystic mood is evoked early in the book. The thick woods around the parsonage were believed by the children to be inhabited by spirits and *ghommids* (Soyinka's term for traditional forest spirits); and Uncle Sanya, brother to J. J. Ransome-Kuti, who also lived at the parsonage, was believed to be an *oro* (a tree daemon). And soon afterward, we encounter that enigmatic child, Bukola, the bookseller's daughter, who is not of this world for she is *abiku*. She can conjure her existence at will out of this world in order to rejoin her mates in the *abiku* kingdom. She plagued her parents with her strange metamorphoses.

Isara is "several steps into the past. Age hung from every corner, the patina of ancestry glossed all subjects" (p. 67); there the rafters are bare, smoky, and mysterious. It is here that the shadowy women traders resume their human identity; much of the aura of mystery that surrounds their person is dispelled, but the image of Wole's grandfather, simply called "Father," sustains the sense of the mystical: "he truly embodies the male Isara for me in its rugged mysterious strength the female counterpart of which I had earlier obtained from the trading women" (p. 139). In *The Man Died* in which Father was recalled, the grandfather retains that image of "mysterious strength": "My grandfather sits gnome-like, chuckling secretively, every chunk of his body pulsing with love and strength."[5] Wole was called upon to taste a bit of that "mysterious strength" in the ankle-cutting ceremony which the old man himself supervised. The atmosphere in the ankle-cutting chamber was weird and eerie. Wole was surprised one early morning by two shadowy apparitions who had been shepherded into his sleeping-room by his grandfather. On the floor were ritual objects—a clay dish, a bottle of palm-oil, tin containers filled with dark powders. The ankle-cutting ceremony initiated him into the paternal care of his family tutelary spirit. At the end of it all, Father tells him: "Whoever offers you food, take it. Eat it. Don't be afraid, *as long as your heart says, Eat*" (p. 147).

The book ends with an account of the events that led to the formation of the Women's Movement led by Mrs. Ransome-Kuti. A meeting of the wives of professionals, which originally began as a welfare task force, became infected with the spirit of national consciousness which was very much in the air in the early 1940s. In time, this welfare assemblage attracted the attention of all Egba women and became a powerful feminist body that defended the rights of women. In one swoop of feminist fury, it besieged the Oba's palace to obtain the abolition of tax for Egba women. The field marshall of the operation was Mrs. Ransome-Kuti, popularly known as "Beere." Wole's mother was one of her lieutenants. Beere's husband, the inimitable Rev. A. O. Ransome-Kuti, popularly called "Daodu," acted as an unofficial political adviser.

The Ransome-Kutis were the most celebrated representatives of genteel culture in the Ake neighborhood. Culturally, they lived in a world apart; they were refined, polite, and enlightened, and supremely human and philanthropic. They inspired Wole with awe and admiration. Daodu, who made the most lasting impression on Wole, possessed an enormous physique and a most prepossessing personality. The bulldog expression on his face reminded Wole of Winston Churchill. He was an educator, a humanitarian, and a disciplinarian. As the principal of Abeokuta Grammar School, he was indefatigable, conscientious, and firm. He did everything with fanfare and in the grand style:

> Everything that Daodu did was not merely larger than
> size, he made trivia itself larger than life and made
> drama of every event. Discipline was turned into an
> adventure. (p. 173)

To what extent can these memories of childhood be considered a work of art? Both autobiography and fiction originate from the same social matrix; and in a sense, much of African fiction is autobiographical. In his interesting study on the autobiographical imagination in African writing, James Olney says of Achebe's fiction that it is "a supra-personal, multi-generational autobiography of the Ibo people." Ououloguem's novel *Le Devoir de Violence*, he added, can be figuratively seen as "a symbolic autobiography of the entire continent and community of Africa."[6] He distinguishes artistic autobiographies from, say, political ones. Artistic autobiographies are organized like novels—they do not adhere too closely to a chronological, biographical arrangement. In addition to organizational skill, Olney isolates one more criterion: value or significance or what Lewis Nkosi has called "literature as revelation";[7] and Olney claims that events recalled from the past assume this significance only when

> a pattern has been discerned, achieved, and imposed,
> out of the author's own internal order, by himself,
> thus acting as an artist.[8]

Olney has three major works in mind in his evaluation of the artistic effectiveness of autobiographical literature. These works are Camara Laye's *The African Child* (1954), Ezekiel Mphalele's *Down Second Avenue* (1959), and Alfred Hutchinson's *Road to Ghana* (1960).

Wole Soyinka's *Ake* can be added to this noble rank of artistic autobiographies. The question of value is subjective and we will return to it later, but the work is artistically organized. Looking back on his childhood after 48 years, Soyinka selected only those events that could mesh childhood recollections into unified pattern. The orchestration of individual episodes is thematic rather than chronological. For example, the accidental explosion of his father's air-gun actually happened at Ake, but it was recalled in the section of the book dealing with Isara, his father's birthplace. At Isara, Wole compared the bare, smoky, mysterious rafters in father's house with the sealed-in ceiling at the parsonage. At the parsonage, ceiling mats were occasionally ruined by the termites, thus revealing the zinc roof, but these holes held no terrors for the childish mind; and there was that other occasion when he made a hole in the ceiling by firing an accidental shot through it. Then follows the story of the explosion.

But by far the most poetic of the chapters is chapter ten. It begins with the nocturnal mumblings of Sorowanke, the mad woman who lives by the mango tree, and the amorous interlude between her and her lunatic lover, Yokolu. Then it speeds on to the flavors of Ibarepa market, edges off once again to the sounds and sights of the Dayisi Promenade, and returns eventually to a final portrait of Sorowanke, whose stomach has begun to bulge as a result of being impregnated by her demon lover, Yokolu.

Ake cannot be said to possess value to the same degree that Camara Laye's autobiography, *The African Child*, does. That autobiography is recognized as an archetypal specimen of African childhood as a whole. Laye's parents are invested with universal qualities. His mother is the totality of African womanhood in miniature, that same womanhood that Senghor celebrates in his poems; his father's technical skill is a tribute to those who have not invented anything. The initiation ceremonies in Laye's novel are no longer personal experiences but ceremonies that must initiate every true African to a state of manhood.

Soyinka's *Ake* does not possess this universal appeal. Soyinka's childhood environment was urban rather than rural, and he was born, as already noted, into an educated family. Tea was served at that home for breakfast as well as bread and butter and omelettes, and Soyinka tells us that he even tried his hand at the piano. Traditional occupations (when they are mentioned) are not perceived from "within" nor even with sympathy. Soyinka goes to the countryside as a Medza in the midst of his Kala countrymen. Laye strikes the same attitude at Tindican, but he sympathizes with his kinsmen there and regrets that he could not truly become

one of them. At Isara Soyinka enjoys his privileges as
"Omo Teacher," the Headmaster's son. When he goes to
the farm with Broda Pupa, it is with amusement that he
condescends to eat snake meat with the natives:

> Nobody eats snakes, I said. He looked at me, a slow
> dawning in his eyes. "Ah, I forgot, Omo teacher. The
> teacher's children don't eat things like that. They eat
> bread and butter." (p. 133)

Ake cannot move us in the way that *The African Child*
moves us because it is the autobiography of a westernized
African. The ankle-cutting ceremony is an initiation into a
private cult not a communal one as is the case with the
various initiation ceremonies in *The African Child*. Even
the evocation of the mystical, which gives Laye's novel
much of its significance, is treated with scepticism in *Ake*.
Here for example is Soyinka's reactions to the old women
he met at the witches' stall:

> From time to time, a wizened hand rose from the dark
> interior of the stalls, fly-whisk in hand, and described
> in a slow circle through the stall. I experienced shock
> at their flat, emptied breasts and remembered suddenly
> that it was wrong to stare, I looked away. Were these
> the witches we heard so much about? No breasts that I
> had seen before had appeared so flat, it did not seem
> human. (p. 42)

The mystical world is made real in *Ake*, but Soyinka is not
a part of that world. It is Laye's full confidence in that
world that has endeared *The African Child* to our memory.

There is however, something to be said in favor of *Ake*:
Soyinka's vision of childhood is objective and realistic. The
book has not retreated into a world of fantasy and make-
believe as has *The African Child*. What we have in *Ake* is a
real world of domestic brutality and, to young Wole's childish mind, of injustice. "There was neither justice nor logic
in the world of grown-ups" (p. 104), he keeps on telling us.
The larger world outside the home is marked by intrigue,
insincerity, and a form of political and economic exploita-

tion against which the Egba women rose in revolt. Only in the episode dealing with his experiences at the Kouroussa primary school did Laye attempt to reveal the brutalities of his childhood world. There at the primary school the big boys beat up the younger ones with the apparent connivance of the headmaster; but this unwholesome glimpse of his childhood world is easily forgotten as the book speeds on to its celebration of the glory. That one-sided image of the African past is one reason why Soyinka disparages the literature of *Negritude*. He appreciates *The African Child* for its genuine insights into the African worldview, but the work cannot be exempt from his general strictures on the inward, introspective narcissism of the *Negritude* movement. "Every creative act breeds and destroys fear, contains within itself both the salvation and the damnation,"[9] Soyinka has said. *Ake* has both. Here is one more example of the damnation:

> Isara was not the most sanitary of places. There were communal *salanga*, deep latrine-pits, usually well-kept. But it seemed to be accepted that children's excrement could be passed anywhere, after which the mongrel dogs which roamed about in abundance were summoned to eat it up. If they were not available, flies swarmed them until they finally dried up, were scattered by unwary feet at night, churned through by bicycles and the occasional motor lorry. And there were uncultivated patches in between dwellings into which faeces were flung or expelled directly by squatting adults. (pp. 130-131)

The considerations of value and pattern, that is, the organization of the artistic material, are not the only factors that give literature its identity. The quality of language in a given work, the humanness of the characters, and the strategies for the engineering of their emotions must also be considered. Soyinka is not known for character portrayal; their emotions do not always mean much to him, and his characters are not always fully developed. His language, however, is generally high-strung, poetic, and metaphysical. These characteristics are more evident in his other works than in *Ake*; here the abstract metaphysical tone moderates, and his language is pedestrian and matter of fact. The opening paragraphs lack the turgidity and the complexity that characterize syntax and diction in the introductory paragraphs of his novels. Diction is simple most of the time, and events are perceived from the point of view of a child:

> On a misty day, the steep rise towards Ikoko would join the sky. If God does not actually live there, there was little doubt that he descended first on its crest, then took his one gigantic stride over those babbling markets—which dared to sell on Sundays—into St. Peter's Church, afterwards visiting the parsonage for tea with the Canon. (p. 1)

But the factual, realistic narrative does occasionally give way to flights of fantasy, and when this happens, Soyinka's language resumes its normal mythopoeic strains. This does not happen too often in *Ake*; only in the description of the deities engraved on the palace walls at the Oba's Palace is Soyinka compelled by the dignity of those images to adopt a more elaborate language:

> This brief, low tunnel, roofed by the upper floor of the offices was a time capsule which ejected (projected?) us into an archine space fringed by the watchful luminous eyeballs of petrified ancients and deities. . . . From the humane succession of bookshop, church, cenotaph . . . we were thrust suddenly on this arc of silent watchers, mounted warriors—single and clustered, kneeling priestesses, sacrificial scenes, royal processions. (p. 204)

The obviously contrived passages strike one as pedantic when Soyinka strives deliberately after poetic effects through the manipulation of alliterated consonants and assonance as in this passage: "The blare of motor horns compete with a high-decibel outpouring of rock and funk and punk and other thunk-thunk from lands of instant-culture heroes" (p. 157), or merely through the use of rhythm for its own sake: "The lines of humanity curled through hidden *agbode* to swell the other throngs on a final approach along the road that led to the gates of the palace" (p. 216).

The language bounds upward in the panoramic overview of the landscapes around the Ake parsonage, but it can equally descend directly to earth when speaking of the most uncanny of terrestrial details. The poet who has an eye for the terrifying objects displayed in the witches' stall (p. 42) or the sensuous delicacies concocted by the Ibarapa market-women (p. 154) can also leap into the heavens:

> We climed at will into overlapping, inter-leaved planes, sheer rock-face drops, undergrowths and sudden hideouts of cultivated fruit groves. The hibiscus was rampant. The air hung heavy with perfumes of lemon leaves, guavas, mangoes, sticky with the sap of *boum-boum* and the secretions of the rain-tree . . . Needle-pines rose above the acacia and forests of bamboos kept us permanently nervous. (p. 2)

There are two areas, as has already been observed, in which the book is not aesthetically satisfying. One is its utter neglect of the pathetic or romantic side of human emotions, and the other is the unwholesome mode of characterization. The book makes no appeal to our emotions. An opportunity for the management of pathos does exist in the account of the sudden death of Folasade, but Soyinka walks over this episode summarily:

> I looked at Tinu who stood there impassively. Wild Christian stood by, a sad sweet smile on her face, saying things which I could not understand, only that we were not to feel sad about anything, because Folasade was now out of pain. (p. 97)

Sentiment for the sake of sentiment is, of course, to be discouraged. The story of the death of Check Omar in *The African Child* is very moving. The essence of loss is made concrete; and consolation comes directly from philosophy:

> Check has gone before us along God's highway, . . .
> all of us will one day walk along that highway, which
> is no more frightening than the other . . . The other?
> . . . Yes. the other: the highway of life, that one we set
> foot on, when we are born, and which is only the
> highway of our momentary exile.[10]

Soyinka also keeps the emotions of love strictly at bay. Wole's attitude to love was rather cavalier. The wife of his father's close associate, Mrs. Odufuwa, would become his future wife because she was "the most beautiful woman in the world." He also entertained uxorious dreams about some of the younger *aroso* women who attended Mrs. Ransome-Kuti's improvised adult education classes. Laye's tender picture of his young love first with Fanta and later with Marie illuminates *The African Child*.

The other weakness in *Ake* (a minor one) is related to characterization. Characters are scantily sketched, which may actually be a flaw of the autobiographical mode itself as the author speaks in his own voice and deals with real characters. The author cannot manoeuvre his characters at will as can the *novelist*. The narrator of a fictional work can intervene between the author and his material, thus relieving the author of the narrative burden. Obviously, the author can switch voices and points of view, and can place characters in situations of psychological or physical conflict in order to further define their nature. In the area of characterization, autobiography resembles history. The autobiographer has no poetic licence.

Ake is further disadvantaged in terms of characterization because characterization is a general weakness of Soyinka. The characters in *Ake* are not fully realized or individualized. Even Soyinka's parents, Wild Christian and Essay, are not permanently engraved upon our memory. Daodu is the one memorable character in the story, the indefigable Daodu who transforms the very business of living into ritual and is manic about music.

Soyinka uses impressionistic mode of characterization in *Ake*. Characters are not seen in action most of the time but are simply described to us. The impressionistic mode is the opposite of the dramatic method of character revelation.

Soyinka's mother is called "Wild Christian," but we never see that wildness. His father is as stern as Daodu, but that sternness is not *dramatized* as Daodu's imperial temperament is. The personalities of Wild Christian and Essay are simply not made very concrete.

The art that guarantees *Ake* a favorable verdict in our consideration of its merits as a work of art is deliberately lacking in *The Man Died*; and because the lack is deliberate, the work's status as literature becomes increasingly problematic. Soyinka was too close to his material to successfully distill the experience into imaginative literature. Early reviewers have commented on the book's uneven quality.[11] It suffers from the artistic weaknesses common to works composed in the heat of emotion. *Equiano's Travels* comes easily to mind. Both *Equiano* and *The Man Died* were written under very strained emotional conditions. The tone is often polemical; the address direct; and digressions that normally would find proper places in the appendix are inserted into the main body of the text. But the attitude of these two writers to their tormentors differs. Ardent as he was in his fight against the injustices of slavery, Equiano nevertheless extended a hand of fellowship and of Christian forgiveness toward the perpetrators of the slavery system. He hoped to win their sympathy through a direct assault on their conscience. Soyinka feels that he is a lone combatant in the fierce struggle for justice, and must return many deadly shots for every bullet fired by the enemy. He vilifies his tormentors and reduces them to odious animals: "These men are the mindlessness of evil made flesh. They are pus, bile, original putrescence of Death in living shapes."[12] The doctor who examined him at a Lagos clinic is an "unctuous toad"; a senior public servant in this establishment is "a gorilla." The gaoler named Polyphemus is "a cicatriced tower of menace" and "the priest of the rites of submission." Another prison guard who makes such awful guttural sounds is nicknamed Hogroth: "You, pig, you with your concrete mixer throat, regurgitating mortar and slag and dung plaster" (pp. 132–33). But there is no rest for Hogroth (or his creator) until he has tasted the full rage of Soyinka's venom. Hogroth becomes a metaphor for all that is odious, loathsome, and vile. Hogroth eats cola-nuts and infects the world with contagious discharges from his diseased body:

> Four yards away a gob of slime hits the grass verge of the gutter, the end of a blurred arc that begins on *ptuh*! and ends in *splat*! The churning in the throat is resumed, preparing the world for another goro-gritty gob. (p. 133)

The language of scatalogy, of polemic, and direct assault on the physical deformities of his tormentors is toned down when these prison experiences become transmuted into such imaginative literature as *Season of Anomy* (1973). There the verbal excesses of *The Man Died* and the author's emotional rage are brought under control, and an aesthetic distance is made to intervene between the author and his material. Soyinka had hoped to forge a new literary technique in *The Man Died*, a technique of "brutal realism" which he wanted to make the style of future African writing. "Brutal realism" would take into account the proximity in real life between ugliness and beauty, the way in which on the African political scene, the "gloved, beautifully be-ribboned leader who has just waved so graciously to the people, who has just wiped with a lace handkerchief the drops of champagne from his lips, has just before that moment given the order for the quiet liquidation of a number of innocent trade-unionists":

> I tried several ways of narrating this experience and making certain indictments. As I said in the Preface, I even thought one time of separating the two things. And then I thought a book if necessary should be a hammer, a handgrenade which you detonate under a stagnant way of looking at the world. . . . I would like to suggest that in another five to ten years with the reality of African politics . . . this sort of style . . . wold become commonplace.[13]

But these negative observations on the literary worth of *The Man Died* need to be qualified. The Lagos episodes (chapters 2–15) mostly record Soyinka's interviews with the agents of the law and are predominantly factual and historical. Soyinka was still in constant touch with the outside world. The process of in-gathering, of the gradual withdrawal of his ego into the inner shell which he often describes as "an insulating capsule" begins in this section, and the passages that focus on this experience share the emotional intensity of the Kaduna sections where he achieved a mystic state of true weightlessness. It is also in this section that the digressions occur, one on p. 112 is a footnote to the Red Cross and the other (p. 117) mocks the spurious atrocities commissions instituted by the Gowon government. But there is one point in favor of these digressions. They perform the same roles as flashbacks in fiction. Events are juxtaposed in these digressions at points so as to make the most emotional and psychological impact, not where they would have appeared according to strict chronology.

The Lagos episodes are less artistically organized because they are made up of police interviews and queries. But one chapter in this section (chapter 12) is largely subjective and, therefore, imaginative, in which Soyinka, assuming his typical Ogun mantle (or is it Nietzsche's?), opts for action rather than withdrawal: "Man can only grasp his authentic being through confrontation with the vicissitudes of life" (p. 87). The existentialist quest for the inner self in *Season of Anomy* is here shown to be tantamount to the individual's abdication of his social responsibility:

> Any faith that places the *conscious* quest for the inner
> self as goal for which the context of forces are mere
> battle aids is utterly destructive of the social potential
> of that self. Except as sources of strength and vision
> keep inner self out of all expectation, let it remain
> unconscious beneficiary from experience. Suspect all
> conscious search for the self's authentic being . . . Let
> action alone be the manifestations of the authentic
> being in defence of its authentic visions. History is too
> full of failed prometheans bathing their wounds and
> spirits in the tragic stream. (pp. 87–88)

Soyinka is saying that the man has not yet died in him, that he cannot withdraw into the cocoon of self-pity, contemplate surrender, or resign himself to his tragic destiny through suicide or self-immolation like Oedipus' escape through blindness. The only way out is direct confrontation with the forces of darkness: "I wanted eyes of hate and fear around me to keep me constantly alert" (p. 223).

The gradual in-gathering that began in the Lagos episodes attains momentum in the Kaduna sections. The breach with the outside world is now complete. Soyinka is the Kronos of the underworld, the King of solitude. He relies primarily on his inner resources for survival. The sentences in this chapter are quarried out of his own entrails. His mental and spiritual agonies, his hallucinations and visions, are experiences felt in the marrow and the blood; and these are communicated to the reader in compelling prose.

> Locked and barred from a more direct communion, a human assertiveness has reached me through the cosmos, a proud, inextinguishable promethean spark among dead bodies, astral wraiths, failed deities, tinsel decorations on barren space. Sign, probe and question I accept you, incandescent human dare. Extension of my restless eye and mind I claim you and absorb you. I transmit you, pore of my skin, electronic core of my will, prowl . . . prowl. (p. 252)

Some of the episodes here are organized as if they were fiction, and many of them possess the potential for becoming great short stories. Some do, indeed, achieve that status, for example, the story of Fajuyi's death (chapter 22), Victor Banjo's Third Force (chapter 23), and the account of the internecine conflicts among the insect world (chapters 36 and 37). Fajuyi's story has pathos and suspense. Adekunle Fajuyi was one more casualty of "history's tramp of feet." He was sympathetic to the Third Force and took a firm stand against an unpopular, corrupt Chief Justice of the former Western Region against General Ironsi's wishes, which action alienated Ironsi. In his last days, the pomp and pageantry of his high office had no more appeal for

Fajuyi; the State House itself was an immense void like Soyinka's crypt, inhabited by a lone prisoner, Fajuyi himself. Fajuyi had premonitions of his impending death; and the end came in the July 1966 countercoup in which he and General Ironsi were both killed.

However, it is not fair to assess Soyinka's prison memoirs as a pure work of art. The book is a sociopolitical document in its own right. Until the sudden publication of the memoirs of the war generals, it was the only book to provide an objective account of the events of the war years and will always be consulted as one of the authentic reference books on the Nigerian Civil War. For the student of literature, it serves as a key to some of the more obscure allusions in Soyinka's second book of poetry, *A Shuttle In The Crypt* (1972). *Season of Anomy* derives much of its material from *The Man Died*. Polyphemus is Suberu, and the Kaduna Prison is Temoko. The hell-gate into the two underworlds carries the same ominous quotation "abandon hope all ye who enter."[14]

Notes

1. Wole Soyinka, *Ake: The Years of Childhood* (London: Rex Collings, 1981), p. 104. Subsequent references are to this edition.

2. T. S. Eliot, "The Use of Poetry and the Use of Criticism," in Frank Kermode, ed., *Selected Prose of T. S. Eliot* (London: Faber and Faber, 1975), p. 91.

3. See *The Interpreters* (London: Heinemann, African Writers Series, 1970), p. 246.

4. *Idanre and Other Poems* (London: Methuen, 1967), p. 67.

5. *The Man Died* (London: Rex Collings, 1972), p. 154.

6. James Olney, *Tell Me Africa: An Introduction to African Literature* (Princeton: Princeton University Press, 1973), p. 17.

7. Lewis Nkosi, "Fiction by Black South Africans," in Ulli Beier, ed., *Introduction to African Literature* (London: Longmans, 1967), p. 212.

8. Olney, pp. 20, 21.

9. "And After the Narcissist?" *African Forum*, Vol. 1, No. 4 (Spring 1966), p. 60.

10. Camera Laye, *The African Child* (London: Fontana Books, 1959), p. 150.

11. See the entries in John Agetua, *When The Man Died* (Benin City: Bendel Newspapers Corporation, 1975).

12. *The Man Died*, p. 225.

13. John Agetua, *When the Man Died*, p. 37.

14. This quotation appears in *The Man Died*, p. 129, and in *Season of Anomy* (London: Rex Collings, 1973), p. 282.

PART THREE

FIVE METAPHYSICAL PLAYS

△ △

7

A DANCE OF
THE FORESTS

DRAMATIC TECHNIQUE

The Soyinka of *A Dance of the Forests* (1963)[1] has not yet evolved fully the sophisticated technique of the "drama of essence" which he was to perfect in *The Road* (1965) and *Madmen and Specialists* (1971). This technique relies essentially on juxtaposition of moods and rhythms rather than on detailed plot development.[2] Only toward the end of *A Dance of the Forests*, in the tumultuous climax, in the Dance of the Half-Child, did Soyinka attempt the method of the drama of essence in which gesture counts more than words. Action is shown rather than related. Prior to this moment, he used certain conventional elements of dramatic exposition: prologue, soliloquy, narrative language.

The language is relaxed and descriptive, and the characters are extroverted in the sense that they keep no secrets from us. They speak openly of their roles, their intentions, and their grievances. Demoke's crime, which in a play like *The Road* would have been couched in a mystic symbolism, is here de-mystified. Demoke himself speaks openly about it. The Prologue (Aronis testimony) provides clues to the dramatic situation as do the two major soliloquies in Part One, spoken by Demoke and his god, Ogun. Demoke's soliloquy confirms Aroni's testimony in the Prologue, is itself couched in the manner of an open testimony like Shakespeare's soliloquies.

> The world knows of Demoke, son and son to carvers;
> Master of wood, shaper of iron, servant of Ogun,

Slave, alas, to height, and the tapered end
Of the silk-cotton tree. Oremole
My bonded man, whetted the blades,
Lit the fires to forge Demoke's tools.
Strong he was; he whirled the crooked wheel
When Oro puffed himself. Oro who was born
With a pebble in his throat, and frightens children
Begging for their tiny hands to pull it out. (p. 26)

Ogun's soliloquy also confirms the testimony of the Prologue, but it possesses its own peculiar dramatic significance—it identifies a mysterious voice heard suddenly in the course of the dramatic action and reveals Forest Father's plan to lure the erring mortals to a remote corner in the heart of the forest for questioning. Ogun tells us who the real villain is in respect of Oremole's death:

Once again, he foiled me, Forest Father,
Deeper still you lead my ward into your
Domain, where I cannot follow. To stay him,
I assumed his father's voice, who follows now.
Hard upon my heels. I'll not desert him.
The crime, if crime it was, lies on my head. (p. 28)

But by far the most detailed exposition is in the Prologue. Soyinka there identifies the characters and introduces us to the dramatic situation. The human community, neighbors of the forest dwellers, are celebrating a feast called the Gathering of the Tribes. They ask Forest Father to send illustrious ancestors to this feast, but Aroni (Forest Father's lieutenant) sends instead two spirits of the restless dead named Dead Man and Dead Woman, both of whom belonged in their previous incarnation to the court of the great African warlord, Mata Kharibu. The Mata Kharibu past has bloody and violent affinities with four of the living generation named Rola, an occasional whore, nicknamed Madame Tortoise in her previous incarnation; Demoke, a carver now but a court poet in his former life; Adenebi, Court Orator today but Court Historian in the Court of Mata Kharibu; and Agboreko, priest and diviner both now and then. The totem and its purpose are conveniently described in the Prologue.

But although the play has made a liberal use of Western dramatic conventions, it is heavily saturated with Yoruba elements. Soyinka wanted to create a truly modern African theatre by fusing the Western conventions with "the idioms of the traditional theatre."[3] The result of this fusion is that elements of the African worldview naturally infiltrate into his imaginative vision. One factor that characterizes this worldview is animistic realism, that is, the interfusion of matter and consciousness in past, present, and future modes, which manifests itself in the cyclic approach to time and in the concept of reincarnation. If time oscillates back and forth and sometimes takes a leap into the future as the African worldview claims, dramatic action can also flash forward into the future or backward into the past. At the command of Forest Father time recedes backward into infinity, ushering us into the Court of Mata Kharibu where we encounter the exact personages engaged in the current drama. Animistic realism accounts for the elements of fantasy and surrealism in the action. Part One is the operation of the conscious psyche; Part Two (which is all dream) the operation of unconscious psyche as symbolized with the motifs of forest and darkness. We need not go to Jungian psychology to explain these concepts—they are all part of the African worldview, as is the mingling of the dead and the living.

Soyinka uses dance, ritual, mime, and masquerade in this play:

> I tried to interpret a modern theme, using one of the idioms of dance or mime. . . . I tried to use a lot of the rites, a number of religious rites, and there is one of exorcism . . . which I tried to use to interpret a theme which is quite completely remote from the source of its particular idiom.[4]

These idioms are interrelated; dance is an element they all have in common. Dance is, after all, the language of ritual. In the rites of exorcism near the end of Part One (pp. 36–37) the set, as Oyin Ogunba says,[5] is complete with flogger, dancer, and acolyte. The flogger clears a space with his whips for the dancer and his acolyte to perform while the dirge-man supplies the musical accompaniment. The complete set forms a backdrop for Agboreko's rites of divination. He warns the living in his usual proverbial language that their ritual can have no influence on the dead: "If they are the dead and we are the living, then we are their children. They shan't curse us" (p. 37). Dance is so important to Soyinka's method in the play that one can correctly speak of the technique of dance.

The word "dance" operates at various levels of meaning in the play, and it is not always associated with agitated body movement. In most of the Yoruba ritual dances, a step or two might be sufficient. We have dance as drama, dance as ritual, dance as the movement of transition, and dance as festival. The entire dramatic enactment itself, as the title of the play implies, is conceived as dance. This is the sense in which Aroni has used the term in the following context:

> The apprentice [Oremole] began to work above his master's head; Demoke reached a hand and plucked him down . . . the final link was complete—the Dance could proceed. (p. 6)

But the rites of the dead themselves in much of Part Two are spoken of as a dance, and they terminate with a particular dance, the Dance of the Half-Child, which is a mimed contest of Ogun and Demoke against Eshuoro and his followers over the fate of the Half-Child.

Dance as the movement of transition leads to a state of possession when communion with the dead is achieved. Gerard Moore, commenting on this form of dance, writes:

> The dance is the moment of trance when the dancer can bridge the gap between the human and the divine, that is to say that he transcends his human state during the dance and attains a higher state in which he can commune with the divine.[6]

The three masked humans—Demoke, Rola, and Adenebi— achieve this state at the dance of welcome, and spiritual illumination dawns upon them.

Dance is also a vital ingredient of the ritual of invocation

or the summoning of the gods. The various dances mentioned in the play include:

> the dance of exorcism
> the dance of welcome
> the dance of the Half-Child
> the dance of the Unwilling Sacrifice
> the dance around the totem.

Soyinka has used these dances to give a local habitation
and a name to his play, while at the same time using them
as dramatic tools.

Through symbolism, a motif is suggested rather than
baldly stated. Soyinka uses both ritual symbols and non-
ritual ones. Dance is a ritual symbol of possession. The
forest, an extension of the grove metaphor, is not only a
ritual symbol of expiation or purgation but also a non-
ritual symbol with multiple connotations. First, the forest
is the abode of an unseen power, the home of the gods.
Soyinka might have inherited this symbolism from Fagunwa's novel that was translated into English as *The Forest of
a Thousand Daemons* (1968). In Fagunwa's novel, the
forest is the home of daemons and ghommids. In Soyinka's
own childhood home at Ake a nearby forest is supposed to
be inhabited by all kinds of spirits.[7] Both in Fagunwa,
Tutuola, and Soyinka, the forest is also a metaphor for the
human world. The inhabitants and the proceedings in the
forest represent the larger world beyond the forest. Finally,
the forest is a maze, a labyrinth impenetrable and unknow-
able, where nothing happens and yet everything is possible. In the rites of the dead in this play, the masked mortals
move round and round in a circle, as in a dance. The stage
directions inform us that the "mask-motif is as their state of
mind" (p. 64). When the impenetrable forest is linked to
darkness, as in this play, they both become a symbol of the
unconscious psyche. The events in the forest are like a
dream to the unconscious mortals.

Other major symbols are the totem and the Half-Child.
The totem is a symbol of continuity. As a very tall flagpole,
the totem is an emblem for man's bestial and criminal
passions routed into the past and piercing through to the

present and the future. Demoke, the author of the totem
says

> Madame Tortoise is the totem—most of it anyway.
> In fact, you might almost say she dominated my
> thoughts—she, and something else. About equally.
> (p. 23)

If Madame Tortoise signifies sexual passion, the other un-
stated obsession is violence. Oremole falls to his death from
the top of the totem, and in the dream action in Part Two,
Demoke also falls from the totem when Eshuoro sets it on
fire, but his fall is intercepted by his patron deity, Ogun.
But if the totem is the symbol of man's criminal and sexual
passions, why should so much praise be lavished on it? "It
is the kind of action that redeems mankind," said Forest
Father, masquerading as Obaneji (p. 10). The point is that
the symbol is different from the reality of what it stands for.
Forest Father praises the amount of work and craftsman-
ship that have gone into the making of the totem, that is,
its artistry, not necessarily what the artifact signifies. "You
have the fingers of the dead," says Forest Father of the hand
that carved the totem (p. 43). As Murete has noted, it was
Forest Father himself who taught man the art of carving
(p. 43).

The most readily acceptable interpretation for the Half-
Child is drawn from the occasion for which the play was
written, that is, the "celebration" of Nigeria's political
independence in 1960. The Half-Child can be viewed as a
symbol of the newly independent Nigeria or, in a generalized sense, the symbol of the newborn states of Africa. In
either case, the new nation is prematurely born if it is only
a "Half-Child" and is doomed to death as the Half-Child
himself has forecast. But there are critics such as Eldred
Jones, who prefer not to limit the play's meaning to Africa.
For these, the Half-Child is a symbol of man's future, a
future of violence and destruction as the spirits of the
future have chorused. But the moment we associate the
Half-Child with "abiku," that is, the child that comes and
goes, it becomes also a symbol for the doom of repetition.
Soyinka frequently links this concept with the image of the
snake. In the poem "Abiku," the *abiku* itself boasts to its

mother that "I'll be the/Suppliant snake coiled on the doorstep/Yours the killing cry."[8] The snake is recalled in such images as circle, coil, rings, and the idea of repetition through spinning motions. In the play, the Half-Child is linked with the snake and with a spinning motion. These images occur in a brief dialogue between the Half-Child and Eshuro:

> Half-Child: I found an egg, smooth as a sea-pebble.
>
> Eshuoro [gleefully]: Took it home with him,
> Warmed it in his bed of rushes
> And in the night the egg was hatched
> And the serpent came and swal-lowed him.
>
> Half-Child: Still I fear the fated bearing
> Still I circle yawning wombs. (p. 70)

The stage directions on this scene read: "The Half-Child begins to spin round and round, till he is quite giddy" (p. 70).

If the Half-Child is the symbol of the doom of repetition, Demoke cannot keep it unto himself, for man cannot stem the tide of destiny. This is the implication of Forest Father's warning that Demoke is holding a doomed thing in his hand. Demoke does the best thing that could be done in the circumstance, that is, he hands the Half-Child over to his mother in order to restore the *act* of fate. The Half-Child, offspring of injured parents (Dead Man and Dead Woman), underscores the repetitive nature of evil. Soyinka has resorted to an element derived from the Yoruba culture (the *abiku*) in keeping with his declared intention to root his imagination to his land and life.

DRAMATIC STRUCTURE

The word "structure" is essentially an architectural term appropriated by literary criticism to designate the developing unity of a work. For example, one may distinguish between the physical structure of a poem and its internal structure. The physical structure is the shape of the poem (the appearance of the stanza and the length of the lines). Concrete poetry relies almost entirely on physical structure for much of its impact. The internal structure is the poem's inner design, the way images and symbols advance the poem's central thought or idea.

Dramatic structure can be defined, then, as the organization of the action into a coherent unity. There are five conventional stages in this organization. The first is *exposition*, which provides essential information about the characters' background and sets the plot in motion. The second is *complication*, which creates a situation in which the conflicting interests of the characters clash with one another. The third is *climax* or the *turning-point*, at which point the dramatic hero has committed himself to an irretrievable line of action. The fourth is the *reversal* or *peripety*, at which point the fortune of the hero suffers a drastic reversal; and the fifth is the *catastrophe* (or denouement in comedy) which presents the consequences of the reversal, ties up loose ends, and allows the audience to experience a catharsis. Structure is essentially an organic concept, and the five stages are interrelated, not separate entities.

The five-part dramatic structure is a natural corollary to the division of a tragedy into five acts, a convention that was applied to plays in Western literature up to the nineteenth century. Modern drama does not fall into such neat categories. Soyinka's plays, for example, do not lend themselves to the conventional five-act pattern, and physical action is sometimes far less important than psychological action. Furthermore, the peculiarities of his dramatic technique are bound to affect the arrangement of his dramatic materials, so that a discussion of dramatic structure will almost certainly overlap with one about technique.

In a rather very broad sense, the structure of a Soyinka play is not linear, but cyclical. The cobweb movement detected in the structure and technique of the novels (*The Interpreters*, especially) appears in the plays as well. In *A Dance*, the action circles round and round in the maze of the forest. Structure, too, has its temporal dynamics; and Oyin Ogunba is correct[9] in observing that the temporal

organization of structure in this play is tripartite, covering
the present, the past, and the future.

But we can also think of the structure in *A Dance* as a
two-part movement, each part terminating in a climax of
action. Such climaxes are convenient devices for rounding
off the events of the separate halves of the overall action
and, as such, are permanent features of Soyinka's dramas.
In a situation where nothing happens or so much happens
at a leisurely pace, all too suddenly the balloon of inertia is
punctured and both audience and cast are shaken up by the
impact of the blast. This approach is Soyinka's favorite
method of organizing the structure of his plays.

In *A Dance* the terminal action in Part One is the sudden
intrusion on the stage of the smoking, dilapidated passenger lorry named The Chimney of Ereko. This action is
preceded by Forest Father's informal interrogation of the
erring mortals during which some of them face up to their
guilt and others recoil from it. The entry of the Ereko is not
quite as unexpected as it seems; we have been sufficiently
forewarned, but its grotesque appearance and its antics
which terminate in a crash create considerable commotion.
Before the crash, the Ereko scatters a band of pious diviners
led by Agboreko and leaves Adenebi dazed. This climax ties
the action in Part One together and prepares us for Part
Two.

Part Two is more eventful than Part One. The climax at
the end of Part One is merely anticipatory, foreshadowing
the final climax in the second part. But Soyinka has over-
worked this device to the point of imbalance. Part Two is
overloaded, and the pace of action is unrelieved from the
moment we are transported by magic to the Court of Mata
Kharibu to the end of the play. From the events at the Court
of Mata Kharibu we move uninterruptedly to the rites of
welcome in which the dead pair are questioned. After that,
seven spirits of nature and triplets present a dreadful image
of the future. This is followed by the tumultuous dance of
the Half-Child in the course of which the crowded action
around the totem is perceived in silhouette.

Soyinka's critics have been dismayed by the rapid pace of
events at the end of Part Two, the more so because the
action is not accompanied with expository dialogue. But

there is some sense in Gerard Moore's observation[10] that the absence of expository dialogue is intentional, for the crucial climax at the end comes at precisely the moments when, in Soyinka's belief, action must pass from words into music.

THE CONSISTENCY OF AS

A Dance of the Forests is the work of a sensitive young man disenchanted with the unverified myths and illusions enthroned as national or racial characteristics. The play was written at a time (the late 1950s to the 1960s) when *Negritude* idealized the image of the African past.

The action at the Court of Mata Kharibu enables the audience to assess the merits and demerits of this past. The proceedings at that Court reveal that the past had its grandeur, its majesty, and its nobility, but it also had bestiality, intrigue, and injustice. Mata Kharibu is an irascible warmongering emperor, his wife a coquettish prostitute, and his advisers are men of questionable character who lack integrity and good sense. But the most disturbing aspect of that past is man's inhumanity to man. The noble warrior was sold into slavery by his own fellow Africans for refusing to fight the war of the queen's wardrobe. The point Soyinka is making is that the slave trade existed in Africa long before the white man arrived on the scene. We cannot, therefore, blame this tragedy on the white man if our own people practised the trade. The Questioner provides more details:

> Three hundred rings have formed
> Three hundred rings within that bole
> Since Mulieru went away, was sold away
> And the tribe was scattered. (p. 62)

The recognition of this unhappy fact is what Soyinka means by the philosophy of self-acceptance[11]—the acceptance of the glory and the indignities of the past. *Negritude* has ignored the bad side, and for that reason Soyinka has subjected that ideology to a constant barrage of criticism.

Comparing *Negritude* with the later emergence of a more realistic vision on the African literary scene, Soyinka writes:

> We whose humanity the poets celebrated before the proof, whose lyric innocence was daily questioned by the very pages of the newspapers, are now being forced by disaster, not foresight, to a reconsideration of our relationship to the outer world.[12]

In this very play, his message is that As can't change: it was, is, and ever shall be. Dead Man confirms this view in his observation that "the pattern is unchanged" (p. 61). As has always been associated in Soyinka with cannibalism, his metaphor for man's inhumanity to man. He himself confessed that it was his theory of the general cannibalism on the part of human beings that inspired the play:

> I find that the main thing is my own personal conviction or observation that human beings are simply cannibals all over the world so that their main preoccupation seems to be eating up one another.[13]

It is Soyinka's belief in the universality of this concept and the consistency with which the theme is handled in Soyinka's work that has caused Abiola Irele to speak of Soyinka's "Voltairean view of history as a record of human follies, of mankind imprisoned within an absurd cycle of blind passions."[14]

Cannibalism and the free play of thought link this play to *Madmen and Specialists*, in which these motifs are more fully developed. Just before he departs from the Court, the Warrior warns Mata Kharibu that "unborn generations will, as we have done, eat up one another" (p. 49). His greatest crime against the emperor was that he possessed and exercised the ability to think for himself. "It was you slave . . . who dared to think," Mata Kharibu says in mockery. And the Warrior accepts full responsibility for this guilt: "I plead guilty to the possession of thought. I did not know that it was in me to exercise it, until your Majesty's inhuman commands" (p. 48). The Mata Kharibu–Warrior conflict anticipates the conflict between Dr. Bero and Old Man.

CRIME AND PUNISHMENT

If Soyinka is not committed to a political ideology as some critics claim, there can be no question about his commitment to a moral one. His works are constructed around a clear-cut moral pattern. Evil might triumph, but our sympathy is clearly demanded of the select few who combat this evil. In *The Interpreters* in which some of the major characters appear to be insensitive to the sufferings of others, Bandele emerges as the voice of thunder reprimanding those who have erred against moral law. In *Season of Anomy*, Ofeyi and The Dentist range themselves on one side in the contest between good and evil. *A Dance of the Forests* is one of the first works to establish Soyinka's reputation as a moralist. It upholds the ethical principle whereby crime is followed by punishment for both god and man. Yoruba mythology is full of stories of gods who have offended against the moral law and had to be punished in order to bring about the eventual re-establishment of cosmic harmony. In the play we witness the trial of three mortals who have offended against moral law—Demoke, Rola, and Adenebi. It is subtly suggested in the play that Mulieru's suffering at the Court of Mata Kharibu might have been a form of penance for a previous error. Forest Father speaks of the Mulieru who was the terror of humanity:

> I know you (Mulieru)
> In the days of pillage, in the days
> of sudden slaughter, and the parting
> of child and brother. I knew you
> In the days of grand destroying. (p. 62)

Forest Father, a benevolent deity, is content to administer a gentle rebuke to the three human offenders. It is enough for him that they should discover their own regeneration through self-condemnation, not through torture. His idea of penance differs from that of Eshuoro, who still

sees hell as a place where "the womb-snake shudders and
the world is set on fire" (p. 43). We learn from Demoke that
Forest Father's strategy achieves its result. At the end of it
all, Rola is no longer identified with Madame Tortoise,
and Adenebi has learnt his lesson:

> We three who lived many lives in this one night, have
> we not done enough? Have we not felt enough for the
> memory of our remaining lives? (p. 73)

The moral regeneration augers well for the future, but it
cannot neutralize the powerful image of destruction which
that future portends. Their change of heart is an individual
experience; it does not indicate a national rebirth and
general renewal.

The play evokes a disturbing image of the supreme arbi-
ter of morality himself, Forest Father. He is a pathetic
figure, tragic and ineffectual, and a prisoner of his high
office. His helplessness in the face of the repetitive pattern
of human and divine folly is delicately suggested even in
the stage directions. At the beginning of the trials, the
tableau reveals him in an attitude of helpless impassivity:
"Forest Father is sitting on a large stone, statuesque"
(p. 60). This impassivity is made more apparent in the
second trial scene both by his own utterances and the stage
directions. After he has made the confession: "I take no
part, but listen," the stage directions say: "Goes to his seat,
impassive" (p. 64). His language reflects a sense of tragic
boredom for his vocation:

> Recognition is the curse I carry with me. (p. 21)

> My secret is my eternal burden. (p. 71)

> The fooleries of beings whom I have fashioned closer
> to me weary and distress me. (p. 71)

Human folly and the stupid acts of lesser gods compound
Forest Father's problems:

> those who tread the understreams
> Add ashes to the hairs
> of Forest Father. (p. 61)

The dilemma of the supreme god springs from man's misuse of his freedom. Man is created in god's image as a free agent, but he cannot escape the consequences of his actions. This fact is even lost on some of the gods. Ogun, interceding for Demoke's crime, pleads: "He has no guilt. I, Ogun, swear that his hands were mine in every action of his life" (p. 59). Forest Father, with his superior awareness of the operation of moral law, dismisses Ogun's claims as "conceits": "Will you all never rid yourselves of these conceits!" (p. 59). Free will and the dilemma which its ironies pose for the supreme deity are the theme of Forest Head's remarks at the end of the end of the play:

> The fooleries of beings whom I have fashioned closer to me weary and distress me. Yet I must persist, knowing that nothing is ever altered. My secret is my eternal burden—to pierce the encrustations of soul-deadening habit, and bare the mirror of original nakedness— knowing full well, it is all futility. Yet I must do this alone, and no more, since to intervene is to be guilty of contradiction, and yet to remain altogether unfelt is to make my long-rumoured ineffectuality complete. (p. 71)

In simpler language, Forest Head is saying that all is futility, for all is predetermined and pre-arranged. It is his privilege as well as his burden to see through the hypocrisies and fooleries of man, and yet he cannot intervene to arrest this recurrent cycle of human stupidity for that would negate the purpose of creating man as a free agent. All that he can do is to pierce through the layers and layers of all the habits that deaden the soul, hoping that in the course of these excavations, he would reach the soul's original purity ("nakedness").

OTHER MINOR THEMES

Gerard Moore has described *A Dance of the Forests* as a treasure house of themes and ideas that Soyinka was to return to and refine in much of his later writing.[15] We have noted the beginning of the philosophy of As in the theme of cannibalism, which is taken up more fully in *Madmen and Specialists*. The deadly Nigerian road and the deplorable condition of its passenger lorries are more fully handled in *The Road*, and the overblown head of the second of the triplets, which presages the emergence of dictators on the African political scene, is explored in some greater detail in *Kongi's Harvest*.

Other minor issues foreshadowed in *A Dance of the Forests* include the theme of artistic creation and that of pollution. The first is expressed through Demoke and the second through Eshuoro. Demoke the artist figure, must liberate himself before he can create through his own physical dissolution or that of a surrogate (Oremole). The paradoxical association of physical disintegration with artistic creativity originates from Soyinka's tragic view of artistic creativity. This concept is given expression quite early in Soyinka's career in the statement: "Every creative act breeds and destroys fear, contains within itself both the salvation and the damnation."[16] This aesthetic principle is a legacy bequeathed to the artist, in Soyinka's view, by Ogun himself, the first tragic artist. Ogun suffered physical dissolution in the abyss of transition, but he emerged whole therefrom through the exercise of that indestructive element within him, the will. After the successful re-assemblage of his disintegrated personality, Ogun bridged the abyss with knowledge, art, and poetry. Ogun's votary in the play, Demoke, felt an upsurge of artistic elation after he had hurled his apprentice to his death. We share this elation in his own confession of the deed:

> and I
> Demoke, sat in the shoulders of the tree,
> My spirit set free and singing, my hands,
> My father's hands possessed by demons of blood
> And I carved three days and nights till tools
> Were blunted, and these hands, my father's hands
> Swelled big as the tree-trunk. (p. 27)

The theme of pollution is brought forth by Eshuoro, Ogun's rival. Eshuoro deplores man's desecration of nature. The gods have been evicted from the forest and the trees uprooted by the wheel of progress. "When the humans preserve a little bush behind their homes," Eshuoro complained, "it is only because they want somewhere for their garbage—dead dogs and human excreta" (p. 41). Houses and roads have been built where forests once stood. Closely allied to the theme of pollution is that of urbanization. The cities are congested, and the economic strains imposed on the city-dwellers by the new cash economy destroy the concept of the family. Rola calls her relations "a pack of dirty, yelling grandmas and fleabitten children" (p. 9). She has nothing but contempt for one of the fundamental virtues of our cultural heritage, the extended family system: "This whole family business sickens me. Let everybody lead their own lives" (p. 9). Forest Father masquerading as Obaneji reminds her that it never used to be a problem (p. 9).

Soyinka attempted to embody in *A Dance of the Forests* far more ideas than he could actually manage. It is as if the playwright was aiming for aesthetic cartharsis within every opportunity provided by this early work. The play thus lacks a central focus. His single-theme plays are more effective as dramatic pieces and are more aesthetically satisfying. In his later works, Soyinka applies his energies towards a comprehensive development of one major thematic obsession in each work.

CHARACTERIZATION

A Dance of the Forests leads us to an awareness of the destiny of divinity. In the whole world of man there is not one human being that is worthy of salvation. This is probably true of the lower order of the divine hierarchy; but we have the actions of Aroni and sometimes Murete's half-hearted gestures of good faith to redeem the gods. On the human plane, on the other hand, the supreme creator looks in vain for one act or good deed that could redeem mankind. Forest Father said of Demoke's totem that it is the kind of action that can save humanity, but it does not actually do so because the totem is rooted in violence. Only the dead man had this opportunity in his previous incarnation, and he is haunted by a lingering remnant of his own guilt. The all-knower who created man in his own image in order, as some say, to escape from his loneliness, finds himself in a more serious dilemma. Forest Father, a long-suffering deity, pathetic in his own wretchedness, incapacitated by his superior knowledge of the futility of existence, strikes a sorry figure in spite of his dignity and his towering personality.

If we view the quarrelsome habits of Ogun and Eshuoro as extensions of human weaknesses, we can say that the major characters are convincing even though they are not drawn in the round. Ogun and Eshuoro are petty-minded and self-centred and too eager to defend the foibles of their human wards. "Soon, I will not tell you from the humans," Forest Head warned (p. 59). Their *deus ex machina* appearances and disappearances at critical moments in the action are part of their supernatural prerogatives; we cannot question them.

Envy, insensitivity to the sufferings of others, and duplicity distinguish the three mortals singled out for chastening. Of the three, Adenebi is the most odious with his Falstaffian sense of honor: "Think, if I, a Councillor, was discovered with her [Madame Tortoise]" (p. 34); followed by Rola with her self-righteous posturings: "I am not a criminal. I don't work in the Council and . . . I have never been to court in all my life" (p. 22). It is given to Demoke to finally reach a self-awareness that will ultimately redeem mankind.

But his own father, Old Man, is denied the wisdom that comes with old age. How could he ever have imagined that he could drive the dead away with petrol fumes? "Baba, will you never believe that you cannot get rid of ancestors with little toys of children," (p. 38) warns Agboreko, the true voice of wisdom. The Old Man's stupidity earned him more punishment on the night of transition than the marked victims: "We have tasted the night thickness of the forest like the nails of a jealous wife" (p. 73).

LANGUAGE

Since *A Dance of the Forests* is a major early work, it is not surprising that it should abound in linguistic experiments. Soyinka has not discovered his "natural" voice at this early stage; but Soyinka's "natural" voice is not neces-

sarily desirable. That "natural" voice is distinguished by
such traits as syntactical jugglery, abstract diction, and
processional symbolism. This style has its virtues when
competently handled, and Soyinka does occasionally prove
himself to be a master of the allusive style. We do not find
traces of this later style in *A Dance*; it begins to appear in
The Road and *Madmen and Specialists*. The language here
is relaxed, tending towards the descriptive rather than the
cryptic, the declaratory rather than the allusive. The immediate influences, in terms of its natural music, its simplicity
and the occasional resurgence of dramatic eloquence (see,
for example, Demoke's speeches, Ogun's soliloquy and
Eshuoro's declarations, pp. 26–28, 43–44) are Shakespeare
and the natural simplicity of colloquial speech. The play
has linguistic affinities with *The Lion and The Jewel*
(1963), but here the language has been purged of its adoles-
cent exuberances and its artificial rhetoric. Only in Adenebi's utterances does artificiality persist for a satirical purpose. The pace and cadence of the language are realistic,
and the diction is colloquial rather than literary. Aroni
tells us at the beginning in such a straightforward way that
he knows who the dead ones are:

> They are the guests of the Human Community who
> are neighbours to us of the Forest. It is their Feast, the
> Gathering of the Tribes. Their councillors met and
> said, Our forefathers must be present at this Feast.
> They asked us for ancestors, for illustrious ancestors,
> and I said to Forest Head, let me answer their request.
> And I sent two spirits of the restless dead. . . . (p. 5)

The Dead Man, too, speaks in a natural poetic rhythm
which is in keeping with the simplicity of his character.
His language contrasts with Adenebi's oily rhetoric. When
Dead Man laments his tragedy, our pity and emotion are
aroused for the sufferings he had undergone both here and
in the world beyond. He tells us that

> When I died, I fell into the understreams, and the great
> summons found me ready. I travelled the under-
> streams beneath the great seas. I flowed through the

hardened crust of this oldest of the original vomits of
Forest Father. (p. 24)

This is poetry pure and unadorned. The word "rhetoric"
has a connotation that links it to artifice, to "clever" language, something put on for show only. Adenebi is a master of artifice and of outward pretences. All these are suggested in his speech: "The accumulated heritage—that is
what we are celebrating. Mali. Chaka. Songhai. Glory.
Empires" (p. 11). He retains this same rhetorical idiom in
his previous incarnation: "War is the only consistency that
past ages afford us. It is the legacy which new nations seek
to perpetuate" (p. 51).

Language is matched to character and situation. This
explains the alternation between verse and prose in the
play. The soliloquies are in verse. In a dramatic soliloquy
the character bares his heart; he speaks out his grievances
and maps out his strategies for future action. This solemn
occasion requires the dignity of verse even though the
speaker may be an individual without dignity. In Part One
Eshuoro holds a dialogue with Murete, and the medium is
prose; but when he begins to utter his grievances in a
soliloquy, he changes over into verse.

Forest Father's language is solemn and weighty like the
language of the earth mothers in *Madmen*, but this is the
case only when he speaks in his true voice. As Obaneji, he
adopts the colloquial diction of everyday speech. The use
of prose in the proceedings at the Court of Mata Kharibu
reflects the general lack of integrity amongst the courtiers,
but verse is the medium for Forest Father's rites of welcome. The noble spirits of nature make their declamations
in verse, while the ignoble triplets speak prose.

Agboreko lends local color to the language with his
proverbs; his language has the easy transparency of
Achebe's proverbs and so does not constitute an obstacle for
the non-native:

If the flea had a home of his own, he wouldn't be out
on a dog's back. (p. 32)

When the crops have been gathered it will be time
enough for the winnowing of the grains. (p. 72)

Certain linguistic mannerisms which Soyinka was to develop more fully in his later work make their first appearance here in *A Dance*. The most obvious example is Old Man's flair for impacted rhetoric in *Madmen and Specialists*, that is, he goes on and on until he has exhausted all possible pejuratives he can pile up on an unfortunate adversary. Murete and Adenebi do this in *A Dance*:

> You mucus off a crab's carbuncle, you stream of fig pus from the duct of a stumbling bat. (p. 43)

> Do you, a mere cog in the wheel of destiny, cover your face and whine like a thing that is unfit to lick a soldier's boots. (p. 51)

Forest Father's language evokes sometimes the resonance (but not the ambiguity) of Professor's language in *The Road*: "My secret is my eternal burden."

The "natural" voice we find in the poems and the prose works is not Soyinka's dramatic voice. His dramatic voice has beauty, simplicity, originality, and pathos; it is generally more homely and more accommodating. It seems that drama is his natural medium.

Notes

1. Wole Soyinka, *A Dance of the Forests* in *Collected Plays*, Vol. 1 (London: Oxford University Press, 1973). The play was first produced in 1960 and published in 1963. All page references are to the collected edition.

2. Quoted from James Gibbs, "My Roots Have Come Out in the Other World: Soyinka's Search for Theatrical Form up to the end of 60," Paper presented at the Second Annual Conference of the Literary Society of Nigeria, University of Ife, February 1982, p. 1. The method of the drama of essence is treated more fully in the essay on *The Road*.

3. Ezekiel Mphahlele, "Interview with Wole Soyinka," in Dennis Duerden and Cosmo Pieterse, eds., *African Writers Talking* (London: Heinemann, 1972), p. 170.

4. "Interview with Wole Soyinka," p. 170.

5. Oyin Ogunba, *The Movement of Transition* (Ibadan: Ibadan University Press, 1975), p. 86.

6. Gerard Moore, *Wole Soyinka* (London: Evans, 1978), p. 8.

7. Wole Soyinka, *Ake* (London: Rex Collings, 1979). See the first chapter.

8. Wole Soyinka, *Idanre and Other Poems* (London: Methuen, 1967), p. 30.

9. *The Movement of Transition*, p. 95.

10. *Wole Soyinka*, p. 39.

11. He preached this philosophy in a very early essay, "The Future of West African Writing," See Bernth Lindfors, "The Early Writings of Wole Soyinka," in James Gibbs, ed., *Critical Perspectives on Wole Soyinka* (Washington: Three Continents Press, 1980), p. 43.

12. Wole Soyinka, "The Writer in a Modern African State," in Per Wastberg, ed., *The Writer in Modern Africa* (New York: Africana Publishing Corporation, 1969), p. 20.

13. *African Writers Talking*, p. 173.

14. *Critical Perspectives on Wole Soyinka*, p. 61.

15. *Wole Soyinka*, p. 37.

16. Wole Soyinka, "And After the Narcissist?" *African Forum* Vol. 1, No. 4 (Spring 1966), p. 60.

———————————— △ △ ————————————

8

THE ROAD

DRAMATIC TECHNIQUE

The major ideas dramatized in a Soyinka play are generally within the intellectual reach of most of his readers; what is more difficult to unravel is the tortuous knots of his dramatic method. Soyinka is by natural disposition an experimental writer. In his novels, poems, and plays he frequently adopts what he calls an "elliptical" style. In the elliptical tradition, the artist tends to play hide and seek with the reader. The game distorts chronology, forestalls organic development of character, and relies instead on fragmentary revelation of expository details. Juxtaposition and counterpoint supercede narrative logic. The purpose is not to court obscurity for its own sake, but to make the reader alert, energize his response, and involve him in the act of creation.

The elliptical method has variously been described as "absurdist," impressionistic, or expressionistic, but it is not necessarily a modernist invention. Soyinka finds its principles operative in the dramatic patterns of Yoruba festivals, especially those of Oshun and Obatala. The drama that stems from these festivals, he often claims, is all "essence."[1] In the essay, "The African Approach to Drama," he boldly labels this theatrical form the "drama of essence."[2] In the drama of essence, as James Gibbs has noted, "the narrative element is obscure and the play makes its impact through the contrast and juxtaposition of different rhythms and moods."[3] This technical device is utilized by Soyinka in *A Dance of the Forests* (1960), and *The Road* (1965).

The Road is difficult because it dispenses with the story element, and relies, instead, on symbolic action, elliptical insinuations, and simultaneous juxtapositions of incidents from the past with those in the present. Flashbacks intrude themselves on the audience, not as memories but rather as immediately realized actions. Soyinka keeps his sense of time fluid so that the past can sweep into the present. The free movement in time is related to the function of the road as the "link." This free movement from past consciousness to present consciousness is what Soyinka means by the term "the movement of transition,"[4] not the social transition from the pre-colonial to the independence era as Oyin Ogunba would have us believe.[5] The term "transition" connotes much more than political evolution and the psychic and social adjustments mandated by social transformation. Soyinka speaks of the transition from life to death, from the divine to the human essence, and the free movement of essences from the past to the present and to the future. The Preface poem, "Alagemo," speaks of the transition from the land of the ancestors (past, death) to the realm of the living (present, life).

First a word about the Agemo cult. Agemo is the deity believed by the Ijebus of Western Nigeria to be the supreme god. The Ijebus, an ethnic community among the Yorubas, consider Agemo as the almighty god instead of Olodumare, who is the major deity among the other communities in the Yoruba nation. Agemo shares certain characteristics with Soyinka's Ogun. He is extremely vindictive when he is offended, but is forgiving as soon as he is placated with rites and offerings. His votaries are essentially men of proven "masculinity," and during his annual festivals he is "god of the road" like Soyinka's Ogun. The spirit speaking in the Preface poem is a messenger or an incarnation of the god, who is uttering strange mythopoeic strains as he passes from the land of the ancestors to the world of the living.

> My roots have come out in the other world
> Make away. Agemo's hoops

Are pathways of the sun.
Rain-reeds, unbend to me, Quench
The burn of earthwheels at my waist!
Pennant in the stream of time—Now,
Gone, and Here the Future
Make way. Let the rivers woo
The thinning, thinning Here and
Vanished Leap that was the Night
And the split that snatched the heavy-lidded
She-twin into Dawn.

Line 1 emphasizes the issue of transition; line 2 is a pun on making "a way," which is what we have at the beginning of line 8. The sun's pathway in line 3 is its daily journey from east (life) to west (death). It is used here as a metaphor for the transition from the realms of death to those of life. The fluidity of time in the Yoruba worldview is the subject of the remaining part of the poem. The demarcations in time (Now, Gone (or the Past), and the Future) are commanded by Alagemo to abandon their individual identity or separateness, so that they can join the common stream of time. Time is later imaged as a river and is urged to absorb into its stream the diminishing Here and the dissolving Night which interposed itself between the two sister entities Dusk and Dawn. We need not go into a line-by-line interpretation of the poem; but it is interesting to note that line 4 is a direct allusion to the popular belief among the Ijebus that Orisa Agemo can command nature: for instance, he can cause and halt rain. The festivals honouring Agemo are performed in the peak of the rainy season (June or July), but the priests can dispel the rains by invoking the power of the god.[6]

The overall theme of the poem is the streamlining of time and the free movement that results. Murano, a child of both the past and the present, has experienced both life and death. He has made the transition as effectively as his god Ogun. Murano is, in effect, the Agemo spirit that speaks in the poem. His roots have come out in the other world. Murano has a multiple personality. He is (a) the Agemo spirit in the Preface poem, (b) the possessed god at the Ogun Festival, (c) the man killed by Kotonu's lorry, and

(d) Professor's palmwine tapper and bartender. We are familiar with this use of a *doppleganger* in Soyinka's works. One character in *A Dance* is both Rola and Madame Tortoise; and in the long poem *Idanre*, Oya is at once Ogun's wife and Sango's and, at the same time, a wine-girl and the girl killed in a road accident. What is most important, however, is that Murano functions as a dramatic *deus ex machina* for arresting time or death and, thus, allows Soyinka to make the scenic transitions from past to present. Critics not familiar with this fluid concept of time, which Soyinka has utilized to its fullest in the play, are bound to raise eyebrows about his use of flashbacks. Thus Martin Esslin says of Soyinka's method in general:

> My only criticism of his dramatic technique concerns his somewhat overfree and somewhat confusing use of flash-back scenes.[7]

The confusion will be clarified by a reading of the plays from "within," that is, from within the context of the Yoruba worldview.

By the time the play begins, several events have already taken place off-stage. Kotonu, of the famous passenger lorry, "No Danger No Delay," had narrowly escaped an accident near a narrow bridge built with rotten timber. Another crowded passenger lorry that overtook Kotonu close to that bridge crashed into the river. Kotonu's father, who was a truck-pusher, had died many years earlier in a road accident, crushed against his own load of stockfish. The memory of his father's death and the shock of his own narrow escape from a road accident combine to strengthen Kotonu's resolve to quit the road.

The accident by the bridge happened severn days before the play began. That same day, Kotonu's lorry knocked down a masquerader possessed by the god of the road, Ogun, who was being honored by his devotees at their annual festival. It was that same day also that Kotonu's colleague, Sergeant Burma, a tanker-driver, died in a motor accident. Burma, a tanker-driver, died in a motor accident. Burma's brakes failed him as he was going down a hill, and his tanker exploded into flames as it crashed, burning

Burma to ashes. Each of these previous events is re-enacted on stage. Soyinka uses the chorus to situate the action in the present. As each tragic death by road is recounted, Say Tokyo Kid and his thugs sing a dirge to commemorate the event. Two of these previous incidents are most tellingly telescoped into the present: Kotonu's dangerous approach to the fatal bridge and the encounter with Murano as an *egungun* possessed by Ogun. We hear the violent screech of Kotonu's brakes as he approaches the bridge; the dialogue situates the action in the present:

> Samson: Don't go too near the edge. The planks are rotten.
> Kotonu: This is a huge hole they've made. And the side is completely gone.
> Samson: For God's sake be careful!
> Kotonu: You are wrong. This hole was never dug for me.
> Samson: Does this wretched bridge look choosy to you? Just be careful that's all.
> Kotonu: I tell you the hole was never dug for me. It isn't one mile since they overtook us remember?
> Samson: Get off the rotten edge.

The second action (the drivers' festival) bursts in on the reader unexpectedly. Only the stage direction—"It is a Drivers' festival"—reminds one that this scene is a restaging of a previous event. The dancers sweep onto the stage like a whirlwind and sweep off as soon as their acrobatics are over. The action then resumes its normal tempo. Their very intrusion looks more like a first performance rather than a re-enactment; but, as such, it is important since it helps the audience to fill the gap in their imaginative reconstruction as to who is knocked down and by whom. Soyinka's stage directions are invaluable to the reader's imaginative reconstruction of the threads of the story. The nuances of the stage setting: "aiding the god's seeming possession" (p. 201) as opposed to genuine possession at the end of the play when Murano has properly resumed his mask. Soyinka's stage direction then reads "The *egungun* has become thoroughly possessed (p. 228).

Soyinka also uses traditional theatrical idioms. He speaks, indeed, of his technique in the early plays as one of integration or fusion of these theatrical idioms into a modern theatre.[8] The traditional forms utilized in *The Road* are those of the dance, mime, masquerade, the chorus, and religious rites and ceremonies.

The elliptical method, or what Soyinka conceives in the context of Yoruba traditional drama as constituting the drama of essence, and the integration of dance and mime combine to give Soyinka's dramatic technique its unique quality.

DRAMATIC STRUCTURE

The Road is divided into two parts, each of which terminates in a psychological climax. Physical action in the sense of connected episodes leading gradually to a climax is rare, and what physical action there is takes the form of violent stampedes motivated by curiosity. In Part One such a movement occurs when Professor forestalls Salubi's curiosity over the identity of Murano. In part Two there are two major dramatic moments: (a) the sudden eruption on the stage of the actors and dancers at the Ogun Festival, which is, in effect, a flash-back with no apparent relationship to previous or future events, and (b) a parody of this festival at the end when Murano dons his Ogun mask at the bidding of Professor. This action triggers the climax that brings the play to an end; and, unlike the climax in Part One, it is motivated not by curiosity but by its opposite: anagnorisis or discovery. In terms of physical action, we have then three dramatic moments occurring toward the end of the two parts of the play. Their positioning corresponds to the psychological climaxes.

"Psychological action" is the characters' response to Professor's adept manipulation of their fear of death or their curiosity over Murano's identity. It is hard to identify psychological actions, nor are they easily classifiable into recognizable patterns for they are, in the main, subjective responses built into the psychology of a given character. The fear of death cripples the will—it leads to inaction; it has paralyzed Kotonu and renders Samson useless by association. Only Say Tokyo Kid can liberate himself from this fear and is, in consequence, to undertake the one major action that rushes the play to a climax—the stabbing of Professor. Professor's death removes the fear and leads to the self-liberation of the rest of the characters.

Structure in the sense in which the term is understood in conventional drama (a beginning, a middle, and an end) cannot be considered meaningfully in the case of *The Road*, for the action is first internalized before manifesting itself physically in the two major episodes at the end of the play.

THE ROAD TO DEATH

The deaths by road enumerated in the foregoing section should be supplemented with Kotonu's roll-call of the latest victims of the road at the beginning of the play. Kotonu's list includes Zorro, "who never returned from the North without a basket of guinea-fowl eggs"; Akani the Lizard, Sigidi Ope, Sapele Joe, Saidu Say, Indian Charlie, Humphrey Bogart, etc. Soyinka sees the road as a deadly phenomenon; in Nigeria, especially, there are an unusual number of accidents. The play is inspired by Soyinka's awareness of the deadly realities of the road in his country. A group of poems in his first book of verse are designated "poems of the road." In one of these poems, all of which concern death on the road, "Death in the Dawn", Soyinka tells how he escaped death, like Kotonu, in a road accident. What assuaged Ogun's thirst for blood on this occasion was the blood of "dawn's lone trumpeter," a cock. The grim reality of death is summed up in the poem's final stanza:

> But such another Wraith! Brother,
> Silenced in the startled hug of
> Your invention—is this mocked grimace
> This closed contortion—I?[9]

The fatal refrain, "May you never walk/When the road waits, famished," occurs for the first time in this poem. It recurs in the long poem *Idanre* where Soyinka invokes the ghosts of all those "who by road/made the voyage home."[10]

The road is invested with human attributes in the play. Apart from Professor, the road is the most fully realized character in the play. The road is a traitor or one who lies in ambush. "May we never walk," say the drivers, "when the road waits, famished" (p. 199), and later on the lay-abouts lament the treachery of the road: "The road played us foul" (p. 213). The most deadly and vivid metaphors about the road occur at the end of the play when the road becomes a viper. Professor urges his men to:

> Breathe like the road. Be the road. Coil Yourself in dreams, lay flat in treachery and deceit and at the moment of a trusting step, rear your head and strike the traveller in his confidence, swallow him whole or break him on the earth. (p. 228)

It is Professor, the prophet of doom, who calls the road a slaughter-house:

> When the road raises a victory cry to break my sleep I hurry to a disgruntled swarm of souls full of spite for their rejected bodies. It is a market of stale meat, noisy with flies and quarrelsome with old women. (p. 159)

Since the theme of death is here uppermost in Soyinka's mind, the road is linked with images of sterility; it is a patient rock and a woman with barren thighs:

> When the road is dry it runs into river. But the river? When the river is parched what choice but this? Still it is a pleasant trickle-reddening somewhat—between barren thighs of an ever patient rock. The rock is a woman you understand, so is the road. They know how to lie and wait. (p. 197)

The vehicles that travel the road inherit the road's association with tragic fatality. The lorry that crashes at the fateful bridge is "pregnant with still-borns" and the passengers are pursued with "the wraith of dust" (p. 196).

The physical road is the road to death; but the metaphysical road serves as the "link." The metaphysical road is not a fully developed concept; it is only casually hinted at in the Author's Note for the producer. The metaphysical road is the channel of transition. The road possesses a mythological significance for the Yoruba which Soyinka has frequently exploited in his writings. The Yoruba god, Ogun, was the first road-maker, celebrated in the Yoruba folklore as the "path-finder." The Yoruba road is the "gulf of transition," the pathway of Ogun, the first darer and conquerer of transition. The road is also the "fourth stage" linking the living, the dead, and the unborn. It is a symbol of continuity, of eternal recurrence and of interterrestrial communication between divine and human essences. The Ageno masquerader who speaks in the Preface poem visits the living through the metaphysical road, and the victims of the physical road join the ancestors by passing along the metaphysical road. As a child of the shadow, Murano's daily voyage takes him along the metaphysical route that runs from dusk to dawn. Professor walks the physical road in his quest for the metaphysical road. The passage of transition, writes Soyinka, includes "the part psychic, part intellectual grope of Professor toward the essence of death" (p. 149). Professor's death at the end is the logical outcome of his quest. He can find the world only through self-surrender or self-sacrifice. He must journey through the road that Murano uses only, unlike Murano, he cannot revisit the living.

THE WORD

Professor learned the Word in the course of his association with the church. He was an active member of a community church where he often read lessons during Sunday services and gave Bible classes to primary school pupils at Sunday School. But he was suspected of deliberately misinterpreting the Holy Writ to the children entrusted to his care. Rather than inculcate moral precepts to his pupils, Professor encouraged them to rethink conventional moral-

ity. For example, he informed the children that the cross of
tender palm fronds which they wore on Palm Sundays was
good evidence that palmwine was good for them:

> Child, I said, my dear child, God painted the sign of
> the rainbow, a promise that the world shall not perish
> from floods. Just as he also carved the symbol of the
> palm, a covenant that the world shall not perish from
> thirst. (p. 222)

In those days of religious fanaticism, Professor's conduct
amounted to downright blasphemy. Soyinka's deliberate
misinterpretation of the Bible and his earlier misappropri-
ation of church funds culminated in his being excommuni-
cated. When he left the conventional church, Professor set
up a rival quasi-religious body close to its premises:
"Through that window, my sight led straight to this spot"
(p. 206). Professor regards the proceedings at his shack (the
sharing of the wine tapped by Murano) as a religious
ceremony. The evening communion with his regular customers he speaks of as "the hour of sacrament" (p. 181).
The customers remind him of his Sunday-School pupils;
the song they sing at their evening carousal he calls a
hymn; and the distribution of wine becomes another form
of the eucharist. Professor dreads the church window because it reminds him of his past. When that church window is thrown open, Professor suffers a great uneasiness.
The church window is a channel connecting the present
with the past that always reminds Professor of his embezzlement of church funds and of his expulsion from the
church.

The Word is the divine Logos which metamorphosed
itself, through the divine fiat, into the world; it is synonymous with truth, light and life. An earlier stage direction
makes this meaning clear:

> The window of the church is thrown open suddenly,
> revealing the lectern, a bronze eagle on whose out-
> stretched wings rests a huge tome. (p. 162)

Professor himself had once understood the Word in this very light:

> If you could see through that sealed window you will see the lectern bearing the word on bronze. I stood often behind the bronze wings of the eagle; on the broad span of the eagle's outstretched wings rested the Word—oh what a blasphemy it all was but I did not know it. (p. 205)

The Word means various things to Professor, depending upon the particular circumstance that warrants his use of the term. The Word is first and foremost the bundle of newspapers and other odds and ends of paper Professor carries about with him. At other times the Word means a road sign. When we first see Professor, he is carrying a road sign bearing the word "BEND." When Professor alludes to the word in this non-biblical sense, the letter "w" is printed in lower case. Of the word "BEND" on the road sign, Professor says:

> A new discovery every hour—I am used to that, but that I should be led to where this was hidden, sprouted in secret for heaven knows how long . . . for there was no doubt about it, this word was growing, it was growing from earth until I plucked it. (p. 157)

Professor sees himself as a gleaner, gleaning loose words from the road. The word in this regard means whatever Professor finds on the road; it includes road accidents, the victims of the crash, and motor spare parts which Professor forages out of a wrecked vehicle. On the one hand, Murano is the Word because when Professor goes out on his scavenging expedition on the road he finds Murano; on the other hand, Murano is the Word in the sense that the Word is death. It is in this sense that Professor can describe the scene of a recent crash as the "latest offering of the Word" (p. 188) or designate the road leading to the scene itself as the "true path to the Word" (p. 159). The bruises or inju-

ries sustained by victims of road accidents in a crash serve
Professor as synonyms for the word. "What's the Ministry's
needle after all," he says to Samson, "except for sewing the
Word together or the broken flesh" (p. 196). Professor
thinks that native medicine men are better healers of road
injuries than the Ministry of Health and implies that the
Ministry is only minimally concerned with human lives,
and centrally concerned with death.[11]

The Word means also football pools. When Professor
saw these pools he called them "cabalistic signs" and made
them the subject of a mystifying monody:

> But these are the cabalistic signs. The trouble is to find
> the key. Find the key and it leads to the Word . . . very
> strange . . . very strange . . . a rash of these signs
> arrived lately . . . that woman of tapa knows some-
> thing, or else she is an unconscious medium. Oh God,
> oh God, the enormity of unknown burdens, of hidden
> wisdoms . . . say the Word in our time o Lord, utter
> the hidden word. (p. 203)

Salubi breaks in at this point and defuses the charged
mystic atmosphere by informing us that the "cabalistic
signs" are only football pools.

Occasionally, the word carries a legal connotation,
when, for example, it means an oral or written evidence to
be tendered before a court of law. Particulars Joe, the unworthy agent of the law, says to Professor after he had
listened to the latter's evidence on the accident at the
bridge, "Is that your last word, Professor?" (p. 221). The
question is charged with an irony that introduces a new
dimension to the meaning of the word. We must see "last
word" here as an ironic foreshadowing of Professor's last
utterance in the play, his valedictory speech at the end of
the play beginning with the exhortation "Breathe like the
road. Be the road. Coil Yourself in dreams, lay flat in
treachery and deceit" (p. 228). Very often, the layabouts
pun on the word. They are aware that the word, so long as
Professor continues to use and abuse it, is incoherent and
meaningless. Salubi dismisses Professor's use of the word

as mumbo-jumbo (p. 176). Earlier he had called the word a
magical incantation or an abracadabra with which Professor cheats and enriches himself (p. 154). At one point in the
play, Professor urges Samson to "find the Word. It is not
enough to follow Murano . . . find the Word" (p. 187).
Samson says in reply:

> Professor, if you could just find one word to persuade
> Kotonu not to give up driving, I would be satisfied
> with that. (p. 187)

The most persistent meaning for the Word in the play is
Death, its mystery and its essence. The search for this meaning, for the secret or essence of death is the purpose of
Professor's quest and his burden. It is a quest that is
fraught with danger as Professor himself acknowledges:

> There are dangers in the Quest I know, but the Word
> may be found companion not to life, but death.
> (p. 159)

His Quest does, in fact, terminate in death. When Professor says that Murano is the Word he means that Murano
has tested death and has gained knowledge of its mystery.

Professor's "vengeance" on the Word sets the tone for the
general irreverence to the church in the play. His language
is virulent and abrasive when he speaks of the church, and
he sees its congregation from a critical perspective:

> The organist is rinsing his dirty face in cold water.
> The pastor is fixing his borrowed collar-stud. And the
> communicants are beating their husbands. (p. 210)

The conventional church carries much of the burden of the
satire ("Dat one no to church, na high society," says Salubi
in mockery of the church, p. 162), and Professor's irreverent allusions to the church encouraged his followers to
scorn that institution. "Give us this day our daily bribe,"
says Salubi in mockery of the Lord's prayer (p. 155) and his
friend, Samson, adds his own cue:

> I go chop the life so tey God go jealous me. And if he
> take jealousy kill me I will go start bus service between
> heaven and hell. (p. 155)

Salubi's jest and Samson's statement are their own attempt
at Professor's brand of wit.

THE STERILITY MOTIF

Critics have observed that there are few references to
women in *The Road*; the play's universe is essentially a
man's world. When women are mentioned, they are seen
not as procreative earth-mothers but as a barren rock, with
sterile thighs, a malicious goddess, or a vampire growing
fat on human blood. Woman is not a happy mother but a
wailing-woman beating her breast in despair after the
death of her husband. Family life is deprived of the joy of
reunion by the fateful road. Woman is a river that drowns,
a road that lies in wait, or a fateful passenger-lorry "pregnant with still-borns."

The river in the play does not renew or guarantee rebirth. The river is dry; it washes lives away and turns red.
The river is not a fountain nor a spring but a trickle. There
is an absence of regenerative waters. The landscape of the
play is a parched land; and the dry, dripping, drowning,
red river recalls, in its destructive rage, the apocalyptic tides
in *A Dance of The Forests*. Creative symbols are deliberately converted into negative ones. The positive aspect of
Ogun's creative-destructive totality does not emerge in the
play. The play's original title, *The Road of Life*, was, of
course, ironical. The play builds up a conscious negation
of positive energies and values, and the passages that
thwart these energies are spoken by the demonic Professor:

> Below that bridge, a black rise of buttocks, two un-
> yielding thighs and that red trickle like a woman
> washing her monthly pain in a thin river. So many
> lives rush in and out between her legs, and most of it a
> waste. (p. 197)

The road, the river, the spider, the bridge, the gods are all predatory monsters or cannibals lying in wait for human flesh, like Moloch. Imagery comments upon, and advances, the theme of death and sterility.

CHARACTERIZATION

The elliptical mode within which the play operates does not permit a rounded view of character. Characters are viewed in flashes, and their backgrounds are revealed only in fragments. Characters are important not in themselves but only in so far as they advance the dramatic action. The layabouts are nearly anonymous and function as a group rather than as individuals. Only Kotonu and his mate, Samson, stand out as individualized beings. But even their presence is submerged by the personality of the road, whose effective human agent is Professor. Particulars Joe is a gleaner of inconsequential facts, and Chief-in-Town is a collector of thugs. They breeze in and out of the play as required. Their impact as characters is minimal; they are important in the context of the play's satirical thrusts on the law and on men of politics. The road and Professor are really the most outstanding characters. Murano is also of importance, but less so.

The road itself is assigned human attributes and even spoken of as a god. Professor, the road's faithful servant, emerges as a magician, a mystic, a necromancer, a pseudo-philosopher, a rhetorician, and a trader. His god, after the road, is money. He gives his age in pounds and shillings and claims that we "cannot neglect the material necessities of life" (p. 200). In spite of the aura of mystery around Professor, there is a comic and sometimes a pathetic dimension to him. One cannot but think of Professor as a lonely, miserable old man like King Lear.

Murano is almost physically absent in the play. He is a child of the shadow or the twilight world, emerging at dawn and disappearing in the day, only to reappear at dusk. He is a creature of two worlds—life (dawn) and death (dusk) with one leg in this world and the other in the world beyond. He is thus a human embodiment of the road as a metaphysical link between the living and the dead. He has travelled to the land of the dead and returned safely like Ogun, but he was struck dumb for spying on the gods. The journey to the land of the dead and his return to earth are what Soyinka speaks of as "a visual suspension of death." Murano was knocked down by Kotonu's lorry when he masqueraded as the god Ogun. He was nursed back to life by Professor, who now uses him as one of his relics of mysteries or wonder. Professor had earlier used the mystery of the Word to cheat and confuse and now exploits the mystery that surrounds Murano for his selfish purpose. By toying with this sacred mystery, he brings the vengeance of the gods upon himself.

Murano serves also as a way to suspend or arrest time. Soyinka overtaxed the reader's suspension of disbelief in *A Dance of the Forests* when twelve centuries were erased in an instant. Soyinka roams in *The Road* from the past to the present through the mystical suspension of time in Murano. We cannot question the logic of his flashbacks and flashforwards. They function by means of an associational logic sanctioned by the Yoruba worldview.

Murano is at the center of those elements of the play that focus on traditional *moeurs*—the question of ancestor worship, ritual sacrifice, reverence for the gods, taboos, and respect for tradition. Here he is at opposite poles to Professor, who is an iconoclast and a religious sceptic. The layabouts respect tradition, unlike Professor; and Say Tokyo Kid, who eventually despatches Professor, does so out of fear of the untold misery which Professor's desecration of a sacred object, the *egungun*, might bring upon his head. "I don't want no curse on my head. . . . Do you want to go blind from things you shouldn't see?" (p. 227). He kills Professor as a service to the gods.

LANGUAGE

Language has degenerated into an incoherent chatter or meaningless rhetoric, and yet language is potent because it spellbinds and charms. Professor is, of course, at the crux of the puzzle posed by language in the play. Is he not after all, a master magician and a grand dialectician, endowed with an enormous capacity for spinning out clever repartee from his intellectual threadmill, and conscious of his power over words? "I offer you sanctuary in my tower of words," he boasts to his subordinates on the road (p. 201). Professor in *The Road* and Old Man in *Madmen and Specialists* (1971) represent two extremes in the use of language—verbosity and reticence—but their language thwarts communication in both cases. The Old Man says little, withholds his thoughts, and amuses himself over the mendicants' attempts to puzzle out the meaning of the Philosophy of As. Professor is wordy, but his verbiage yields little meaning.

Language, like Murano, has mystifying potential, which Professor can exploit in order to cheat. Dialogue between him and his followers operates on different wavelengths, and Professor relishes the confusion he inflicts through his mastery of words. Rhetoric or fluency of speech seems to be more important to Professor than communication. Toward the end of Part One, he confronts Samson with a threnody on the mystery of the Word:

> But you couldn't have known the Word could you? A gravestone turns slow and gentle on the hinge; angels trapped by day in illusions of concrete rise in night's parole; the dead earth opens at your feet—my friend, confronted with the Resurrection would you know the Word? (p. 182)

Samson responds with amazement: "Would I what what Professor?" And Professor goes on:

> Daylight marble lies! Oh mocking God! To think that even worms were given the Word—else why do they hold our flesh in such contempt? (p. 183)

Samson, as yet unvanquished, dares the suggestion:

> Do you mean for instance, if Kotonu died now and I met him at night?

Professor insists that his (Samson's) knowledge of the Word is the point at issue: "Would you know the Word?"

Samson surrenders at last with his layman's understanding
of the Word:

> Well I don't know which word. But I might try Our
> Father which art in Heaven and take to my heels.
> (p. 183)

After Professor, Samson is the most thoughtful character.
His confused response to Professor's rhetoric is a measure
of the gap in communication between Professor and the
other customers of the road under his protection.

Professor's first speech (p. 182) needs to be carefully examined. His three analogies based on (a) gravestone, (b) angels, and (c) dead earth have no apparent bearing on his
central concern—knowledge of the Word. And what does
he mean (p. 183) by "daylight marble"?

Professor picks his words carefully, weighs their effects
on his audience, invests his speeches with liturgical solemnity, and deliberately steers them toward the eschatologi-
cal:

> If you think I do this from the kindness of my heart
> you are fools. But you are no fools, so you must be
> liars. It is true I demand little from you, just your
> presence at evening communion, and the knowledge
> you afford me that your deaths will have no meaning.
> . . . But understand that I would live as hopefully
> among cattle, among hogs, among rams if it were
> Ramadan, I would live as hopefully if you were ant-
> heaps destined to be crushed underfoot. But I suppose
> you my friend, would dare to call this also, accident?
> . . . But I thank you all who hasten the redeeming of
> the Word. You are important I promise you. Everyone
> here is important. Your lives whittle down the last
> obstacle to the hidden Word. (p. 221)

Notice in the above passage some of Professor's tricks: his
fondness for spurious logic and his flair for puns and word-
play. The assumption that all those who are not fools are
liars is an obvious illogical leap. Thus, from the mention
of "rams," Professor's mind jumps senselessly to "Rama-

dan." Earlier, he has turned "arm" and "army" to similar
pun-yielding profit: "You may be the devil's own army but
my arm is powered with the unbroken Word" (p. 157). The
substance of the speech is meaningful only to Professor
himself. In what ways, one wonders, have the lives of his
subordinates on the road whittled down the last obstacle to
the Word?

When Professor lifts his magician's mask, his language
is sober even though it never ceases to be rhetorical; but he
now speaks in his own voice and not as a magician. Such is
the case in Professor's last speech already cited and in his
confession of what Murano means to him:

> And should I not hope, with him to cheat, to antici-
> pate the final confrontation, learning its nature bar-
> ring its skulking face. (pp. 223–224)

Professor takes delight in administering verbal shocks to
his audience as befits his role as an iconoclast. He deliberately thwarts conventional associations of language in
order to inject his own linguistic idiosyncrasies. A minor
example of this habit is Professor's allusion to the sound of
a road crash as "a victory cry" or his giving his age in
pounds and shillings. A more serious example of Professor's deliberate inversion of accepted linguistic usage is the
suggestion that the church is not a prayer house but a place
where husbands and wives go to settle scores: "the com-
municants are beating their husbands" (p. 210). If the
church is the proper place for settling domestic scores,
Professor would have us believe that his "aksident store"
guarantees spiritual fulfillment to his followers: "That
shop sustains our souls and feeds our bodies" (p. 195).
Another example of Professor's inversion of conventional
associations of language is the insinuation that prophets
are liars: "You lie like a prophet," Professor tells Samson
(p. 207).

Professor's experiment with language is part of his deliberate effort to be eccentric and obscure, and he does
become incomprehensible by resorting to metaphysical images. He deliberately stretches his images, impacts and
compacts them, yoking by violence ideas that are appar-

ently unlike. In one breath, in the second part of the play,
the road is a river with red trickles, then a barren rock, and
finally a woman with sterile thighs. Professor's rapid
switches from one image to another recall the intellectual
agility (and toughness, too) of metaphysical imagery:

> Below that bridge, a black rise of buttocks, two un-
> yielding thighs and that red trickle like a woman
> washing her monthly pain in a thin river. So many
> lives rush in and out between her legs, and most of it a
> waste. (p. 197)

The charge of incoherence against Professor is not difficult to substantiate. Some of the passages already cited
embody much of that incoherence. At the beginning of the
confession scene, Professor works himself into making a
grand disquisition on the biblical aphorism that the wages
of sin is death; but after proclaiming the words "sins and
wages and sin," Professor comes to an abrupt end. The
stage direction reads: "Stops. Turns and faces the church"
(p. 205). After executing those ritual movements, Professor
goes into the story about his embezzlement of church funds.
He builds up gradually to the peak of his rhetorical flour-
ishes and ends the confession on a note of "bathos," betray-
ing a concern which is not in tune with his god-like posturings:

> It is, I think, likely that I left the church coffers much
> depleted . . . but I remember little of this. Have you
> heard anything? (p. 206)

Irony hangs heavy over many of Professor's utterances. It
looks indeed as if Professor has foreseen his own death or
the futile outcome of his quest. His speeches focus increasingly on this futility and point inexorably to his tragic
destiny:

> a.   "But you must not think I accept all such manifes-
>   tations as truth. It may be a blind. I know this is
>   not the Word, but every discovery is a sign-post
>   . . . eventually the revelation will stand naked,

    unashamed . . . the subterfuge will be over, my
    cause vindicated." (p. 160)

b.   "He'll come at the evening communion hour.
    When that shadow covers me in grace of darkness
    he will come." (p. 186)

c.   "Have I spent all these years in dutiful search only
    to wind up my last moments in meaningless state-
    ments." (p. 195)

The correspondence between example *b* and what actually
does happen to Professor at the moment of his death is
oracular. The stage direction etches a graphic description
of the scene:

    Still upright in his chair, Professor's head falls for-
    ward. Welling fully from the darkness falling around
    him, the dirge. (p. 229)

Professor's personality dominates the play, but the spell he
casts over his followers (the subterfuge) is broken at the end
when his cause is not vindicated.

Notes

1. Wolf Soyinka, *Myth and Literature*, p. 152.

2. Quoted from James Gibbs, "My Roots Have Come Out
in the Other World: Soyinka's Search for Theatrical Form
up to the end of 60," Paper presented at the Second Annual
Conference of the Literary Society of Nigeria, University of
Ife, February 1982, p. 11.

3. *Ibid.*, p. 1.

4. Wole Soyinka, *The Road*, in *Collected Plays*. Vol. I
(London: Oxford University Press, 1973), p. 149.

5. This is the point argued in the introductory remark to
his book *The Movement of Transition* (Ibadan: Ibadan
University Press, 1975).

6. For more information on the Agemo cult, see Oyin Ogunba, "The Agemo Cult in Ijebuland," *Nigeria Magazine*, No. 86 (1965), pp. 176–186, and "Agemo: The Orisa of the Ijebu People of Southeastern Yorubaland," Paper presented at the Conference on the Orisa Tradition, University of Ife, June 1981, pp. 1–31.

7. Martin Esslin, "Two Nigerian Playwrights," in *Introduction to African Literature*, ed., Ulli Beier (London: Longmans, 1967), p. 262.

8. "Wole Soyinka Interviewed by Ezekiel Mphanlele," in B. Dennis Duerden and Cosmo Pieterse, eds., *African Writers Talking* (London: Heinemann, 1972), p. 170.

9. Wole Soyinka, *Idanre and Other Poems*, p. 11.

10. *Ibid.*, pp. 64 and 65.

11. Elaine Fido, "*The Road* and Theatre of the Absurd," Paper presented to the First Ibadan Annual African Literature Conference, July 1976, p. 11.

—————————— △ △ ——————————

MADMEN AND SPECIALISTS

DRAMATIC TECHNIQUE

Madmen and Specialists (1971) is the most puzzling, the most challenging, and the most elusive of Soyinka's expressionist dramas. This technique is used in *The Road* and *Kongi's Harvest*, but Soyinka is at his most demanding and even burdensome in *Madmen*. Nothing is named or explained directly in this metaphysical drama, only hinted at through allusion or insinuation. Theme replaces plot as the dynamic of the play, and characters are sketched rather than fully developed.[1] The play dispenses with Soyinka's favorite technique, the flashback. Pessimism and cynicism have been nurtured to a point in both Soyinka himself and the characters that discussion and meaningful exchange are thought to be unnecessary. Dialogue is esoteric and cryptic, and comprehensible only to the initiated; words reach down to an unspoken reality which is more potent than the surface meaning. That tendency in modernist drama defined by John Fletcher and James Mcfarlane as the "aesthetics of silence,"[2] has here been stretched to its limit. Who is Old Man? What was he before the war and what did he do at the front? What is the place constantly referred to as "out there" and "the other place"? Who are "they" and what are the "faces"? What is meant by "As"? And where are all these things happening?

The play contains answers to all these questions and herein lies Soyinka's skill as a dramatist—his plays are self-contained units operating consistently and logically within

the ambit of their own universe—but at no point are these
answers provided by direct exposition. What we know of
the characters' past and of their present roles come to us in
their casual remarks and jokes to one another.

Madmen and Specialists is one of Soyinka's works that
communicate his reaction to social anomie. This reaction
began with the October poems of his first verse collection,
Idanre and Other Poems (1967), in which he mourned the
casualties of the social upheavals of 1966. There were at
least two military coups in Nigeria during that year. The
coups and countercoups entrenched military dictatorship
in Nigeria after the country had endured a civil war. To
Soyinka, the period of military dictatorship and the civil
war will always remain Nigeria's darkest moment. He was
critical of the abuse of power and privileges during the era
of civilian administration, but those abuses attained an
unprecedented climax in the military era. He also suffered
personal humiliation under the military, being imprisoned
in August 1967, for his effort to organize a Third Movement. This Movement would have taken advantage of the
weakening of the power base in the Federal structure during the war years and staged a socialist military coup. Old
Man in *Madmen and Specialists* is Soyinka's alter ego,
reacting against the sadistic military dictatorship in the
Nigeria of the war and post-war periods. His counterparts
are Ofeyi and the Dentist in *Season of Anomy* (1973). All
three subvert the status quo, but they differ in their methods. Ofeyi operates through moral conversion, the Dentist by guerilla violence, and Old Man by the cult of the
absurd, which manifests itself through mockery, self-dis-
gust, and cynicism.

The play's immediate target (that is, the system whose
efficient operation is obstructed by "cysts" like the Beros) is
Nigeria of the post-war era. But the significance of the
play's message can be extended to all police states. However, it is obvious that the place "out there" or the "other
place" in the play is one of the war fronts of the Nigerian
Civil War. Close to these war fronts are make-shift hospitals for the wounded. Old Man is employed in one of these
convalescent hospitals as a rehabilitation officer, but instead of healing the wounded physically, he indoctrinates

them with subversive ideas. They are victims of a senseless war, he tells them, fighting for no ideology except that which ministers to the interests of what Soyinka called "the alliance of corrupt militarism and a rapacious Mafia."[3]

The appearance of the Priest in the first part of the play is a dramatic sleight of hand, neat and adroitly managed. It is through the Priest that we have the first clue to Old Man's role at the war front. The Priest tells us in his jerky language that Old Man was doing "recuperative work among some disabled fellows" (p. 239).[4] This information is later fully confirmed by Dr. Bero. He tells Si Bero that

> Father's assignment was to help the wounded readjust
> to the pieces and remnants of their bodies, physically.
> Teach them to make baskets if they still had fingers.
> To use their mouths to ply needles if they had none, or
> use it to sing if their vocal chords had not been shot
> away. Teach them to amuse themselves, make some-
> thing of themselves. Instead he began to teach them to
> think, think, THINK! Can you picture a more treach-
> erous deed than to place a working mind in a mangled
> body? (p. 242)

Dr. Bero's character shows through his langauge. We can-not mistake the arrogant swagger and his indifference to the sufferings of others. This passage also discloses Old Man's abnormal crime against the system: he has dared to place a working mind in a mangled body.

We later learn from Bero that because of Old Man's daring attempt to make the mangled bodies think, he was certified insane, that is, "dangerous," and was therefore incarcerated in a crypt, the cellar. Before his imprisonment, Old Man was interrogated by "them"—the military sadists whose drooling faces he mocked in one of his cryptic ex-changes with Dr. Bero: "Your faces, gentlemen, your faces. You should see your faces. And your mouths are hanging open. You're drooling but I am not exactly sure why" (p. 254). The arrest of Old Man, his mock trial, and his sentence for protective custody all happened a day or two before the play begins.

The Priest provides us with foreknowledge of Old Man's

character: He might be noble but he is somewhat queer and stubborn. The actual word used by the Priest is "strange." Ironically, however, the oddity of his character derives from its very nobility. Because the war caused too much massacre and waste of human life, according to Dr. Bero's letter to Old Man during his sane days, Old Man thought in his Swiftian logic that it would be better indeed to legalize cannibalism, for that, no more no less, was what was happening at the front. This is the beginning of Old Man's philosophy of As, one of whose precepts is that human flesh should be eaten. According to As, war brutalizes the human soul. The Priest also says: "You know, it's strange how these disasters bring out the very best in man—and the worst sometimes" (p. 239). The Priest appears to be a buffoon; his entry is casual and unexpected, yet within that brief dramatic moment he is able to introduce us to the major issues at stake in the action.

The Mendicants tell their own story in bits and pieces. They are the victims of the war, having been maimed, blinded, or emotionally and psychologically wrecked by the bombshell referred to in the play as "the blast" (p. 250). Goyi is a rubber ball—he lost all his fingers at the front. The Blindman lost his sight, the Cripple, his limbs, and Aafaa, his emotional equilibrium. Aafaa, who is the cleverest of them all, is similar to Old Man in his penchant for verbal wit and cryptic humor. Before he began to suffer from his spasms, he was deployed at the front as an army chaplain. As he says, "it was my job to go round comforting the poor fools—or burying them" (p. 250). His spasms began with the shock he received from a bombshell:

> They told me up there when it began, that it was something psy-cho-lo-gi-cal. Something to do with all the things happening around me, and the narrow escape I had. It's not so bad now. I still remember the first time. I was standing there just like this, blessing a group of six just about to go off. They were kneeling before me. Then—well, I can't say I heard the noise at all, because I was deaf for the next hour. So, this thing happened, no signal, no nothing. Six men kneeling

in front of me, the next moment they were gone.
. . . That was when I began to shake. (pp. 256–257)

When he began to shake, Aafaa was "referred" to the rehabilitation center where he came into contact with Old Man
for the first time. He was Old Man's most brilliant pupil
and was so thoroughly indoctrinated with As that he could
challenge both Old Man himself and Dr. Bero with impunity.

The Mendicants' immediate assignment in the play is to
watch over Old Man, to keep him "safe" in his protective
custody in Dr. Bero's surgery in town. Before the play
began, the Mendicants had smuggled Old Man out from
the front under cover of darkness down to Dr. Bero's house.
They needed to be discreet because Dr. Bero wanted to
prevent Old Man's daughter, Si Bero, from knowing what
was happening to Old Man until Dr. Bero judges it appropriate for her to know.

Dr. Bero is first introduced in one of the jokes the Mendicants have formed the habit of cracking on the subject of
"specialization" and of being "a specialist." The specialist,
as they have come to understand the term, is one who has a
solution to all problems just as the military dictators claim
to: "He is a specialist. Amen. That takes care of everything" (p. 222), says Aafaa half-seriously. And when Dr.
Bero make his first entry on the stage, he is greeted with a
chorus of: "the specialist." And the stage direction states:
"Standing there is Bero, uninformed, carrying a holdall"
(p. 230). Aafaa, who dares to take liberties with the specialist, earns the wrath of his swagger stick. The stage-direc-
tion continues: "Bero cuts him across the face with his
swagger stick" (p. 233). That is followed by Bero's line:
"That should remind you I do know how to slap people
around." We next see Bero in a conversation with Si Bero.
He hushes her excitement over his safe return from the
front: "Be quiet! I don't want my return announced"
(p. 233). He dismisses her solicitations about his patients in
a most offhand manner and calls them "corpses." When
she inquires about her father's safety, Dr. Bero reveals that
his new profession makes it easier for him to keep an up-

to-date dosier on all those enlisted at the front. He has
gathered intelligence information on Old Man's mental
condition that reveals that he has become insane. This is
intelligence he would not have gained had he remained with
the medical corps, so this new profession has its advantages
after all: It has enabled him to be of extra "use" to the family.
Bero explains:

> The specialist they called me, and a specialist is . . . a
> specialist. You analyze, you diagnose, you prescribe.
> (p. 257)

From the hints we have gathered from Bero's conversation
with Si Bero (one cannot say his "sister," because As acknowledges no blood relationships), we can surmise that
Bero was a medical officer before he became a military
intelligence officer, which profession he finds even more
congenial than his long-standing career as a medical doctor. While Bero was away, Si Bero stood in for him at the
surgery. She sought the aid of the natural healers, the Earth
Mothers, the witches who introduced her to the secrets of
medicinal herbs. But these secrets are bought at a dear
price. Before she could be introduced into the witches'
sorority, Si Bero had to pawn her own life or the life of a
dear one. She might have pawned her life, but when the
time comes for settling accounts, the Earth Mothers select
their own victim—Dr. Bero himself.

These then are main points that the audience must understand before it is able to follow the Mendicants' antics
and the irony in Old Man's utterances. The Yoruba elements of Soyinka's theatre works have been pared down.
There is no room here for masquerades, dancing, singing,
or proverbs. What we have in their place is parody.

The parodies operate very much like the flashbacks, for
they intrude upon the reader unannounced. When Aafaa
begins to act like Dr. Bero, the rest of the Mendicants slip
into the roles of the subordinate agents of the system with
ease. They parody the mock-trial sessions in an As system
(p. 220), Dr. Bero's sadistic enjoyment of the sufferings of
his victims in the torture chamber of As (p. 223), the visit of
the First Lady to the home of the disabled (p. 260), the

soldiers' make-believe stunts to persuade the people that
their continued stay in power is by popular will (p. 220-
21). They even parody Oid Man's lectures on the philosophy of As (p. 243) and their own begging sessions (p. 218).
In each of these parodies, the rest of the Mendicants know
by instinct what role to assume once any one of them has
begun the mimicry. In the passage that follows, the Mendicants mimic the way As deals with a common offender and
with a trustee who is found to have been guilty of subversion. Blindman represents the two categories of crime. In
every case, As deals summarily with the enemy. Some are
stripped naked and flogged to death; others have their
limbs amputated; others have their eyes removed. The Mendicants go into this parody after recalling the way Si Bero
shouts orders at them as they pick her herbs (Blindman
plays the role of both victim and the agent of As):

Goyi:	First the roots.
Cripple:	Then peel the barks.
Aafaa:	Slice the stalks.
Cripple:	Squeeze out the pulps.
Goyi:	Pick the seeds.
Aafaa:	Break the pods. Crack the plaster.
Cripple:	Probe the wound or it will never heal.
Blindman:	Cut off one root to save the other.
Aafaa:	Cauterize.
Cripple:	Quick-quick-quick, amputate! (Blind-man lets out a loud groan.)
Aafaa:	What do you mean, Sir; How dare you lie there and whine?
Goyi:	Cut his vocal chords.
Aafaa:	"Before we operate we cut the vocal chords."
Blindman:	That's only for the dogs.
Cripple:	Your case is worse. You are an under-dog.
Goyi:	Rip out his vocal chords. (Blindman lets out another scream).
Aafaa:	We don't want you in this fraternity.
Cripple:	Fool! You should see the others and thank your stars.

Blindman:	I can't see them to thank.
Aafaa:	(Snatches his stick): Shall I put them on his head? He can have them in all colours.
Cripple:	Leave him for now, we'll simply expel him (p. 228).

DRAMATIC STRUCTURE

The action of *Madmen and Specialists* is organized into a two-part movement, each of which terminates in an intensified rhythm of agitated gesture, verbal in Part One and physical in Part Two. Generally, however, physical action in the sense of connected episodes leading gradually to a preconceived climax is rare. Like *The Road*, *Madmen* is a drama of non-event. Even *The Road* has more agitated, more tumultuous, action than *Madmen*. In that play, we have, for example, the tumultuous entry of the Ogun devotees at the Drivers' Festival, the commotions of the dancing masqueraders, and the Yankee exhibitionisms of Say Tokyo Kid and his men. There is little such action in *Madmen* except for the Mendicants' quick verbal repartee. What is more significant in a consideration of structure here is the timing of each entry and exit of the actors in the drama of words. We have mentioned the dramatic significance of the unannounced but supremely managed integration of the Priest into the sequence of events in Part One. The other characters or groups of characters are switched in and out of the stage in successive transitions with certain cues (in Part Two) serving the dramatist as transitional signatures. This smooth transition from one scene to another is what Oyin Ogunba has called the "dovetail technique."[5]

The verbal duel in Part One consists of nine scenes:

1. The Mendicants among themselves.
2. The Mendicants and Si Bero.
3. Si Bero and the Old Women.
4. Si Bero and the Mendicants once more.
5. Bero, the Mendicants, and Si Bero.
6. The Old Women among themselves.

7. Si Bero, Bero, and the Priest.
8. Si Bero and Bero.
9. Si Bero, Bero, and the Mendicants talking As.

In Part One, the action idles along until the very end when the Mendicants are called upon to perform for Si Bero. At this point they quicken their verbal dramatization of the philosophy of As, which brings the section to an end.

Part One speaks of As and its methods. In Part Two, we see As itself in the person of Old Man and further parodies of its method. A breakdown of the action reveals the following scenes:

1. The Mendicants and Old Man.
2. Old Man and Bero.
3. Bero and Si Bero.
4. Old Man and the Mendicants, with the Mendicants singing the ballad of the visit of the First Lady to the Home of the Disabled.
5. Old Women and Bero.
6. The Mendicants and Old Man, with the Mendicants finishing up their ballad and taking up a new song "Pro Patria Mourir."
7. Bero and Old Man.
8. The Mendicants, Old Man, and Bero.
9. The Old Women take up the cueword "Abuse."
10. The Mendicants taking up the cueword "Abuse" with Old Man acting for a while as a silent observer.
11. The Old Women looking for Si Bero.
12. The Mendicants and the Old Man once more.

The action proceeds leisurely to its climax as in Part One, with subtle transitions between scenes. Scene 6 is a continuation of 4. The action is not disrupted but only subdued to accommodate the brief exchange between Dr. Bero and Old Woman in scene 5. In a similar manner, scene 10 is temporarily interrupted by 11 and runs out its full course in 12. The internal ordering of the action in Part Two is more sophisticated.

Scene 8 ends with Old Man's mockery of the attempts of

mere mortal man to play god. Dr. Bero cannot do a flood or
dodge lightning, yet he apes the non-existent one who can.
He himself, Old Man thinks, is even closer to god than the
Beros, for at least he can foretell the future.

His bleak horoscope of the future reveals "A faithful
woman picking herbs for a smoke-screen on abuse"
(p. 276). The word "*abuse*" is a cueword signalling the
entry of the Old Women in the next scene. Scene 9 opens
with Iya Agba screaming "Abuse! Abuse! What do we do?
Close our eyes and see nothing" (p. 276). The scene itself
ends with Iya Agba herself insisting on paying earth her
dues in time. "We pay our dues to earth in time. I also take
back what is mine" (p. 268). The word "due" connects the
present scene to the next. When the Mendicants make their
entry in scene 10, they take up the theme of dues:

> I want my dues
>
> Not promises
>
> I want my dues
>
> Not promises. (p. 268)

The concluding climax in Part Two is more uproarious
than the end of Part One, being in itself an apocalyptic
finale to the entire drama. As Old Man, possessed by the
god of As, insists on operating on the Cripple, Dr. Bero
shoots him down. Meanwhile the Old Women have judged
that the opportune moment to invoke an armageddon of
fire upon the Bero household. The ensuing conflagration
is a cleansing ritual that returns the earth infested by the
Beros to its original purity.

THE PHILOSOPHY OF AS

As is the ability to bend nature to one's will (p. 237). But
even if Dr. Bero had not afforded us this insight, the Mendicants are there to help us. Throughout the play they do
nothing else but demonstrate through parody the method
of As. Old Man is evasive all along but at the end of the
play, he throws off his ironic mask and wants to *demon-*

strate by practical example the way As actually operates. "Let us taste just what makes a heretic tick," says Old Man. That is the voice of As, the language of its agents. As is the radical excision of the cysts that obstruct the efficient working of a socio-political system. In the republic of As, all who dare to protest against the system are heretics who must be guillotined at the altar of As. Such is the lesson to be derived from Old Man's determination to operate upon (the expression in the play is "practice") the Cripple who insisted on being *heard*. Old Man's parody nearly spills over into reality through his excessive reaction to As as a machinery of oppression. The audience should see his action as the climax of all the antics in the play that burlesque the method of As.

As is not really a new concept for Soyinka. His works are one long protest against As in its various manifestations. The warrior in *A Dance of the Forests* who was sold into slavery and was later murdered because he would not fight an unjust war was a victim of As. Eman in *The Strong Breed*, himself a burnt offering on the altar of custom, is a victim of As. Prophet Jeroboam in the Jero plays has perfected all strategies for making his converts victims of the religious As. *Kongi's Harvest* is one more critique of political As. In *Madmen and Specialists*, however, As has become an overriding theme. In this play, As protects the group interest of a military cartel that Soyinka has called the "alliance of a corrupt militarism and a rapacious Mafia." Dr. Bero, a one-time medical practitioner now turned military intelligence officer, represents the military wing of the alliance. In Chief Batoki and Zaki Amuri of *Season of Anomy*, Soyinka presents the civilian arm of the alliance. *Madmen and Specialists* concentrates on the operations of the military wing of the alliance just as *Season of Anomy* focused on the tactics of the civilian power elite. The antics of the new arrivistes to perpetuate their positions are identical in both works. Old Man sees through it all and refuses to be deceived like the rest of humanity. As is his petword for the cartel itself and its tactics. It stands for all forms of dictatorship, oppression, exploitation, social injustice, blind pursuit of self-interest, opportunistic expediency, etc.

The Old Man's disciples are the Mendicants, whom he
elevates above their station by letting them share his insights into human nature. After their indoctrination, the
Mendicants begin to *think* and to rationalize. Even the
blind ones among them are made to see through human
nature with their mind's eye. Blindman, speaking of his
own brainwashing, recalls one of his conversations with
Old Man:

> You can see me, he said, you can see me. Look at me
> with your mind. I swear I began to see him. Then I
> knew I was insane. (p. 243)

The Old Man's constant target during his numerous As
sessions with the Mendicants is the political power elites.
Election manifestos and political speeches are empty talk.
Behind this political rhetoric languish the real victims, the
suffering humanity who choke in silence. This is the "underdog," the "Us," the Dentist talks about in *Season of
Anomy*.[6] Old Man's doctrines are extremely popular with
the Mendicants. Their mangled bodies are, after all, living
testimonies of the reality of As. Old Man's philosophy has
helped them turn their attention away from their misfortunes to society itself. They scorn self-pity and convert
what otherwise would have become a destructive self-dis-
gust into a disgust with society. At one point in the play the
Mendicants mimic the antics of military dictators who
promise to relinquish power if the people so desire only to
then stage manage a vote of confidence for themselves.
Aafaa, assuming the role of a military chief executive, intones:

> If there is any one who does not approve us, just say so
> and we quit. I mean we are not here because we like it.
> We stay at immense sacrifice to ourselves, our leisure,
> our desires, vocations, specializations, et cetera, et cet-
> era. (p. 220–221)

The Mendicants demonstrate the operation of the judicial
system in an As regime. Accusations are concocted against
a chosen victim who is subjected to a mock trial. At the end

of it all, the victim, now a chastened man, is grateful to his tormentors. In the passage that follows, the victim is Goyi. The rest of the Mendicants play Dr. Bero and his aids:

Aafaa:	Did we try him?
Cripple:	Resurrect, you fool. Nobody tried you yet.
Aafaa:	You are *accused.*
Blindman:	Satisfied?
Cripple:	Fair enough.
Blindman:	Bang!

      (Goyi slumps)

Aafaa (rinsing his hands):
      Nothing to do with me.

Blindman:	Fair trial, No?
Aafaa:	Decidedly yes.
Blindman:	What does he say himself?
Goyi:	Very fair, gentlemen. I have no complaints. (p. 220)

Because these parodies are not explicit, it was important that the audience be familiar with the decoded attributes of As. Aafaa satisfies this need in his alphabetical definition of As (see the section on language).

As has a long history. It was, is, and ever shall be. Dr. Bero aptly calls it a god that is both new and old. The satire in the play is directed against the machinations of political As; but there are other forms of As. Old Man names these as scientific As, metaphysical As, sociological As, the economic, recreative, and ethical As (p. 271). As changes slightly here, that is, from the machinery of oppression to the machinery of psychological exploitation: All creeds and dogmas that enslave the mind of man are born of As. This is also true of all excuses for man's violation of moral codes.

However, the main emphasis of As in the play is political. It is in the political context that As's relationship to cannibalism becomes immediately meaningful. As seizes human reason and forces man to slaughter his fellowmen, thus providing As with its favorite dish, human flesh. Man's history is riddled with wars and rumors of wars

which have been fought for political ends. If so much
slaughter is to be permitted in the name of war, so goes Old
Man's Swiftian logic, then we might as well legalize cannibalism. After all, Old Man says, "all intelligent animals
kill for food" (p. 254). The cannibalism theory is Old
Man's logical protest against the senseless wastage of
human lives in the name of war. Dr. Bero, who himself has
tasted human flesh, sees the act as the end of all inhibitions,
the conquest of the weakness of man's all-too-human flesh
with all its sentiment. Cannibalism then is the ultimate
goal of As. It was prophesied in *A Dance*[7] that unborn
generations would eat one another. That prophecy is pain-
fully fulfilled in *Madmen*.

Old Man's use of As as a means of protesting against a
corrupt establishment is ineffective, for in practical terms
As, as we know it in *Madmen*, is the end result of cynicism
and nihilism, the final retreat of the ego into an obscure
corner. Soyinka's Marxist critics have denounced this approach to the ills of society as being superficial, defeatist,
and negative. They charge Soyinka with diverting the revolutionary potential inherent in the masses in his works
with ritual and mysticism, rather than organizing this potential into an active fighting force for the improvement of
human society. This criticism is best articulated by Lewis
Nkosi in *Tasks and Masks*: (1982):

> Soyinka's greatest achievement has been to find theat-
> rical forms and idioms varied enough to dramatize the
> frustrations of a certain group in African society; his
> weakness has been his constant striving after meta-
> physical formulas which merely mask these frustra-
> tions.[8]

CHARACTERIZATION

Madmen and Specialists is a drama of ideas; as such, the
ideas appear to be more important to the dramatist than the
characters. The characters are more effective in their collective identity than as individuals. The Mendicants belong to
one group; the Old Women to another; and the Beros form
yet a separate group. Only Old Man stands alone and above

these other groups as the essence of wisdom. He has the penetrating gaze of a sage and can pierce through all disguises and all barriers into the very quintessence of personality itself like the sage Apollonius in Keats's poem *Lamia*. Old Man indeed embodies the Apollonian instinct for reason and self-knowledge. He is paired at one point in the play (p. 262) with the Greek sage Socrates. He evokes all the good associations of old age: wisdom, foresight and insight, knowledge, and the gift of prophecy. That he represents a type rather than an individual is apparent from the fact that he has no proper name but is only called "Old Man." The contempt he radiates toward the demigods whom he recognizes to be midgets hurts them more than open abuse. Old Man's action at the end—his determination to operate upon the Cripple—has puzzled many a reader. He has carried his contempt for the system too far, but his action can be understood if one sees it as a parody that runs the risk of overspilling into actuality.

The Old Women (Iya Agba and Iya Mate) resemble Old Man in being incarnations of wisdom, but theirs is a mysterious wisdom gained at a great peril to the knower while Old Man stands for a pure, disinterested wisdom. Si Bero is introduced to the mysteries of the Old Women's wisdom in exchange for something else—something that is dear to her, which could be either her own life or the life of a dear one. "I warned you when we took you in the fold. I said this gift is not one you gather in one hand. If your other hand is foul the first withers also," they tell Si Bero (p. 274) when the time comes for her to fulfil her pledge. Oyin Ogunba sees these earth-mothers as *aje*, that is, witches in the Yoruba sense in which witches are not especially evil. The *aje* are:

> Women who are acknowledged to be close to the ultimate source of human life and can influence individual lives for good or ill.[9]

In addition to embodying the mysteries of Earth, the Old Women are also agents of karma. "We put back what we take, in one form or another," they tell Dr. Bero. "Or more than we take. It's the only law" (p. 260). Iya Mate is more

maternal, more human than Iya Agba. But the Old Wom-
en's strict insistence on "duty" is compelled upon them by
forces beyond their control. "Nothing we can do, daughter,
nothing but follow the way as we met it" (p. 274).

Dr. Bero is the character in whom the reality of As is
personified. Knowing him as synonymous with knowing
As, for he is its most devoted apostle. It is doubtful if real
life could furnish us with an individual as inhuman, as
conscienceless, and as ruthless in the pursuit of his own
interests as Dr. Bero. Could anyone actually be so wholly
committed to a cause that he not only hates his natural
father for being opposed to this cause but will entertain no
qualms about having him murdered? It seems as if Soyinka
is creating a monster in Bero. "Even on the road to damnation a man must rest his foot somewhere," the Old Women
say (p. 260). But not Dr. Bero. The other characters have
some redeeming qualities that make them kin with us. Dr.
Bero is an unredeemed and unredeemable incarnation of
evil.

The Mendicants share a common destiny as cannon
fodder for the ogre, As. They represent the masses, the
wretched of the earth, eternally engaged in the battle for
survival. They have learned to stake their dearest resources
(their bodies) in that battle in spite of their meagre divi-
dends. The Mendicants make their impact as a group
rather than as individuals: Their reflexes, their speeches,
actions and psychologies are identical and derive from a
common mentality—the mentality of the oppressed. Aafaa,
who aspires toward individuality by his quick-wittedness
and outspoken directness, does not quite attain that status.
He is not quite differentiated enough from the others.
Blindman's speech at the end sounds like an utterance from
Aafaa. One suspects that the Mendicants' anonymity is
deliberate, for the system denies them individuality.

LANGUAGE

The play's most outstanding achievement is its language. Both Old Man and the Mendicants possess an immense facility with language. Their language is not always

as rhetorical as Professor's speeches in *The Road*, but it is terse, cryptic, and yet profound and far-reaching in its allusions. The ability to wring the nuances from each word does not belong to Old Man alone but is common to the Mendicants as a whole. They have perfected the art of double-talk, which they have learned from Old Man, and have mastered his gift for poetry, his flair for verbal wit, and his ability to form new words from existing ones.

Aafaa relishes the resourcefulness of his imagination in the attempt to relate As to the alphabet. His attempt stops at the letter "I," but that is no mean feat, considering the poetry of the attempt and the appropriateness of its diction. "A" is acceptance. Adjustment of Ego to the acceptance of As. "B" is blindness in As. As is all-seeing; All shall see in As who render themselves blind to all else. "C" is for contentment. "D" is for Divinity, Destiny, and Duty: Destiny is the Duty of Divinity (D-D-D). "E" is for Epilepsy; "F" for fulfilment, and "G" for Godhead: As is Godhead. Aafaa is himself conscious of his power over words. By the time he comes to the letter "H" he is fully inspired. "H" is for Humanity: Humanity the ultimate sacrifice to As, the eternal oblation on the altar of As.

Aafaa distinguishes himself as the most accomplished acolyte of his master, Old Man. He calls himself "the quickest of the underdogs" (p. 255). His wit is at its most intensely sustained moment in the one long speech he makes near the end of the play on the history of ecclesiastical schisms:

> . . .there was no hole in the monolithic solidarity of two halves of the priesthood. No, there was no division. The loyalty of homosapiens regressed into himself, himself his little tick-tock self, self-ticking, self-tickling, self-tackling problems that belonged to the priesthood spiritual and political while they remained the sole and indivisible one. Oh! look at him, Monsieur l'homme sapiens, look at the lone usurper of the ancient rights and privileges of the priesthood . . . look at the dog in dogma raising his hindquarters to cast the scent of his individuality on the lamp-post of Destiny! (pp. 273–274)

We can hear Old Man, the grand rhetorician and eloquent poet in his own right when he means to be in Aafaa's verbal jugglery. Old Man dismisses all enemies of As as:

> the cyst in the system, the splint in the arrow of arrogance, the dog in dogma, the tick of a heretic, the tick in politics, the mock of democracy, the mar of marxism, a tick of the fanatic, the boo in buddhism. (p. 275)

Old Man's trick is to fragment his words into syllabic units and then convert the most accentuated of the vowel sounds in those units into an independent sound unit which he juxtaposes with the parent word. In another instance, he piles up concatenations of rhyming verbals:

> . . . do you not defecate, fornicate, prevaricate, when heaven and earth implore you to abdicate (pp. 271–272).

In every case, the intention is to exploit words for their musical and rhythmic effects. In Aafaa's long speech cited earlier, he appears at one point to have lost touch with the main trend of his argument, floating only on the waves of sound: "The loyalty of homo sapiens regressed into himself, himself his little tick-tock self, self-ticking, self-tickling, self-tackling problems that belonged to the priesthood."

It is, however, in the skill for verbal theatrics that the Mendicants excel. These verbal theatrics entail much more than the Mendicants' ability to make puns, of which there are many examples in the play. "Rem Acu Tetigisti," for instance, gives us "R. A. T." and "rat." "Official rat is what I smell," says Aafaa, which implies that all along the Mendicants suspect foul dealing in high places; "dog" gives us "underdog," "watchdog," and "dogma." "The end," Old Man says, "justifies the meanness" (p. 267); "disabled" gives us a more serious deformity, "de-balled." The more obvious case of verbal theatrics emerges in the situations where words are continuously extended into other dimensions of meaning where they become relevant to As.

Thus, when the Mendicants remark that when things go wrong, it is the lowest who get it first, they recall, too, that they are at the bottom of things. The meaning of the word "bottom" is immediately extended into As: "bottomless account." That reminds us of the embezzlement of public funds by highly placed public officials, a phenomenon Soyinka has satirized elsewhere:

> Ever-ready bank accounts
> Are never read where
> Children slay the cockroaches for a meal.[10]

Certain words such as "smoke," "flood," and "elections" serve the Mendicants as cue words whose meanings are to be extended into As. "Smoke" gives us "smoke-screen," and Old Man says that the election manifestos, the charades and the pious pronouncements are all smoke-screens: "At the bottom of it all humanity chokes in silence" (p. 265). When he looks into the future, Old Man sees "a faithful woman picking herbs for a smoke-screen on abuse" (p. 267). "Flood" gives us its counterpart in As: "running-water" by which Old man means "running progress," "faucets," and "pipes." The Cripple, who cannot reach the new innovation (the tap water), says: "too high," and Old Man translates even this secondary motif into As: "too high like the price" (p. 265). High price does not merely imply the high cost of living, which has made begging even a less profitable concern, but the high price (death) that As exacts from its victims.

But the motif of running water recalls the running mouths that heap election promises on the people. The word "elections" in its own turn gives us "electricity," which in As translates into "electrocution" and the electric chair. Dr. Bero might not have had access to an electric chair, but whatever means he uses to eliminate his victims Old Man calls "Electrodes on the nerve-centre, the favourite pastime of As" (p. 266).

When Old Man evokes the high ideal of patriotism as contained in the Latin aphorism "Dulce et decorum est pro patria mori," we are meant, of course, to contrast this high ideal with what goes on in the republic of As. It is more

becoming and more appealing in As not to die for one's
country but to exploit it. The word "corum" which is
formed from "decorum" translates into As as: "quorum."
"Quorum" reads for some of the Mendicants as a corruption of "corum," but when they have seen through the
irony (that is, when they have perceived its As relevance), it
becomes another occasion for "rem acu tetigisti." "No quorum, no quorum, that's the damned trouble," says Goyi,
and the Cripple approves: "Yes Sir, you've banged the
hammer on the nail" (p. 261). The word-play on "corum"
and "quorum" points to the increasing emphasis on "quorum" even in our national legislatures. Because legislators
are absentee law-makers, bills depend on the formation of a
"quorum" for their passage. That recalls Old Man's favorite lesson on civic responsibility. "In ancient Athens
they didn't just have a quorum. Everybody was there! That,
children was democracy" (p. 261). The word "quorum"
trails off later into the Mendicants' euphemism for the seat
of political power (the parliament) were the "national
cake" is shared, and they express a desire to be members of
that "quorum":

> Before I Join
> The saints above
> Before I join
> The saints above
> I want to sit on that damned quorum (p. 261).

Certain ethical concepts, especially those connected with
duty, choice, and truth, lose their conventional connotation when appropriated by As. In the very first scene in Part
One, the Mendicants' ironic insistence on the word "duty"
indicates that this word carries a meaning that is peculiar
to As. "You may say he is . . . dutiful," says Goyi, speaking
to Dr. Bero. Right away the Cripple relates the word to its
conventional association: "Him a dutiful son? You're
crazy." Thereafter, Blindman returns the word to its true
meaning in As: "I know what he means. Bang! All in the
line of duty!" (p. 220). The stage direction points to an
imaginary victim of As, Goyi, clutching his chest as he
drops dead on the floor. To be dutiful in As is to decapitate

all suspects, and in the case of Dr. Bero, to subordinate one's own filial duty to that duty demanded of him by As. Soyinka is careful to situate the tragedy in a domestic context in order to demonstrate the extent to which As can dehumanize and de-personalize its agents. Dr. Bero does not, indeed, hesitate to assassinate his own father in the service of As.

The meaning of the word "choice" is also transformed in As. He who chooses is an enemy of As, an agent of subversion. "As chooses, man accepts," says Aafaa. This adage is illustrated in a mini-comedy performed by the Mendicants toward the end of Part One. The Cripple has just swallowed a fat bug which he picked from his rags, and Aafaa challenges him on the choice of that particular specimen:

Aafaa:	Did you choose it?
Cripple:	It chose me.
Blindman:	Chose? An enemy of As.
Aafaa:	Sure? Not a disciple.
Blindman:	An enemy, subversive agent.
Aafaa:	Quite right. "As chooses, man accepts." (p. 234).

In the Old Man's mockery of freedom of choice in As, he suggests to Dr. Bero a list of alternatives he can conjure up to mask his denial of freedom of choice to his victims.

Shall I teach you what to say? Choice! Particularity! What redundant self-deceptive notions! More? More? insistence on a floppy old coat, a rickety old chair, a moth-eaten hat which no certified lunatic would ever consider wearing. . . . A perfect waterproof coat is rejected for a patched-up heirloom that gives the silly wearer rheumatism. Is this an argument for freedom of choice? (p. 252)

As in "choice," the word "truth" has a meaning that is peculiar to As. "Truth" is whatever confessions that are extorted from the victim in the torture chamber of As. This

kind of truth, the Old Women tell Dr. Bero, is easy to come
by: "Truth is always too simple for a desperate mind"
(p. 259). The Mendicants have learned to make a mockery
of Dr. Bero's torture-chamber truth: "Think not that I hurt
you but that Truth hurts. We are seekers after truth. I am a
specialist in truth" (p. 223). This truth is to be contrasted
with the truth which Old Man stands for, the truth that
politicians are liars. One recalls that Old Man calls himself
"the one and only truth" (p. 242).

The language of the Old Women has a solemnity that is
lacking in the Mendicants' verbal casuistry. Their speech is
weighty and their cadence measured: "We move as the
Earth moves, nothing more. We age as Earth ages" (p. 259).
Their very personality is identified with Nature herself,
which indeed supplies them with the ingredients of speech.
The herbs and seeds they stockpile in Dr. Bero's surgery
enjoy an identity with the human body:

> Can I sleep easy when my head is gathering mould on
> your shelves? (p. 274)

> But my head still fills your room from wall to wall
> and dirty hands touch it. (p. 274)

Their language has its own ironies and paradoxes, but
these are of a more sober kind than the Mendicants' verbal
gimmickry: "You never can tell of seeds. The plant may be
good; but we'll know, we'll know" (p. 235). The new worthless seed (Dr. Bero) is here contrasted with the good parent
stalk (Old Man), whose humanity will only be redeemed by
the propitious seed (Si Bero). This contrast is more obvious
in Iya Agba's remark: "I haven't burrowed so deep to cast
good earth on worthless seeds" (p. 235). Dr. Bero metamorphoses rapidly from a "worthless seed" to a leaking sieve
that cannot even hold the grain before it has a chance of
being separated into seed and chaff: "Let him watch it. I
haven't come this far to put my whole being in a sieve"
(p. 236). The Old Women are natural healers, agents of
life-giving forces. It is therefore easy for them to link Dr.
Bero to butchery and bloodshed:

Don't look for the sign of broken bodies or wandering
souls. Don't look for the sound of fear or the smell of
hate. Don't take a bloodhound with you; we don't
mutilate bodies. If you do, you may find him circle
back to your door. (p. 260)

But by far the most persistent imagery in the play is the
religious metaphor, which establishes As as a deity. "D"
stands for Divinity in the alphabetical definition of As, and
"I" for "I am I," a corruption of the biblical attribute for
God, "I am that I am." If As is a religion, the biblical
diction used by its apostles is most appropriate: "I say this
unto you, As is all-seeing. All shall see in As who render
themselves blind to all else." The statement "I am the one
and only truth" stands both for Old Man's truth and the
false truth claimed by As. All those who are opposed to the
new religion are heretics. Dr. Bero worries that the Mendicants are provided with a creed, but they still talk heresy
(p. 263).

The play's language is primarily biblical in its diction;
but within that diction there are two speech patterns: the
solemn, measured language spoken by the Old Women,
which is soaked in grain imagery and animal metaphor
when Dr. Bero is the subject of their discourse, and the
staccato language spoken by the Mendicants. Since the
bulk of the satire is directed against political As, the Mendicants' language derives its force from its being rooted in
current cant.

Notes

1. Susan Yankowitz, "The Plays of Wole Soyinka," *African Forum*, Vol. 1, No. 4, (Spring 1966), p. 130.

2. John Fletcher and James McFarlane, "Modernist Drama:
Origins and Patterns," in Malcolm Bradbury and James
McFarlane, eds., *Modernism* (Harmondsworth: Penguin,
1976), p. 507.

3. Wole Soyinka, *The Man Died* (London: Rex Collings, 1972), p. 182.

4. Wole Soyinka, *Madmen and Specialists* in *Collected Plays* Vol. 2 (London: Oxford University Press, 1974), p. 239. Subsequent references are to this edition.

5. Oyin Ogunba, *The Movement of Transition* (Ibadan: Ibadan University Press, 1975), p. 219.

6. Wole Soyinka, *Season of Anomy* (London: Rex Collings, 1972), p. 104.

7. Wole Soyinka, *A Dance of the Forests* in *Collected Plays* Vol. 1 (London: Oxford University Press, 1973), p. 49.

8. Lewis Nkosi, *Tasks and Masks* (Burnt Mill: Longmans, 1981), p. 191.

9. *The Movement of Transition*, p. 211.

10. Wole Soyinka, *A Shuttle in the Crypt* (New York: Hill and Wang, 1972), p. 81.

10

———————— Δ Δ ————————

THE BACCHAE OF EURIPIDES

BACKGROUND TO THE PLAY

That Soyinka should be more sympathetically disposed toward Euripides rather than to his predecessors Aeschylus and Sophocles should not surprise those familiar with Soyinka's revolutionary temperament. Both in art and life he tends to champion revolutionary protagonists; and the one experimental dramatist in classical antiquity is Euripides. If Aeschylus and Sophocles are to be regarded as Apollonian dramatists, Euripides proves himself in his last play to have been the one spokesman for Dionysian contradictions. Also, the character of the god celebrated in *The Bacchae*, Dionysus—the ritual agonies he suffered, Nietzsche's later effort to link him with the birth of Greek tragedy, his role as an embodiment of contradictions, and as a vegetation deity—these are some of the traits that link the Greek god with Soyinka's patron deity, Ogun.

Euripides was born at Salamis at about 484 B.C. and died in exile in Macedonia in 406 B.C. He was the third of the three great Attic tragedians, the others being, of course, Aeschylus (525–456 B.C.) and Sophocles (496–406 B.C.). He knew Athens in its glory and witnessed the final plays of Aeschylus, notably the *Oresteia* in 458 B.C. He made his own debut in 455, a year after Aeschylus' death but did not win the first of his very few victories in dramatic competition until 441. He is said to have written 92 plays, of which only about eighteen survived.

Euripides was an iconoclast from the beginning as is

evident in his theatre. His plays share certain characteristics that set them apart from the work of his predecessors. He disregarded the Aristotelian notions of responsibility, tragic flaw, and heroism. He questioned the myth of a rational universe upon which the *Poetics* was founded. His own plays are inscribed within a universe devoid of order and moral law, so that the conduct of his characters or the fate that befalls them need not be determined by the imperatives of moral law. The good ones often suffer ill and the bad ones go unpunished. A typical example is the case of Heracles, who is tortured and tormented in the play that bears his name and yet his demeanor is totally free of "tragic flaw."

The language of his plays is often lyrical, but it does not always soar to the height of eloquence that distinguishes the utterance of the Promethean heroes and demi-gods who people the Aeschylean/Sophoclean stage. This linguistic low profile (the use of common speech) is the direct consequence of the one major innovation for which Euripides will always be remembered: He is credited with bringing realism to the Greek stage. This he accomplished by peopling his stage with ordinary men and women, rather than with Titans or monumental archetypes. "In place of the classical kings and battles," wrote Erich Segal, "Euripides brought to the stage familiar things. The living room replaces the throne room."[1] "Through him," says Nietzsche, "the common man found his way from the auditorium onto the stage."[2] And when Nietzsche accuses Euripides of killing tragedy, he means Euripides' debasement of the traditional notions of heroism.

But Euripides, enigmatic dramatist that he was, reverses some of these trends in his most uncharacteristic work, *The Bacchae*. In this final dramatic testament, language is occasionally elevated, men of royal blood re-enter the stage, and the distribution of punishment is dependent upon the law of nemesis. "Let every man's actions save or damn him," says Dionysus at the beginning of the play (p. 242).[3]

In *The Bacchae*, Euripides abandons Apollo in order to pay homage to Dionysus. The two Greek gods, Apollo and Dionysus, represent two complementary impulses in every man—rational, somber and austere as opposed to liberal,

easy-going, and cheerful. Milton's sister poems, "L'Allegro" and "Il Penseroso," have attempted to encapsulate the
basic psychology of these two contradictory instincts. Dionysus is the remote ancestor of L'Allegro, the cheerful man.
But he is also the god of nature, the spirit of fertility; his
season is harvest and fruitfulness.

Classical mythology records two versions of Dionysus'
genealogy.[4] He was a god who was born twice, of different
mothers, but fathered in each instance by Zeus. In the
Orphic version of the legend, the god is called Zagreus, and
his first incarnation is associated by Orphism with the
creation of man. According to this version, Zagreus is the
son of Zeus and Persophone. Hera, Zeus' legal wife, insti-
gated the Titans to destroy the infant god. They tore him to
pieces and devoured him, but Athena saved the baby's heart
and took it to Zeus, who burnt up the Titans with his
lightning. From their ashes sprang up the race of men,
who, Orphism claims, have in them some portions of the
divine spark. Zeus swallowed the heart of Zagreus and out
of it was later born a new Dionysus Zagreus, son of Semele.
Zagreus literally means "torn to pieces."

In his second incarnation, Dionysus enjoyed a mixed
parentage. His father continues to be Zeus but his mother
was a mortal woman, Semele. He was born at Thebes
during the reign of Kadmos, founder of Thebes. Kadmos
had four daughters: Semele, Ino, Autone, and Agave. The
first of these, Semele, fell in love with Zeus and bore his
baby, who was to have been born as Dionysus. But fate,
acting through the agency of Hera, once again intervened
to frustrate the child's normal gestation period within his
mother's womb. Disguising herself as Semele's aged nurse
Beroe, Hera told the expectant mother that she, too, could
become immortal if her divine lover appeared to her in his
true splendor as the god of thunder. Wishing herself to be
immortal, Semele begged the favor, which was granted. But
when Zeus appeared to her as the god of lightning, her frail
mortal frame could not withstand the blazing fierceness of
the great manifestation. Before she dissolved to ashes, Zeus
snatched the unborn child from his mother's womb and
sewed him into his thigh. When the gestation period was
over, Dionysus was born from Zeus' thigh. In order to

protect the divine child from further harassment from Hera, Zeus changed Dionysus into a ram and brought him up in a cave. Here, the myth goes on, the father of the gods himself charged the Sage Silenus with the boy's upbringing. Silenus helped him to discover the secrets of nature and the art of making wine. When Dionysus grew to manhood, he traversed the Eastern world teaching humanity his mysteries and asserting his divinity. In Euripides' *The Bacchae*, Dionysus returns to his native land, Thebes, journeying through Phrygia and Lydia to the Isles of Crete. He has come to Thebes to re-assert his divine authority.

KADMOS AND THE FOUNDING OF THEBES

Thebes was the principal city of Boeotia, a district to the northwest of Attica in which Athens was located. The city was equipped with seven gates and located beside the great mountain, Kithairon, and a number of famous rivers, including Dirce and Asopus. The mythical origin of the city is that when Kadmos' sister Europa was stolen by Zeus in the form of a white bull, his father, Agenor of Sidon, sent Kadmos and his brothers to search for Europa. After various adventures, Kadmos, led by Athena, set out to establish a city. Led by a cow chosen by the goddess, he came to a spring where he was to establish the city. When most of his men were killed by a serpent who lived there, Kadmos killed the serpent and, again following the instructions of the goddess, sowed its teeth. From the teeth sprang up armed men who began fighting among themselves until Kadmos stopped them by throwing a stone into their midst. These "sown men" and their descendants became the great families of Thebes. Among them was Echion, the father of Pentheus. The various allusions in the play to a race of dragon spawn refer to Kadmos' first act of peopling his city with a race of sown men.[5]

THE WORSHIP OF DIONYSUS

Dionysus' military successes throughout the world of classical antiquity established his supremacy as a powerful deity. There emerged a religious cult known as Dionysianism, which held sway in many parts of ancient Greece for many centuries. The essence of the god's worship was not related to war or military conquest but to agricultural magic, that is, to the bringing forth of the life-renewing energies of nature through physical contact with the supreme incarnation of the spirit of vegetation himself or by recognition of his presence in the midst of nature, for Dionysus, as has already been noted, was a male fertility god. His symbol is the phallus and his votaries are women, called Maenads or Bacchae. In the original ceremony the Maenads dressed up in fawnskin and brandished their *thyrsi* as they marched up to the mountain to meet Dionysus. There they indulged in sexual orgies in order to communicate with the spirit of fertility. This ceremony was commemorated periodically in the Dionysian festivals. George Thomson recalls one of the earliest recorded accounts of the revels:

> Every other year, in many Greek towns, it is the custom for women to gather together in companies of Bacchus, the girls carrying the thyrsus and worshipping the god with wild, ecstatic cries, while the married women sacrifice in groups, indulge in Bacchic revels, and in general sing hymns to Dionysus in imitation of the Maenads, his ancient ministers.[6]

In later-day rituals men were admitted into the cult, but this change might not have been related to agricultural magic but rather to individual sublimation of erotic fantasies.

The actual ceremony in the original ritual consisted of three stages. The first is the representation of Dionysus by one of his favorite totems: the bull, the lion, the goat, or the snake. The second is the frenzied dancing and reveling in the mountains (accompanied with liberal distribution of wine), and the third (which is the climax of the proceedings) is the tearing to pieces of the sacrificial animal known as the *sparamagnos*, and the eating of its raw flesh, otherwise called the *omaphogia*. The dancing and the wine bring the celebrants into a state of possession which reaches its climax in the dismemberment of the sacrificial animal. This violent action re-enacts the passion of Dionysus who was torn to pieces by the Titans. The very act of tasting the raw flesh of the god-surrogate enables the votary to partake of the god's divinity.

The Dionysian festivals were celebrated once every two years when Apollo, the god of sanity, yielded the crown to Dionysus, the god of frenzy. This compromise was worked out in recognition of the need for man to occasionally indulge the dark irrational forces within his psyche.

The kinship between Dionysus and the Yoruba god, Ogun, exercises an irresistible fascination for Soyinka. Dionysus' thyrsus and ivy recall Ogun's stave and palm; both gods are associated with wine, harvest, and the fruitfulness of the seasons. The phallus is consecrated to both gods in recognition of their attribute as fertility gods. Also Dionysus' agony in the hands of the Titans anticipated Ogun's physical disintegration in the abyss of transition. In acknowledgment of Ogun's affinities with Dionysus, Soyinka has worked some lines from Ogun's hymns into Dionysus' theme songs. In the following lines from Soyinka's version of the *Bacchae*, the slave leader evokes Dionysus in a liturgical utterance whose imagery and metaphors use the familiar vocabulary of Ogun's archetypal attributes:

> Come, god
> Of seven paths: oil, wine, blood, spring, rain
> Sap and sperm O dirge of shadows, dark-shod feet
> Seven-ply cross-roads, hands of camwood
> Breath of indigo, O god of the seven roads
> Farm, hill, forge, breath, field of battle
> Death and the recreative flint. (p. 295)

The ceremonies associated with the cult of Dionysus in its unadulterated phase came later to be linked with meaningful implications in the dynamics of rituals and political evolutions of society.

THE RITUAL FACTOR

George Thomson[7] has attributed certain conventions of primitive fertility rituals to the cult of Dionysus. One of these is the belief in sympathetic magic, that is, the practice whereby the human community fertilizes itself by a simple act of physical contact with the fertility of nature. In most primitive societies, his evidence goes, virgins are believed to be capable of becoming mothers by contact with sacred rivers. The spring festivals of ancient Chinese peasantry are marked by ribaldry and sexual licence typical of the Dionysian orgies. Also the motif of symbolic or physical death followed by resurrection, which is basic to rites of initiation or of passage, has its origin in the agonies of hero-gods—Dionysus, Christ, and Ogun, who confronted death physically in the interest of their community's well-being. The human counterpart of the ritual archetype is the carrier or the scapegoat whose suffering is an extended version of the passion of the hero-gods. Tragic drama in general enacts this paradigm, either specifically or in disguise. In *The Bacchae*, Pentheus dies the death of the scapegoat. He goes out into the wilderness, here the mountain Kithairon, where he is torn to pieces by the Maenads as an embodiment of Dionysus who was torn to pieces by the Titans; and by his death he purges the guilt of Thebes for its failure to recognize the new god, Dionysus. Soyinka had earlier exploited the motif of the carrier in *The Strong Breed* (1964) and used it as the main metaphysical ideology in *Death and the King's Horseman* (1975). His first encounter with the Euripidean version of the theme must have been a fascinating experience.

THE POLITICAL DIMENSION

Dionysus is a collective force that unites all nature in a dance of communion. All oppositions are reconciled and all contradictions annulled in his rites. The individual experiences this reconciliation on a personal level in the very suppression of his inhibitions in the wake of religious ecstasy, while on the communal level he is at one with his fellowman, with nature, and with the god. The slave leader pays tribute, in Soyinka's adaptation, to the god's role as a force that reconciles all antinomies: "His mesh of elements/Reconciles a warring universe" (p. 251). Nietzsche has captured the spirit of universal harmony that is generated by the god's presence in nature:

Not only does the bond between man and man come
to be forged once more by the magic of the Dionysian
rites, but nature itself, long alienated or subjugated,
rises again to celebrate the reconciliation with her
prodigal son, man. The earth offers its gifts voluntarily, and the savage beasts of mountain and desert approach in peace. The chariot of Dionysus is bedecked
with flowers and garlands; panthers and tigers stride
beneath his yoke. . . . Now the slave emerges as a
freeman; all the rigid hostile walls which either necessity or despotism has created between men are shattered.[8]

Nietzsche's theory begins and ends with Dionysus' potential as a revolutionary deity who is capable of challenging
existing social and political organizations. In any society
wherein capital is sustained by labor, Dionysus is apt to be
embraced by the underprivileged as a patron saint. This
was the case with Greek society of the fifth century B.C., in
which slave labor was exploited in the mines, the farms,
and the aristocratic households. In Euripides' time the
slaves, the helots, the women (who were completely con-
troled by the men) welcomed the god as the spirit of liberty.
This aspect of Dionysus is not highlighted in Euripides'
Bacchae for obvious reasons (the play could not encourge
insurrection openly), but Soyinka gave it prominence in
his own version. The slaves, encouraged by the prospects of
the god's imminent annunciation, are openly rebellious.
Dionysus was to liberate them from bondage, so they hailed
him as the priest of restitution. At the end of the play,
authority was overthrown and the spirit of equity restored.
Kadmos, who assumed control over the affairs of state after
Pentheus' death, shouted orders to the slaves but no one
paid him heed.

The Theban experience is fraught with ominous lessons
for modern states. The god's coming marks the inaugura-
tion of a new order that runs counter to the old, and the
new order's birth trauma shatters the foundations of the old
society. W. B. Yeats stated that a new age emerges from the
ashes of the old every two thousand years. This was a
concept of Blake's—the theory of flux, which asserts that

without contraries [there] is no progression. Blake's theory of contraries can not only be applied to one individual's desire for self-realization but to the healthy development of society. This is a dialectical process: The confrontation between the rebel and authority causes a crisis, out of whose ruins emerges a new order. By the time Dionysus has established his authority over Thebes, Pentheus and his palace lie in ruins.

The structure of both the original *Bacchae* and Soyinka's version is determined by the logic of the dialectical pattern, but this is more self-consciously the case with Soyinka. He overemphasizes the apocalyptic imperatives of the dialectic. The god is truly heralded in footsteps of earthquake. The slaves are too expectant of the dawn of the new order. The myth of the god is a self-conscious factor in the revolutionary dynamics for social change.

DIONYSUS AND LITERARY MODERNISM

The revolutionary tendencies inherent in Dionysus have their consequences in art and literature. Dionysus stands for the necessity of change, for the virtues of experimentation in art; he has been invoked, as a result, as the appropriate symbol for literary modernism. Monroe Spears writes in his influential inquiry into the nature of modernism in twentieth-century literature:

> Dionysus presides metaphorically over most of the recent trends in theater, from cruelty and absurdity to audience participation, nudity, and the tribal rock musical. On or off the stage, he is apparent in two contemporary figures: the black militant, violently releasing dark and repressed forces both in society and within the psyche, and the rock musician, with his female devotees and his orgiastic cult of collective emotion.[9]

But the god's presence in literature was felt much earlier. It has been suggested that English literary history can be seen in terms of the alternating reigns of Apollo and Dionysus. The neo-classical concern for order in life and art is clearly

Apollonian, whereas the Romantic impulse for the free expansion of the human spirit in life and art is unquestionably Dionysian (or Ogunian). Modernism in literature is an extension of the romantic spirit in its preoccupation with bold experimentation. But before the emergence of the moderns, the presence of the god was noticeable in the life style and literary posturings of the English aesthetic and decadent movement that immediately preceded the modernist era. The aesthetes of the nineties in both England and France are the sons of Dionysus who manifested himself to them through Eros and their addiction to opium. Like Dionysus, they were critical of the bourgeois suppression of the dark forces in the name of prudence and conventional morality. When Pentheus examines Dionysus, he sees the familiar figure of the aesthete:

> You are not at all bad-looking
> Quite attractive I am sure, to women
> Long hair, all nicely curled. (p. 266)

The major innovations introduced by modernism into literary technique are Dionysian in the sense that they are strongly influenced by the cult of the irrational and the illogical in both form and content. The cult of the irrational may be remotely related to the art of dislocating language, which is characteristic of modernist writing; but it manifests itself supremely in the vogue for the juxtapositional technique and in the use of myth. In much modernist writing, syntactical and chronological sequence is given up for a structure that depends on the perception of relationships between disconnected word-groups or historical experiences which must be juxtaposed and perceived simultaneously. A deliberate effort is made to thwart the inherent connectiveness of language and to frustrate the reader's normal expectation of a sequence.

The use of myth in modernist literature recognizes the hidden forces of the psyche, for there are areas of experience that cannot be comprehended by rational cognition. Eliot, the supreme myth-maker of the modern age, has described the modernist method as the continuous manipulation of the parallel between consciousness (the present) and the unconscious (the past).

But the moderns also recognize the relevance of Apollo to literature. Thus Yeats criticizes those innovations of Pound's that he considers obstructionist. He blames Pound's "unexplained ejaculations," his "unbridged transitions," on the fury of the savage gods.[10] Eliot returned to the domain of Apollo when he declared himself in 1927 to be classicist in literature, royalist in politics, and Anglo-Catholic in religion. He and other moderns like him have achieved a compromise between Apollo and Dionysus. Dionysus would ask for no more.

SOYINKA'S INNOVATIONS

Soyinka's version of the *Bacchae* follows closely the main features of the myth of Pentheus and his tragic encounter with Dionysus: the arrival of the god at Thebes, his rage for vengeance, the opposition mounted by Pentheus, Dionysus being taunted, questioned and imprisoned by Pentheus, the god's miraculous escape from prison, Pentheus' gradual surrender to the hypnotizing powers of the god, his journey to the mountain as a sacrificial victim, escorted thither by the god, and his ultimate death, torn to pieces by the Maenads.

All these elements of the myth are painstakingly recapitulated in Soyinka's adaptation, but he brings the reader closer to the meaning of Dionysus' role as a ritual archetype, that is, Dionysus as the prototype of the hanged god who suffered physical disintegration so that nature may be renewed. Soyinka is fascinated by this phenomenon because of his familiarity with the Yoruba god, Ogun and the Christian god, Christ. The old seer, Tiresias, reveals the meaning of the sacrifice undergone by dismembered hero-gods. In a casual conversation with Dionysus, Tiresias speaks of the death of gods and heroes as the sacrifice which nature demands for its own regeneration:

> Dionysus: And if you have been flogged to pieces at
> the end, like an effigy?

> Tiresias: Then I shall pass into the universal energy
>   of renewal like some heroes or gods I could
>   name. Isn't that why you all seem to get
>   torn to pieces at some point or other?
>   (p. 243)

At the end of the play, when Pentheus has paid the supreme penalty on behalf of Thebes, Tiresias speaks of the
ritual implication of the sacrifice:

> Understanding of these things is far beyond us. Per-
> haps . . . perhaps our life-sustaining earth Demands
> . . . a little . . . sometimes, a more than token offering
> for her own needful renewal. (p. 306)

This view is corroborated by the old slave at the end of the
play: "We know full well that some must die, chosen/To
bear the burden of decay, lest we all die" (p. 300). Dionysus
and Pentheus are ritual archetypes in Euripides, but these
roles are not as strongly emphasized as they are in Soyinka
because Euripides' audience was familiar with the main
facts of the story.

Soyinka's metaphor for that universal regeneration con-
sequent upon the death of the hero is communion. He,
therefore, needed to revise the end of the play. In Soyinka's
version, the severed head of the ritual archetype, Pentheus,
inundates the earth with blood that is transformed into
wine, which is shared by all. We have in this metamorpho-
sis the combined potency of blood as a fertilizing elixir and
of wine as a magic potion that unites. In Soyinka's play,
Dionysus leaves the stage the moment he has delivered
Pentheus to his enemies. He did not re-emerge as he does in
Euripides to mock Pentheus' bleeding head or distribute
further punishment to the house of Kadmos. The image of
Dionysus as a vengeful god contradicts his traditional reputation as a collective force. The transformation of the bleeding head into a fount of wine suggests that the god's own
sacrifice, or that of Pentheus who re-enacts it, is altruistic.
Pentheus is struck down so that the whole of Thebes might
be cleansed with the blood of the slain hero.

But the theme of communion is developed on two levels. There is the ritual, or religious, sense of communion (man's fellowship with nature) and there is the sociopolitical dimension (man's communion with his fellow men). The ritual aspect establishes Dionysus as the god of plenty. Its mysteries release the productive energies of the earth. Thebes is blessed with abundance of harvest upon the god's arrival at the city. The Herdsman explains:

> The vines went mad . . . they were not themselves. Something seemed to have got under the soil and was feeding them nectar. The weight that hung on the vines even from the scrubbiest patch, each cluster pendulous breasts of the wives of Kronos, bursting all over with giant nipples. (p. 237)

This testimony establishes an obvious analogy with the Yoruba god, Ogun, who is also the god of harvest. In his theme song in Soyinka's *Idanre*, we have these lines:

> He comes, who scrapes no earth dung from his feet
> He comes again in Harvest, the first of reapers.[11]

The theme of harvest runs concurrently with the sociopolitical aspect of communion. The medium through which this second motif is sustained is slavery. The idea of slavery embraces in this context all forms of social injustice: forced labor, racial or sexual discrimination, emotional repression. For obvious reasons, as already noted, Euripides suppressed this factor, but Soyinka has given it prominence in his own work. Right from the beginning of the action, the slaves are shown to be restive and intransigent. Their leader associates the hills and the vines with freedom and Thebes with death and sterility. His thoughts are muffled, his sentiments not fully expressed; but he is more threatening in what is left unsaid than in his open confessions: "Surrounded by walls one can only dream. But one day, one day" (p. 236). He speaks of "my buried longings," and questions the injustice of the system that sup-

plies scapegoats only from the class which benefits least
from the ritual:

> Why us? Why always us? The rites bring us nothing!
> Let those who profit bear the burden of the old year
> dying. (p. 237)

He acknowledges the god openly, for Dionysus has helped
him to overcome his fears: "Welcome the new god! Thrice
welcome the new order" (p. 239). Later, he explains the
meaning of the moment to the slower members of his
bonded fraternity:

> You hesitant fools! Don't you understand?
> Don't you *know*? We are no longer alone—
> Slaves, helots, the near and distant dispossessed!
> This master race, this much vaunted dragon spawn
> Have met their match. Nature has joined forces
> > with us. (p. 240)

Toward the end of the play, the slaves, the helots, and the
Bacchantes constitute themselves into one formidable front
against Pentheus' government. The slaves involve the Bacchantes in a ritual dance of liberation, which signifies the
casting off of their long vassalage in the house of Pentheus.
Soyinka accords the slave motif a significant place in the
action. The stage direction states that a corner of the stage
at the beginning of the play is heaped with the bodies of
crucified slaves, mostly in the skeletal stage.

The second structural change Soyinka effected on the
Euripidean plot is superfluous: the insertion of two wedding scenes at the critical moment when Pentheus is beginning to submit to Dionysus and to acknowledge the hopelessness of his position as an apostle of reason. The
introduction of the mysteries of Eleusis is a minor innovation, but one that is much more effective than the wedding
scenes because the Eleusinian religion is counterposed to
the cult of Dionysus. It is an elitist religious cult, sponsored
by the state and dominated by the priests; its mysteries are
revealed only to select initiates. The Dionysian religion
provides an avenue for spiritual self-fulfillment for the un-

derprivileged of society who are excluded from the closed cult of the Eleusinian mysteries. The priests were, therefore, opposed to the new god because his worship threatened to break their monopolistic hold on revealed religion. When Dionysus comes down to the Eleusinian procession, the priests' first reaction is terror, but they later accord the god a grudging recognition.

DRAMATIC TECHNIQUE

Soyinka reworked the *Bacchae* with the same dramatic devices that Euripides utilized, but he complements these with some of the idioms of his own theatre. The Euripidean conventions he has retained include the use of the prologue, the chorus, off-stage representation of violent actions, and irony as a means of foreshadowing the denouement. Euripides is unique in the extensive use he has made of the prologue as a dramatic device. His own *Bacchae* begins with Dionysus addressing the audience in a soliloquy that functions as a prologue. Dionysus introduces himself to the audience, tells us where he has come from, and discloses his grievance against Thebes and the objectives of his present mission. Soyinka follows Euripides' example by prefacing the action of his own adaptation with a soliloquy by Dionysus.

The chorus is useful to facilitate dramatic exposition. In the Euripidean version, the chorus of Asian Bacchae provide additional information about Dionysus' ancestry:

> Zeus it was who saved his son;
> With speed outrunning mortal eye,
> bore him to a private place,
> bound the boy with clasps of gold;
> in his thigh as in a womb,
> concealed his son from Hera's eyes.[12]

However, the main function of the Greek chorus is to provide a running moral commentry on the action. Soon after Pentheus had vented his ill-humor on the new Dionysian converts (Tiresias and Kadmos), the chorus of Asian women intervenes to judge his action:

> Do you hear his blasphemy against
> the prince of the blessed, the god
> of garlands and banquets Bromius,
> Semele's son?[13]

Thereafter, they comment on the philosophical implications of the sin of pride:

> A tongue without reins,
> defiance, unwisdom
> their end is disaster.
> But the life of quiet good,
> the wisdom that accepts
> these abide unshaken
> preserving, sustaining
> the house of men.[14]

The Asian women are simply designated "Bacchantes" by Soyinka, and their role as chorus is supplemented with the more outspoken indictments from the chorus of slaves. Both choruses play nearly the same kind of role as does the Euripidean chorus. When Pentheus hits the old slave, for example, his action provokes this response from the slaves:

> We are strangers
> But we know the meaning of madness.
> To hit an old servant
> With frost on his head
> Such a one as has stood
> at the gateway of mysteries. (p. 264)

And when he has clamped Dionysus into prison, the Bacchantes lament his action:

> A fiend, murderous to the bone
> This thing means to shut me up
> To plunge me in the darkness of his mind!
> I am not his. I belong to Dionysus. (p. 272)

But the slaves are more interested in interpreting Dionysus as a spirit of liberty than in registering a moral interpretation of the theme on a grand scale as the Euripidean chorus does.

The Greek sense of deceny was revolted by the representation of violent actions on the stage. Yet the attitude of Euripides the iconoclast to this convention remains ambivalent. Pentheus' violent death and the confrontations between the Maenads and royal emissaries happen off stage, yet the palace of Pentheus is toppled in front of the audience. Soyinka is faithful to these Euripidean strategies as he is to the reproduction of the moments of dramatic irony that we encounter in Euripides. When Pentheus submits himself gradually and yet inexorably to the charm of the Dionysian magic, he accepts a cup of wine from the god and drinks it, thereby accepting his fate as a scapegoat as Dionysus explains:

> Yes, you alone [qualify to]
> Make sacrifices for your people, you alone
> The role belongs to a king. Like those gods,
>   who yearly
> Must be rent to spring anew, that also
> Is the fate of heroes, (p. 293)

and the god's observation that "There are risks/A king must take for his own people" (p. 287) foreshadows that destiny. And finally, Dionysus anticipates the exact manner of the king's return journey to the palace: "Your mother will bring you back in triumph" (p. 288).

But Soyinka has worked the idioms of the traditional theatre into the action. Dionysus is, after all, an Oriental deity whose rituals and ceremonies have reminded Soyinka of the nature mysteries of his own society. He uses the idioms of the processional, the drum, mime, ritual, and dance and music. The dance and music are a combination of African and Oriental rhythms. The music is a strange mixture, evoking nostalgia, violence, and death. It is played by ritual drums and timbrels, with a curious admixture of song, chant and ululation. There is always something ugly, writes Soyinka, about the overall emotion released by such music, but the few faces of intensely energized rapture that stand out in the melee indicate some-

thing of the awesome depths which this music can reach
(p. 249).

The wedding scenes (pp. 285–287) employ mime, and
the Eleusinian episode utilizes the processional. The stage
directions are detailed as to the order of the proceedings.
The Master of Revels leads the way, followed by the high
priests of Thebes who are followed by the vestal virgins.
The old man in whom the old year is personified and his
tormentors, and floggers, bring up the rear. As the procession tours the city, rites of cleansing are performed at
strategic locations.

A final point to be noted is the way in which Soyinka has
resolved the conflict through the symbolism of the communion wine. At the end of the play, Pentheus' severed
head becomes a rotating fount of wine flushing the immediate vicinity with sprays of wine. Everyone around (including Agave) rushes to the fountain to slake his or her
thirst. The wine reconciles Agave to Dionysus after she has
regained consciousness, unlike the Euripidean ending in
which she is alienated. The communion wine becomes the
final testimony of collective participation that Dionysus
encapsulates; and it is on this note, most appropriately,
that the play ends.

STRUCTURE, LANGUAGE, AND
THE CHARACTERS

Greek plays are not divided up into acts and scenes,
which build up as in a Shakespearean structure into climax
and anticlimax. But the dramatist must still submit himself
to a subtle form of order which guides him in his own
construction. There are two dramatic moments in the Pentheus–Dionysus conflict. The first is the physical imprisonment of Dionysus, and the second is the psychological
imprisonment of Pentheus. The second imprisonment is
indeed the climax of the whole story to which the subsequent death of Pentheus, and the various forms of punishment inflicted by Dionysus on the house of Kadmos (in the
Euripidean plot) can be viewed as various levels of an
unfolding denouement. Soyinka accepts this rhythm in the

progression and organization of his own action. The self-surrender of Pentheus is the peak of the entire action. But, considering Soyinka's penchant for a two-part structure, this self-surrender ought to have marked the beginning of a gradual denouement which moves rapidly to the crisis in which the transformation of Pentheus' bleeding head into a fount of wine should have been an appropriate climax. But the play is not strictly patterned along these lines.

Soyinka's version subtly organizes the action into an undemarcated two-part movement, each part of which terminates, as is typical for Soyinka, in scenes of intensified action. The first such movement begins slowly with the entry of Dionysus and continues through his dialogue with Tiresias, his temporary disappearance from the stage (which creates an opportunity for the exchange between Tiresias and Kadmos), to the entry of Pentheus and the debate between him and the two elders (Tiresias and Kadmos). This section is climaxed by the imprisonment of the god and the miraculous upheavals that lead to his escape. These upheavals are specified—darkness, thunder, flames, and the roar of collapsing masonry (p. 275).

The hypothetical second movement begins with the god manifesting himself a second time beside the tomb of his mother, Semele. He is revealed, as the stage directions disclose, "as first seen standing on the charred ruins of the grave of Semele. The flames are higher round his feet, the Bacchantes and the chorus are down on their faces" (p. 275).

The god's miraculous escape is reinforced by the report of the Maenads' miraculous exploits on Mount Kithairon. Then Pentheus surrenders himself to Dionysus and he is torn to pieces by the Maenads, Agave experiences deliriums and then self-recognition, and the miraculous transformation of the severed head into a fount of wine takes place. The production directions specify the gradual build-up of intensified action, which properly brings this movement to an end. Dionysus' theme music wells up slowly at first, only to fill the stage later with the god's presence. Then there is a sudden outburst of a powerful red glow from within the head of Pentheus which renders it luminous.

The stage is now bathed in this red glow. And the audience
sees the miracle itself: red jets of wine spring from every
orifice of the impaled head.

Language reflects the basic polarities in the dramatic
conflict. Dionysus uses prose, the language of the common
man, while elevated speech or poetry is the language of the
court. Pentheus, the apostle of reason, declaims in measured iambic pentameter lines upon his first entry on the
stage:

> I shall have order! Let the city know at once
> Pentheus is here to give back order and sanity.
> To think those reports which came to us abroad
> > are true!
> Not padded or strained. Disgustingly true in detail.
> If anything reality beggars the report. It's
> > *disgusting*! (p. 256)

His officers and attendants understand the art of rhetorical
declamation. The Herdsman, reporting the exploits of the
Maenads to the king, must address him in the language of
the court (p. 278). When Pentheus is around, Tiresias and
Kadmos speak the language of the court, but they revert to
prose when they discuss Dionysus among themselves. At
Court, Dionysus imitates the speech of kings. Thus, his
exchange with Pentheus when the King is at the height of
his power is couched in fragmented verse, but as he gains
control over Pentheus, he reverts to his natural medium
(prose), carrying the King along with him. It is a measure
of Dionysus' absolute control over Pentheus that he very
easily abandons his original declamatory style the moment
he begins to feel the influence of the god and adopts the
god's own mannerisms. Euripides did not observe these
linguistic subtleties to the same extent that Soyinka does.
The modulation of prose and verse passages upon character and circumstance harnesses language to theme.

Soyinka introduces contemporary catchwords and
echoes of twentieth-century technology.[15] Dionysus' thyrsus is fitted with collapsible gadgets, and Kadmos contemplates for a while the possibility of staging a military
"coup d'etat," if only to save Thebes from Pentheus' folly.

Pentheus, in turn, is bent on preserving the "territorial integrity of Thebes" at all costs; and all those who are opposed to his plans are "agents of subversion for some foreign power" (p. 284).

The language is steeped in agricultural imagery. The slaves and the Asian chorus celebrate Dionysus as the god of ripeness. Their theme song is informed by images of grape and grain:

> Our feet at the dance are the feet of men
> Grape-pressing, grain-winnowing, our joy
> Is the great joy of union with mother earth. (p. 265)

Even the carnage on the mountain is spoken of in terms of harvest:

> The news found us here
> Of this unseasonable harvest reaped upon
> the mountains. (p. 303)

The characters with individuating traits are the principal personages of the drama, that is, Dionysus himself and the members of the house of Kadmos. The rest of the characters, especially the slaves and the Asian chorus, remain anonymous, subordinating their individuality to their choric roles. The audience concentrates its attention and emotion on the members of the tragic household. Only Pentheus, Kadmos, and Agave even have proper names. Tiresias is an ubiquitous phantom who appears also in Sophocles. The name designates an office rather than an individual.

Pentheus is the most important member of the Kadmos lineage. He is Kadmos' grandson and assumed office as king after Kadmos abdicated for reasons of age. Euripides is silent as to Pentheus' father Ichion, who ought to have succeeded his own father as king. His omission might be deliberate, since the dramatist can then highlight Pentheus as an inexperienced young man, who sticks doggedly to his own views in spite of all evidence to the contrary. For Pentheus betrays a stubborn temper that is inhuman. Not even his grandfather's pleadings nor Tiresias' reasoning can persuade him to reconsider his stand on Dionysus. His tragic flaw is his rigid commitment to principle, whereas balance is said to hold the key for human life. "The secret of life is balance," says Dionysus (p. 277). The lack of balance in Pentheus is a manifestation of pride. The chorus accuses him of committing the sin of pride (translated here as "glory"):

> Unwise are those who aspire,
> who outrange the limits of man.
> Briefly, we live. Briefly,
> then die. Wherefore, I say,
> he who hunts a glory, he who tracks
> some boundless, superhuman dream,
> may lose his harvest here and now,
> and garner death.[16]

Kadmos has achieved this balance, but he strikes us, nevertheless, as a cowardly old man who has no mind of his own. He accepts the god not because he believes in him, but because Dionysus' claim to divinity enhances his family name. Euripides brings out more clearly than Soyinka this opportunistic side of Kadmos:

> Even if this Dionysus is no god,
> as you assert, persuade yourself that he is.
> The fiction is a noble one, for Semele will seem
> to be the mother of a god, and this confers
> no small distinction on our family.[17]

The Tiresias of the play is not a man of honor, as in Sophocles. He brings a Machiavellian taint to the honorable office or seer, so that the name, "Tiresias" comes to connote not wisdom but astute clearsightedness. He harnesses casuistry to his role as a devil's advocate. The chaste woman will not be corrupted in the rites of Dionysus, he claims; and pouring libation, even in the worship of Apollo, means using Dionysus as an intermediary for winning the favor of heaven. It is part of Euripides' historical image as an anti-traditional amoralist and stage sophist to discredit the traditional image of Tiresias as a man of integrity.

Agave deserves our pity rather than our scorn, for she is not responsible for her actions. Dionysus shows himself as a heartless deity by the manner of his revenge against the house of Kadmos. The old slave (the one man from whom we least expect an objective appraisal) is horrified by the god's cruelty:

> Oh this is a heartless
> Deity, bitter, unnatural in his revenge.
> To make a mother rip her son like bread
> Across a banqueting board! (p. 300)

But Dionysus is capable of doing good. He describes himself as a "gentle, jealous joy," and the Asian chorus acclaims him as a god who offers ample reward to those who do his biddings: "Hard are the labours of a god/but his service is sweet fulfilment" (p. 247).

Notes

1. Erich Segal, ed., *Euripides: A Collection of Critical Essays* (Englewood Cliffs: Prentice-Hall, 1968), p. 9.

2. Friedrich Nietzsche, *The Birth of Tragedy*, trans. Francis Golffing (New York: Doubleday, 1956), p. 70.

3. Wole Soyinka, *The Bacchae of Euripides* in *Collected Plays*, Vol. 1 (London: Oxford University Press, 1973). All references to Soyinka's version of the play are to this edition.

4. I am indebted for the account of the myth of Dionysus that follows to Philip Mayerson's compilation of Greek myths in his *Classical Mythology in Literature, Art, and Music* (Lexington: Xerox College Publishing, 1971).

5. This account of the origin of Thebes is borrowed from Carl E. Bain et al., eds. *The Norton Introduction to Literature*, Combined Shorter Edition (New York: W. W. Norton, 1973), p. 785.

6. George Thomson, *Aeschylus and Athens* (New York: Grosset and Dunlop, 1968), pp. 138-139.

7. See the chapter on Dionysus in *Aeschylus and Athens*, pp. 121-139.

8. *The Birth of Tragedy*, p. 23.

9. Monroe K. Spears, *Dionysos and the City* (Oxford: Oxford University Press, 1970), p. 35.

10. In his introduction to his anthology, *Oxford Book of Modern Verse* (Oxford: The Clarendon Press, 1970), p. xxv.

11. Wole Soyinka, *Idanre and Other Poems* (London: Methuen, 1967), p. 62.

12. *The Bacchae* as translated by William Arrowsmith in *Euripides: The Complete Greek Tragedies*, Vol. IV, ed., David Grene and Richmond Lattimore (Chicago: The University of Chicago Press, 1974), p. 547.

13. Arrowsmith, p. 557.

14. *Ibid.*, p. 558.

15. This point is also noted by E. J. Asgill. See his essay, "African Adaptations of Greek Tragedies," *African Literature Today*, 11 (1980), p. 187.

16. Arrowsmith, p. 558.

17. *Ibid.*, p. 556.

11

――――――――――――― △ △ ―――――――――――――

DEATH AND THE
KING'S HORSEMAN

DRAMATIC TECHNIQUE

If *Death and the King's Horseman* (1975) were always published with the Author's Note, the play would be deemed to have three familiar features: a prologue, revelatory dialogue, and allusive language. The Author's Note fulfills the functions of a prologue: It informs us as to the specific historical episode on which the play is based and introduces us to the major historical personages involved in the action. The note recommends sources for further reading and discusses Soyinka's own work.

But if the play appears in print without the Author's Note, the reader must rely (as the audience does) on the dialogue and allusions for the exposition. The allusive language here is less esoteric and less obscure than the total breakdown in communication in *The Road* and *Madmen and Specialists* as a result of excessive reliance on ellipses. In *Death and the King's Horseman*, Soyinka speaks of things without actually naming them, and yet there is no ambiguity for the allusions are self-evident, self-explanatory, and easily penetrable. When the Praise-singer speaks of "the dwellers of that place," the context makes it clear that he is referring to his ancestors or the dead: "Far be it for me to belittle the dwellers of that place" (p. 10).[1] Elesin Oba can also speak of a dance that is no longer of this world in an allusion to the dance of death. The use of allusions in this play is very different from the obscure references to "faces," "the other place," or even to "As" in

Madmen. The significance of these allusions (and this is important for dramatic exposition) is that they are functional: they define the action. The references to "journey," "voyage," "crossing," and the act of going underscore the theme of ritual passage. This is true also of Soyinka's metaphor for the act of passage: dance. "Let me dance into the passage," says Elesin Oba (p. 41).

The use of allusive language supplements the principal means of dramatic exposition: dialogue. The dramatic situation is sufficiently established by the dialogue even without the benefit of the author's prologue. The theme of ritual death is implied in the various exchanges between Elesin and two of the major characters—Praise-singer and Iyaloja. When Iyaloja calls Elesin "the intercessor of the living in the other world" (p. 21), the nature of Elesin's rite of passage is made obvious; and he himself speaks of the role the womenfolk will play in the ritual: "This night I'll lay my head upon their lap and go to sleep. This night I'll touch feet with their feet in a dance that is no longer of this earth" (p. 10). He speaks of his desire to meet his great forebears: "Let the Alafin know I follow swiftly" (p. 41). He also tells a little story in which he discloses the degree of intimacy that had existed between him and the dead Alafin:

> My master's hand and mine have always
> Dipped together and, home or sacred feast,
> The bowl was beaten bronze, the meats
> So succulent our teeth accused us of neglect.
> We shared the choicest of the season's
> Harvest of yam.
>
> ....
>
>   Our joint hands
> Raised houseposts of trust that withstood
> The siege of envy and the termites of time.
> But the twilight hour brings bats and rodents.
> Shall I yield them cause to foul the rafters?
>   (pp. 14–15)

What has been too obviously hinted at in the dialogue between Elesin and two of his aids, Praise-singer and Iyaloja, is exposed directly in Sergeant Amusa's report to the District Officer:

> I have to report that it come to my information that one prominent chief, namely, the Elesin Oba, is to commit death tonight as a result of native custom. Because this is criminal offence I await further instruction at charge office. (p. 26)

The District Officer's houseboy, Joseph, and his ward, Olude, provide more details. We learn from these characters that the king died some thirty days before the play began, and Olude has come home to bury his father who, as custom requires, must follow his master.

For the exposition itself, Soyinka depends upon dialogue, and, to supplement the action, he uses ritual, dance, the drum, the processional, and the ceremonial from Yoruba traditional drama. These idioms are subtly integrated into the action; they are not simply superimposed on it. The whole play is a ritual performance. A king is dead, and we are called upon to watch the ritual ceremonies of his burial. The ceremony begins in a converted stall in the market where the Elesin is decked out with proper attire for the occasion. The floor leading up to the entrance of the stall is covered in rich velvets and woven cloth. All await the glorious emergence of the voyager. The Praise-singer calls the tune, the drummer supplies the music, and Elesin moves in a slow rhythmic procession to the heart of the market. The members of the Osugbo cult (a secret masonic organization) will meet him at the appropriate time as indicated by the moon. They, too, will have toured the town in a musical procession before meeting the Elesin at the market. Elesin dances majestically towards the center of the market until he has worked himself into a trance. Dance is the movement of transition: "Let me dance into the passage", says the Elesin, and Soyinka tells us in the dedicatory note that his own father danced and joined the ancestors. Soyinka has spoken repeatedly on the function of music in tragic ritual. Music alone is the sole companion of the tragic hero in the abyss; it attunes the will to action and rescues the hero from total extinction:

> At the charged climactic moments of the tragic rites
> we understand how music came to be the sole art form
> which can contain tragic reality. The votary is led by
> no other guide into the pristine heart of tragedy.[2]

Elesin is able to put himself into a trance, but his allegiance to the call of life is such that it neutralizes his will for action.

There are other forms of dance in the play. Before the ritual begins, Elesin communicates his displeasure at what he considers the women's neglect of his well-being in a dance of protest, which Soyinka describes as a "half-taunting dance" (p. 11); and later he dances the story of the Not-I-Bird (p. 11). Elesin's dance is purposeful, solemn, regal and graceful, and it contrasts with the ballroom antics of the colonials that have only an entertainment value. Their dance is not anchored to a worldview. Some couples wear fancy dress and others amuse themselves by wearing *egungun* costumes. Soyinka's contempt for the colonial amusement is reflected in satirical asides in the stage directions. The tango, we are told, is played by an old hand-cranked gramophone; the local police brassband spews forth a sorry version of "Rule Britannica," and the orchestra's waltz rendition is said to be of a very low order.

The final stage of the proceedings is the invocation. This is an incantation or ritual watchword to be spoken over the dead body of the king's horseman, so that the soul of the dead king may travel home peacefully. If the Elesin had died at the proper moment, his son, Olude, would have spoken the word, but as the son has preceded the father, it is Elesin's responsibility to utter the word. In this ritual, the mourners form a semi-circle round the body of the king's horseman. The Praise-singer and the drummer stand on the inside of the semi-circle. The drum is silent, but the drummer intones a tune under the praise-singer's invocations. Elesin whispers the ritual watchword from his cell. At the conclusion of this ritual, Iyaloja speaks in an Epilogue directed at Elesin's Bride:

> Now forget the dead, forget even the living.
> Turn your mind only to the unborn. (p. 76)

Critics often ignore the occasional evocation of atmosphere in Soyinka's plays especially the moments of silence and stillness during sombre moments in the dramatic action. Soyinka insists upon stillness for other reasons than the creation of a mood of solemnity. Silence often evokes a sense of space that, in ritual theatre, operates as a fearful reminder of man's helplessness in that disturbing environment that he defines variously as void, emptiness, or infinity. In *A Dance of the Forests*, stillness is useful when Soyinka strives after an effect of timelessness or infinity when Forest Father begins the ritual for liberating the pregnant woman from a burden which she has borne for eight hundred years. The stage direction takes us back to the origin of time:

> Back-scene lights up gradually to reveal a dark, wet, atmosphere, dripping moisture, and soft, moist soil. A palm-tree sways at a low angle, broken but still alive. Seemingly lightning-reduced stumps. Rotting wood all over the ground. A mound or two here and there. Footfalls are muffled. First, there is total stillness, emphasized by the sound of moisture dripping to the ground.[3]

In *Death and King's Horseman*, an atmosphere of stillness is the prelude to tragic inevitability. It creates a mood of tension and suspense at a point when nothing and everything is possible. It is at this moment (p. 75) that Elesin fulfils the role that has long been expected of him.

Soyinka also uses folklore and of symbolism in the story of the Not-I-Bird, which emphasizes the fear of death and proposes Elesin to us as a bold voyager who is not afraid of death.

AS A DRAMA ON TRANSITION

Death and the King's Horseman (1975) derives its material from history, but it is not a historical document. An artist can appropriate relevant elements of an area's history without binding himself to the chronology and the verisimilitude of such historical evidence. The creative artist can use facts and figures to manipulate emotions to a point where they resolve themselves in catharsis. In the present play, Soyinka subordinates relevant elements from history to his goal of effecting a resolution of emotional crisis in the audience. In the original story, the District Officer successfully prevented the Elesin from taking his own life; but such an ending would not suit Soyinka's artistic purpose. Furthermore, the historical Elesin did not have to rely on an emotional intermediary, the femme fatale (his bride), in order to fail in his mission. And upon the evidence of Duro Ladipo's earlier dramatization of the same episode, his son Dawodu, who redeemed the honor of his family by dying in place of his father, was a trader in Ghana. These historical details do not intrigue Soyinka. His own Elesin is tied to a bride and is the father of an enlightened son, Olude, pursuing medical studies in the Whiteman's country. For purposes of dramaturgy, Soyinka has altered historical details so that his own plot and action would corroborate his own idea of art.

It is not the truth of history that Soyinka is concerned with but with the validity of a basic metaphysical question—transition:

> The confrontation in the play is largely metaphysical, contained in the human vehicle which is Elesin and the universe of the Yoruba mind—the world of the living, the dead and the unborn, and the numinous passage which links all: transition.[4]

Soyinka's cosmology (the Yoruba worldview) is made up of three worlds: the worlds of the living, the dead, and the unborn. Linking these worlds together is the fourth area of existence—the fourth world or fourth stage—which Soyinka constantly refers to as the area of transition. The area of transition is the "territory of essence-ideal," the staging ground for cosmic monsters, the source and origin of life corporeal and non-corporeal. This area is to be distinguished from the numinous passage constructed on its vast surface by the sheer will of the protagonist of transition, Ogun, the first road-maker. The "numinous passage" is a narrow pathway, a channel that permits inter-cosmic contact between the different worlds. It is also a channel of continuity. Essences from one area of the three worlds travel to another through the passage of transition, and the constant passage of essences through each territory guarantees continuity. The dead, for instance, influence the living and determine who among the unborn should visit the living. Furthermore, the numinous passage is the orbit of actualization for the matter and non-matter that lie dormant in the fourth area of existence. These essences of matter and non-matter travel to their various spheres through the narrow neck of passage.

For a diagrammatical representation of Soyinka's cosmology, see Chapter 12, p. 297. *Death and the King's Horseman* attempts a human representation of this cosmology using related members of the *dramatis personnae*. Elesin's bride represents the world of the living; the seed implanted into her womb is a visitor from the world of the unborn. The dead Alafin, the "King" of the play, has gone to the world of the dead, and Elesin himself is a creature of the twilight world of passage. The relationship between the three worlds (announced in the Author's Note to be the theme of the dramatic action) is restated somewhat melodramatically by Iyaloja in the play. At the end of the action, she urges the Bride to "forget the dead, forget even the living. Turn your mind only to the unborn" (p. 76). Both the play's metaphors and its action assert the same message. From Iyaloja once again is the injunction:

> Let grain that will not feed the voyager at his passage drop here and take root as he steps beyond this earth and us. Oh you . . . who now bestride the hidden gulf and pause to draw the right foot across and into the resting-home of the great forebears, it is good that your loins be drained into the earth we know, that your last strength be ploughed back into the womb that gave you being. (p. 22)

And when Elesin disappoints her expectations, she questions his hubristic arrogance: "Who are you to open a new life when you have dared not open the door to a new existence?" (p. 67). When the word, "transition," is used in

conjunction with the term "abyss", it generally serves
Soyinka as a metaphor for (a) a vacuum of despair that
engulfs every individual in his moments of stress, (b) a
feeling of spiritual hollowness and of cosmic rejection
which the individual experiences when separated from the
gods. Tragic consciousness originates from these feelings.
In this play, however, "transition" stands for a channel
which permits movement from one area of existence to
another; this, in itself, is a metaphor for the loss of self in a
ritual action.

The present play illustrates by his own work Soyinka's
views on (a) drama and the African worldview and (b) the
nature of Yoruba tragedy. His dramatic theories are tested
here. These theories are first articulated in the essay "The
Fourth Stage" (1969), subtitled "Through the Mysteries of
Ogun to the Origin of Yoruba Tragedy." Two subsequent
essays—"Morality and Aesthetics in the Ritual Archetype"
(1976) and "Drama and the African World-View" (1976)—
reinforce the ideas enunciated in "The Fourth Stage."[5]

In these essays, Soyinka draws us into the African conception of the universe as a hermetic world in which the
cosmos has not lost the essence of the tangible, of the
immediate, and the appeasable. The universe is untouched
by the "attenuation of terrestrialism" bequeathed to the
modern world by the Platonic-Christian tradition and dialectical materialism. The cosmos, in the African imagination, is a looming reality, still threatening in its immensity.
In this environment, man maintains a close contact with
Nature, but his life is a life of fear: fear of ferocious beasts,
fear of the anger of the gods, fear of an unwitting infraction
of the law of Nature, the taboos, and the social mores that
bind society. His life is regulated by codes of conduct that
he meticulously observes. The goal of life is that harmony
that can only be guaranteed through constant communion
with the gods. Soyinka allows us an insight into what this
harmony or moral order consists of:

> Where society lives in a close inter-relation with Na-
> ture, regulates its existence by natural phenomena
> within the observable processes of continuity—ebb
> and tide, waxing and waning of the moon, rain and

drought, planting and harvest—the highest moral
order is seen as that which guarantees a parallel continuity of the species.[6]

Life in this agricultural community is a ritual, in the
sense that every human endeavor—farming, harvesting, the
activities of birth and death—follows a prescribed pattern.
Soyinka holds the traditional view that drama originated
from these ritualized activities and, as such, cannot be
separated in its communal import from ritual. The first
ritual actors are the primordial deities, Ogun, Obatala,
Sango, whom Soyinka calls "the ritual archetypes," and
the first drama was a ritual enactment. This was the drama
of the primordial deities, who are represented by the passage-rites of hero-gods, projections of man's conflict with
forces that challenge his efforts to harmonize with his environment. Their symbolic roles are those of an intermediary
quester and an explorer into territories of essence-ideal
around whose edges man fearfully skirts.[7]

The passage-rites of Ogun are most fully developed in
Soyinka's ritual essays. Ogun is the first hero-god; his
passage-rites lead to tragic consequences for him. He suffered physical disintegration on behalf of humanity in the
abyss of dissolution but was able to reassemble his dismembered body through the activation of his indestructible
will. The first dramatic enactment in the Yoruba mythology is thus a tragic experience, and Ogun is its protagonist.
His passage has the three-part structure basic in rites of
passage—entry into darkness (or preparation), followed by
ritual death, which leads to a rebirth.[8] The rebirth or regeneration is the goal of the ritual. The protagonist submits
himself to a ritual death on behalf of his community.
Soyinka defines ritual drama as a potent enactment with "a
cleansing, binding, communal, recreative force."[9] It takes
the form, in its mythic origin, of a symbolic struggle with
chthonic presences, the goal of the confict being a harmonious resolution for plenitude and the well-being of the
community.

Yoruba tragedy originates from Ogun's agony. Its peculiar characteristic is the courage (will) to dare the abyss of
dissolution. The protagonist must confront death and an-

nihilate his being. But since Ogun was able to reassemble his dismembered body through the agency of the will, the physical annihilation is only temporary. His soul attains plenitude of being in death. In suffering physical disintegration, he saves his soul. This salvation or resurrection is the rebirth, and when his rite of passage has been successfully completed, his community experiences additional regeneration—physical, psychic, or spiritual: harmony in the community, continuity of the species, abundance of harvest, rain, and sunshine all befalling the community in their due seasons.

Death and the King's Horseman is structurally based upon Ogun's rites of transition. Elesin's ordeal parallels Ogun's passage, and it has the same three-part structure of preparation and ritual death followed by rebirth. Although the play has five parts, the essence of the action can be reduced to the three movements of the ritual pattern. Part I is the preparation, Part III is the ritual death (which is aborted in the present play), and Part V is intended to be the movement for the celebration of rebirth. In the play, however, it becomes an elegy for the death of the community:

> Elesin, we placed the reins of the world in your hands yet you watched it plunge over the edge of the bitter precipice. You sat with folded arms while evil strangers tilted the world from its course and crashed it beyond the edge of emptiness. . . . Our world is tumbling in the void of strangers. (p. 75)

Parts II and IV merely accommodate the "colonial factor." Soyinka has dismissed the colonial factor as being merely an incident, a catalytic incident to the major confrontation in the play which is metaphysical.

Part I, the preparatory stage for the ritual, is a moment for sober reflection and for abstinence. But rather than mortify the body, Elesin Oba indulged it. His sexual passion for the young Bride, who has already been betrothed to a lawful suitor, offends the moral codes of the community. This indicates the extent to which corruption and crime have eaten into the fabric of an erstwhile sacred society, and it is in itself an act of hubris. The penalty comes when the gods denied the ritual actor the will to annihilate his being. Instead of dying a ritual death, Elesin dies an ignoble one. He who had been associated with images of nobility and of honor becomes identified with those of shame:

> We fed you sweet meats such as we hoped awaited you on the other side. But you said No, I must eat the world's left-overs. We said you were the hunter who brought the quarry down; to you belonged the vital portions of the game. No, you said, I am the hunter's dog and I shall eat the entrails of the game and the faeces of the hunter. . . . We said, the dew on earth's surface was for you to wash your feet along the slopes of honour. You said No, I shall step in the vomit of cats and the droppings of mice. (p. 68)

The climactic moment of tragic ritual obliterates within the hero all traces of his links with the living. It is at such moments that transitional memory takes over, and intimations rack him of that intense parallel of his progress through the gulf of transition, of the dissolution of his self and his struggle and triumph over subsumation through the agency of the will.[10] Elesin Oba's memories of his tryst with the young Bride linger in and sap his will for action. He tells Iyaloja who arranged the meeting: "You were part of the beginnings. You brought about the renewal of my tie to earth" (p. 69).

In a mythic reading of Achebe's *Arrow of God*,[11] Soyinka noted that the moral dynamics of the African worldview are not emphasized in that novel. The gods are shown to be incapable of influencing events; and individuals guilty of hubris are spared the penalty for their daring. Thus, Ezeulu could with impunity equate his personal whims with the wishes of his god. And when he who is said to be half-man and half-god goes into exile, the cosmic repercussion of the priest's experience of exile are not visited upon his community. Soyinka commends[12] J. P. Clark's *Song of a Goat* for its elicitation of the authentic values of the African worldview. *Death and the King's Horseman* is probably written with this same purpose in view, but the cosmic implications of Elesin's betrayal of his community are asserted rather than shown. The consequences of Elesin's failure of nerve are not felt in the course of the action. "Our world has fallen on emptiness," laments Iyaloja, but we do not see it happen. In *Macbeth* there is universal evidence of the general dislocation of the cosmic order on the night of King Duncan's death. The consequences of that unnatural act were felt in nature and through nature. The night was unruly and darkness entombed the earth, says Lennox. We do not experience a similar eruption of cosmic upheavals in *Death and the King's Horseman*.

LANGUAGE AND CHARACTERIZATION

Language here is distinguished by two rhythms: the musical or the poetic when the ritual characters speak, and the staccato or the colloquial, when we listen to the colonials. Amongst the ritual characters language is a ritualized utterance, a musical speech which is in consonance with the playwright's purpose, for he tells us that *Death and the King's Horseman* can only be fully realized through an evocation of music from the abyss of transition. Both the Praise-singer and the high priestess of the proceedings, Iyaloja, are possessed mediums, uttering visions symbolic of the transitional gulf. Language reverts to its pristine essence, Soyinka tells us, in religious rites, and the movement of words is the very passage of music and the dance of images:

> Richly, richly, robe him richly
> The cloth of honour is *alari*
> *Sanyan* is the band of friendship
> Boa-skin makes slippers of esteem. (p. 17)

Or, consider this other testimony from both the Praise-singer and Iyaloja:

> Gracefully does the mask regain his grove
> at the end of day.
> Gracefully. Gracefully does the mask dance

> Homeward at the end of the day
> Gracefully, gracefully does the horseman regain
> The stables at the end of day. (p. 43)

There is a feminine grace in the language, a tenderness that is supposed to enthrall and lull Elesin into a trance in which he will die the "death of death" on behalf of his community. Even when the theme is a lament, the language still retains its musical charm. The tension within Elesin's personality (a man torn between two worlds) is not allowed to disrupt the mellifluous quality of the language:

> The night is not at peace, ghostly one.
> The world is not at peace. You have
> shattered the peace of the world for ever.
> There is no sleep in the world tonight. (p. 62)

The only exception to the musical language is the speech of the colonials. Sergeant Amusa, a servant of the colonial establishment, breaks the spell with a smattering of the Whiteman's language: "I am order you now to clear the road" (p. 35). But Amusa's position is a curious one. His official duties compel an allegiance to the colonial crew, whereas spiritually he is in imaginative sympathy with his kith and kin: "How can man talk against death to a person in uniform of death?" (p. 25).

Other peculiarities of language are located in the functional imagery, which underscores Elesin's changing destiny—from the role of a redeemer to that of a betrayer. At the beginning of the play, he wears garments of honor; his bearing is royal, his personality resplendent, and his courage is undoubted. Even his food reflects the assumed nobility of his position: It is made of the sweetest meat and wine. Toward the end, when he has fallen from grace, it is the culinary metaphor reflects the reality of his ignoble position:

> I came with a burden I said. It approaches the gates
> which are so well guarded by those jackals whose
> spittle will from this day on be your food and drink.
> (p. 69)

He is gone at last into the passage but oh, how late it
all is. His son will feast on the meat and throw him
bones. The passage is clogged with droppings from
the king's stallion; he will arrive all stained in dung.
(p. 76)

A cluster of such images as cockerel and snake emphasizes Elesin's sexual prowess and cunning: "What tryst is
this the cockerel goes to keep with such haste that he must
leave his tail behind?" (p. 9); and again, "Who would deny
your reputation, snake-on-the-loose in dark passages of the
market!" (p. 19).

The characters are thinly drawn; they are not fully invested with distinguishing characteristics. The play has not
escaped the common predicament of all dramas of ideas;
that is, it tends to subordinate detailed portraiture of character to the more urgent task of beaming out the dramatic
idea. The idea in this case is the subject of transition, whose
major exponents are the African characters. But these characters are nearly anonymous individuals. It is not Soyinka's
intention to develop them beyond what is necessary to the
definition of the theme of transition. They are more important in their group identity than as individuals. They are
guardians of tradition or praise-singers, urging Elesin to
the tragic gulf. In this regard, Iyaloja (mother of the
market) and the Praise-singer recall the group responsibility of the Old Women in *Madmen and Specialists*, another
play in which development of character is subordinated to
the development of an idea. The African characters don't
always have proper names, except, of course, for the key
character Elesin Oba who is the focus of the dramatic
action.

The European characters are also conceived as types but
are more interesting as dramatic creations because they are
frequently caught up in funny and memorable situations
that will remain with the audience for a long time. The
image of Mrs. Pilkings restraining her husband's manic
darts as he masquerades as the Mgbedike *egungun* remains
one of the high points of the play. Apart from this episode,
the Pilkings are involved in a second level of action which
they perform creditably. They embody European preju-

dices against Africa. Their responses to the disquieting rhythms of the ritual drums, their mastery of the psychology of the native, their high sense of duty, and even Mrs. Pilking's inimitable demonstration of her humanity (she cannot understand Olude's calm acceptance of his traditional responsibility) are in character and commend Soyinka as a close observer of human idiosyncracies.

Notes

1. Wole Soyinka, *Death and the King's Horseman* (London: Methuen, 1975), p. 10. Further references to the text are to this edition.

2. *Myth and Literature*, pp. 146–147.

3. *A Dance of the Forests*, p. 60.

4. *Death and the King's Horseman*, Author's Note, p. 7.

5. For more information on these essays, see *Myth, Literature and The African World* (Cambridge: The University Press, 1976). This work is cited in this study as *Myth and Literature*.

6. Wole Soyinka, "Drama and the African World-View," in *Myth and Literature*, p. 52.

7. *Myth and Literature*, p. 1.

8. For more information on the structure of rites of passage, see Hans H. Penner, "Ritual," *The New Encyclopaedia Britannica*, Vol. 15, 15th ed., 1978.

9. *Myth and Literature*, p. 4.

10. Ibid., p. 149.

11. Wole Soyinka, "Ideology and the Social Vision: The Religious Factor," in *Myth and Literature*, pp. 87–96.

12. Wole Soyinka, "Drama and the African World-View" in *Myth and Literature*, p. 50.

PART FOUR

THE LITERARY ESSAYS

———————— △ △ ————————

SOYINKA AS A
LITERARY CRITIC

The bulk of Soyinka's achievement as a literary critic is contained in the book, *Myth, Literature and the African World* (1976), which assembled his most important literary essays and was edited by Soyinka himself. The title is indicative of Soyinka's major preoccupation as a critic. He is fascinated with myth as a phenomenon with unlimited appeal for the imagination, manifesting itself in the literature, culture, folklore, and the worldview of a people. He is himself a manipulator of myth, and his critical statements on works in the mythic mode are bound to throw some light on his own writings.

What is myth? Soyinka does not answer this question directly in his critical utterances, but we can imply from his writing that the term connotes a people's worldview and the moral system of that worldview as reflected in stories of the origin of the world, of gods, and of man. Among his own people, the Yoruba, this view of myth is reinforced by the one-life theory in the Coleridgean sense, which binds man to the gods and to nature for the psychic well-being of the universe. Hugh Holman gives us a more pertinent definition. He distinguishes between the traditional definition of myth and the modernist extension of this definition. In the traditional sense of the word, myths are

> Anonymous stories having their roots in the primitive
> folk beliefs of races or nations and presenting super-
> natural episodes as a means of interpreting natural

events in an effort to make concrete and particular a
special perception of man or a cosmic view.[1]

In the modernist re-definition of the word, myth is seen as
containing

> Vestiges of primordial ritual and ceremony, or the
> repository of racial memories, or a structure of un-
> consciously held value systems, or an expression of the
> general beliefs of a race, social class or nation or a
> unique embodiment of a cosmic view.[2]

These definitions are relevant to Soyinka's use of the term
"myth," both in his own works and in his literary essays.
His essays touch naturally upon other areas of general
interest, for example, the question of authenticity in character conception and presentation and of probability in
plot execution in the criticism of fiction. But his later
excursions into sociological analysis of literature are the
direct outcome of the ideological controversy between him
and his Marxist critics.

For convenience, we will consider Soyinka's essays under
four subheadings: Incidental Essays (1960–1966), Ritual
Essays (1976), Essays on Ideology and Social Vision (1976),
and Controversies (1975–1980). The early essays referred to
as Incidental Essays are not reproduced in their original
form in *Myth, Literature and the African World*, but the
substance of their arguments is worked into the extended
framework of the essay on literature and social vision with
little or no modification. We will discuss them here sepa-
rately in recognition of their merits as literary essays and
also to consider other issues of critical interest that might
have been left out in Soyinka's summary of their contents
in the third and fourth chapters of *Myth and Literature*.

Soyinka's literary essays are, to some extent, one large
essay. His critical prejudices were formed quite early in his
career, and both the early and later essays are crisscrossed by
related threads of thought. The war over *Negritude* rages
still, even though the first shots were fired in the 1960s.
Apart from his objection to *Negritude* on the basis of its
addiction to self-glorifying narcissism, we can detect in

Soyinka's opposition to that movement the beginnings of his later aversion to literary ideology in general. His consistency is a mark of Soyinka's maturity as a critic, which implies that his views are considered carefully before they are offered to the public.

INCIDENTAL ESSAYS

Three essays will be discussed in this section: "The Future of African Writing" (1960), "From a Common Back Cloth" (1963), and "And After the Narcissist?" (1966). The first essay, written probably during Soyinka's student days at Leeds, was published in the University of Ibadan poetry magazine, *The Horn*, founded by J. P. Clark and Martin Banham. Since this essay is not readily available, I reproduce Bernth Lindfors' summary of Soyinka's main argument in the essay. According to Lindfors, Soyinka argues that

> . . . the real mark of authenticity in African writing was indifferent self-acceptance rather than energetic racial self-assertion. Early African writing . . . was dishonest because it either imitated literary fashions in Europe or pandered to European demands and expectations for the exotic and primitive. The first West African writer to produce truly African Literature was not Leopold Senghor but Chinua Achebe.[3]

Here is part of the essay as reproduced by Lindfors and Martin Banham, who was the first critic to notice Soyinka's initial attempts at literary criticism:

> The significance of Chinua Achebe is the involvement, in West African writing, of the seemingly indifferent acceptance. And this, I believe, is the turning point in our literary development. It is also a fortunate accident of timing, because of the inherently invalid doctrine of "Negritude." Leopold Senghor to name a blatant example. And if we would speak of "Negritude" in a more acceptable broader sense, Chinua Achebe is a more 'African' writer than Senghor. The

duiker will not paint "duiker" on his beautiful back
to proclaim his duikeritude; you'll know him by his
elegant leap. The less self-conscious the African is,
and the more innately his individual qualities appear
in his writings the more seriously he will be taken as
an artist of exciting dignity. . . . Senghor seems to be
so artistically expatriate . . . and he and poets like him
are a definite retrogressive pseudo-romantic influence
on a healthy development of West African writing.[4]

Soyinka is rather hard on Senghor and *Negritude* in this
essay; his own writings are equally guilty of some of the
charges he levels at Senghor. His novel *The Interpreters* is
influenced by James Joyce, and his poetry reflects the
"toughness" of the neo-metaphysical poets such as Eliot
and Pound. But Soyinka is no less an African poet because
of his response to these Western influences. The joke about
"duiker" and "duikeritude" graduated to the celebrated
adage about "tiger" and "tigritude" at the African Writers'
Conference at Kampala (Uganda) in 1962. On the whole,
Soyinka is objective in his assessment of works by African
writers. The same Achebe who is praised for his "African-
ness" in "The Future of African Writing" is gently reprimanded in "From a Common Back Cloth" for succumb-
ing to a slight touch of improbability in the resolution of
the plot in his first novel *Things Fall Apart* (1958). The
accidental explosion of Okonkwo's gun, contributing as it
does to the novel's tragic denouement, is, in Soyinka's
view, a narrative expedience rather than an organically
integrated episode. On the other hand, Achebe is praised
for anticipating in the novel some aspects of the traditional
African philosophy which Soyinka will later regard as vital
elements of the African worldview—the mysterious relationship between a man and his *chi*, the mysteries of initiation and of guilt and purification whose ethics, says
Soyinka, "are not those of a court of law but of the forces of
Nature cycle, of the living and the dead." The logic of this
phenomenon is the "philosophy of acceptance. Not blind,
slavish acceptance but a positive faith, an acceptance of
forces that begin where the physical leaves off."[5]

"From a Common Back Cloth" is an assessment of the

African literary image in the novels of the 1950s and of the treatment in those novels of a common theme, the encounter between tradition and change. Soyinka labels both of these considerations the "common back cloth." In the hands of lesser writers like Onuora Nzekwu, the "back cloth" breeds sociological novels. For writers like Alan Paton, Peter Abrahams, and William Conton, the "back cloth" gives birth to dumb, wooden, servile character-types masquerading as human beings. The African characters of these writers lack human attributes because they were not conceived from within, that is, from the "dignity and authority of self-acceptance." Their portraiture is dictated largely by Western stereotypical prejudices originating from what Soyinka calls "a misconceived Christian forgiveness." It is only in the works of writers like Chinua Achebe, Mongo Beti and the South African novelist, Alex La Guma, that African characters appear as fully individuated human beings. Mongo Beti achieved this rounded portraiture by seeing Africans in the first place as individuals composed, like every other human being, of cunning and compassion. His is not the *Negritudinist*, one-dimensional mode of characterization, but a rounded view of both the African and his traditional society. "Hospitality is not, as we are constantly romantically informed that it is, nearly so spontaneous. There is a mercenary edge, and this, alas, is not always traceable to that alien corrupt civilization!"[6] Paton, Abrahams, Conton, and *Negritude* will be discussed later in the essay on ideology and social vision, where they will serve to buttress Soyinka's arguments against literary ideology.

An important writer mentioned in "From a Common Back Cloth" is Amos Tutuola, whose "back cloth" is a shade different from those of his contemporaries. Soyinka finds Tutuola more original than his fellow African writer–intellectuals because his imagination is constantly creating new syntheses. The atom bomb and the magical egg of plenty both find a place in his world. The difference between him and other manipulators of the "back cloth" is the difference between a natural imagination and an "intellectual" imagination. Tutuola is "a story teller in the best Yoruba tradition, pushing the bounds of credibility

higher and higher and sustaining it by sheer adroitness, by
a juxtaposition of analogous experience from the familiar."[7] He is best understood as "the contemporary imagination in a storytelling tradition."[8]

In the third essay ("And After the Narcissist?"), Soyinka
insists that the supreme narcissist in African writing is
Leopold Senghor. Narcissism is the literature of self-wor-
ship or of self-hypnosis, in which the self is "most clamant
in its own adulation." Too much emphasis on the self
breeds stasis, and, thus, stasis becomes an extension of
narcissism. And this is the sense in which writers like
Achebe of *Arrow of God* (1964) and Gabrrel Okara of *The
Voice* (1964) qualify as narcissists. In these works movement is not translated into action: Ezeulu neither dares nor
ventures forth, nor does Okolo, the hero of Okara's novel.
There is no communication in the latter "of the psychic
drive which sets a man on a course of single-minded enquiry into the heart of matter or existence."[9] Okolo's passivity contrasts with the questioning and the daring insistence of Soyinka's own quest-hero Ofeyi, who is equally
engaged, like Okolo, in an enquiry into the heart of existence. The psychic unrest that impels Ofeyi makes him
prone to introspective reminiscences and self-doubt.

Soyinka distinguishes between narcissism and self-exploration. Self-exploration is the burden of the tragic/
subjective artist, the Soul's descent into its own world,
which, as Hegel says in a different context, has been urged
upon the artist by "a severance of mind from world, soul
from circumstance, and human inwardness from external
conditions",[10] whereas narcissism is self-manipulation.
Soyinka's metaphor for it is "a fascination for the womb,"
where there is no distraction and there is no opportunity
for action. But the true poet ventures forth, confronts experience, realizes that

> . . . hot sterilizing pads sealed the cord at birth but
> that such discouraging facts need not condemn the
> poet to exile. And so exploration begins from the
> acceptance; the poet rejects the navel's fascination,
> seeks his path through experience, through liberation,
> through self-surrender.[11]

The work that best illustrates Senghor's narcissistic indulgence leading to inaction, is his dramatic poem, *Chaka*. Chaka, the legendary man of action, appears effeminate, says Soyinka, as a result of Senghor's misapprehension of the proper functions of poetry. Chaka's narcissistic passivity implies that, for Senghor, "poetry is not a force for violence or an occasional instrument of terror";[12] whereas, for Soyinka, "every creative act breeds and destroys fear, contains within itself both the salvation and the damnation."[13] That is, Soyinka sees the artist as the destroyer and the preserver. The Irish dramatist, John Synge, articulated the cardinal ideology of such an aesthetic as the mingling of beauty with brutality. Synge is reported to have warned Yeats that before poetry could be human (beautiful), it must learn to be brutal. The combination of beauty and ugliness in Yeats's later verse, which is so different from the fantasy world of his early verse, is often credited to Yeats's encounter with Synge. Perhaps Senghor should have followed Synge's advice to Yeats in *Chaka* if Chaka was to have been more masculine and energetic. As it is, Senghor's poem is sentimental and negative escapism rather than a vigorous tragic resolution of conflicts through the will for action.

Soyinka returns to this same theme of the passive acceptance (rather than of tragic engagement) inherent in Negritude, in the essay "The Fourth Stage." "The principle of creativity," writes Soyinka, "when limited to pastoral idyllism as negritude has attempted to limit it, shuts us off from the deeper, fundamental resolutions of experience and cognition."[14] Soyinka offers Senghor the example of his god Ogun, who embodies the creative principle:

> In explication of the real problem of Senghor in the interpretation of *Chaka*, which cannot be solved by the poetic self-identification, the example of Ogun, the Yoruba god of war and the creative principle, probably offers the best assistance. . . . Primogenitor of the artist as the creative human, Ogun is the antithesis of cowardice and Philistinism, yet within him is contained also the complement of the creative essence, a bloodthirsty destructiveness. Mixed up with

the gestative inhibition of his nature (is) the destructive explosion of an incalculable energy.[15]

As a corrective measure to Senghor's dull rendition of the
Chaka legend, Soyinka has himself embodied the myths of
Ogun and Chaka in two epic poems (*Idanre* and *Ogun
Abibiman*) distinguished by their conscious cultivation of
the aesthetics of action.

THE RITUAL ESSAYS

The core of the ritual essays is Soyinka's attempt in "The
Fourth Stage" to define the origin and meaning of the
tragic myth in the context of the Yoruba worldview. This
essay was written in honor of Professor G. Wilson Knight,
Soyinka's teacher at Leeds and an eminent Shakespearian
scholar and critic in the ritual mode who aided Soyinka
significantly in his understanding of myth and ritual.[16]
"The Fourth Stage" is Soyinka's first pronouncement on
what he later calls "morality and aesthetics in ritual archetypes" and on the role of drama in the African worldview.
The other two essays on those subjects, "Morality and
Aesthetics in the Ritual Archetype" and "Drama and the
African World View", merely enlarge upon the issues
raised in "The Fourth Stage." "The Fourth Stage" established Soyinka's reputation as a myth critic, a drama theo-
rist, and a master of language. The citation conferring upon
Soyinka the honorary degree of Doctor of Letters from Yale
University acknowledges these attributes:

> Poet and playwright in a language metaphorical and
> lyrical, you have redefined modern tragedy through a
> synthesis of Yoruba and Western tragic forms.[17]

Like Nietzsche's *The Birth of Tragedy* which inspired it,
"The Fourth Stage" was written by a young man, so its
language is explosive, lyrical, and emotional. It is as emotionally charged as Soyinka's prison memoirs, *The Man
Died*, (Chapter XII). In his later literary essays Soyinka's

language is more sober, more controlled, and less mytho-poeic.

"The Fourth Stage" enquires into the origin of Yoruba tragedy. Tragedy, in the Yoruba worldview, originated from the gods' consciousness of their own incompleteness or what Soyinka has called "the anguish of severance." The idea of severance takes us back to what Soyinka refers to elsewhere as "the principle of complementarity",[18] that is, the need for the gods to continually experience the human in them and a parallel urge in man to reassume his divine essence. The interaction of the divine and the human in god and man leads to a complete personality, a unity of being, which fosters what Soyinka terms, in a larger con-text, "cosmic totality." In physical terms, the gods once lived here on earth with the humans, and their partnership was marked by camaraderie and mutual regard for each other. However, either through sin or default, an estrange-ment occurred, and the gods withdrew into the upper re-gions of ether. The estrangement is symbolized in meta-physical or religious terms as the thick undergrowth of matter and non-matter, which Soyinka, borrowing a phrase from Nietzsche, calls "the chthonic realm." Soyinka's god, Ogun, battled with the forces of the chthonic realm, bridged the gap between man and god, and, thus, re-estab-lished the principle of complementarity. "Into this univer-sal womb plunged and emerged Ogun, the first actor, dis-integrating within the abyss" (p. 121). Ogun's pathway through the abyss of being and non-being is "the gulf of transition." And Ogun was able to confront and overcome the dark forces of the abyss because he was the embodiment of the will, for only the will can dare the abyss and emerge therefrom unscathed. The first actor in the Yoruba drama was Ogun, the first darer and conqueror of transition, and the first art was the tragic art (p. 123).

Tragic consciousness in Yoruba drama is the protago-nist's awareness of his parallel progress through the abyss of transition; for "Yoruba tragic drama is the re-enactment of the cosmic confict" (pp. 149–150). Tragic destiny, in general, is man's re-enactment of Ogun's rite of passage. Individual misfortune and tribulations are viewed as per-sonal reflections of the god's agony:

> On the arena of the living, when man is stripped of
> excrescences, when disasters and conflicts (the mate-
> rial of drama) have crushed and robbed him of self-
> consciousness and pretensions, he stands in present
> reality at the spiritual edge of this gulf, he has nothing
> left in physical existence which successfully impresses
> upon his spiritual or psychic perception. It is at such
> moments that transitional memory takes over and in-
> timations rack him of that intense parallel of his prog-
> ress through the gulf of transition. (p. 149)

In prison, Soyinka experienced an agony parallel to his
god's and was able to overcome the dark forces within the
"abyss of transition" through the agency of his own will.
On the other hand, Elesin Oba in *Death and the King's
Horseman* skirted round the abyss but lacked the courage
(will) to make the perilous plunge.

The will, in Soyinka's thinking, is the tragic hero's
greatest asset in the abyss of transition; and music is the
expression of the will. Soyinka marries the two (will and
music) in his theory, taking his cue from Schopenhauer
who had asserted that music is the "direct copy of the will
itself":[19]

> If we agree that, in the European sense, music is the
> "direct copy or the direct expression of the will," it is
> only because nothing rescues man (ancestral, living or
> unborn) from loss of self within this abyss but a titanic
> resolution of the will whose ritual summons, re-
> sponse, and expression is the strange alien sound to
> which we give the name of music. (p. 149)

Soyinka goes beyond this Western definition of music as
the manifestation of the will by relating music properly to
ritual and drama. In his view, music is the tragic hero's sole
companion at the charged moment of his self-individua-
tion:

> This masonic union of sign and melody, the true
> tragic music, unearths cosmic uncertainties which per-
> vade human existence, reveals the magnitude and

> power of creation, but above all creates a harrowing
> sense of omnidirectional vastness where the creative
> intelligence resides and prompts the soul to futile
> exploration. The senses do not at such moments inter-
> pret myth in their particular concretions; we are left
> only with the emotional and spiritual values, the es-
> sential experience of cosmic reality. The forms of
> music are not correspondences at such moments to the
> physical world, not at this nor at any other moment.
> The singer is a mouthpiece of the chthonic forces of
> the matrix and his somnabulist "improvisations" . . .
> are not representations of the ancestor, recognitions of
> the living or unborn, but of the no man's land of
> transition between and around these temporal defini-
> tions of experience. (p. 148)

However, Soyinka's explanation of the function of music
in ritual drama is not so different from Nietzsche's view as
he claims. The insight into the magnitude of creation
which dawns on the tragic hero through music is the counterpart of the retreat into the maternal womb of being or
Original Oneness which, Nietzsche claims, is brought
upon the Dionysiac artist by the magnetic spells of music.[20]

Ogun's pathway, the gulf of transition, is the fourth
stage. The word "stage" underscores its connotation as a
scene of action; but the fourth stage implies much more
than an arena of action. Soyinka's imagination waxes
philosophical in the course of the essay. The "anguish
of severance," for instance, is translated in philosophical
terms as the "fragmentation of self from self, of self from
essence, and of essence from itself." Religion is man's symbolic effort to halt the separation. We must view the fourth
area of experience as a physical, metaphysical, and symbolic reality. As a physical definition of space, the fourth
stage is a synthesis of Miltonic Hell and the Yorubas'
conception of the original abode of cosmic forces. Soyinka
calls it "the seething cauldron of the dark world will and
psyche" (p. 142). Still, Soyinka resorts to Jungian psychology to further clarify his definition of the fourth space. One
might view it as a symbolic representation of the Jungian
"collective unconscious," for it is also defined as "the vor-

tex of archetypes and kiln of primal images" (p. 36).
Soyinka is at pains to define the exact nature and topography of the fourth area of experience: he calls it

1. the womb of origin or of universal Oneness.
   (pp. 30, 153)
2. the territory of essence ideal. (p. 1)
3. the unconscious. (p. 153)
4. the matrix of cosmic creativity or of essence.
   (p. 153)
5. the creative cauldron of cosmic powers. (p. 145)
6. the deep black whirlpool of mythopoetic forces.
   (p. 153)
7. the source of creative and destructive energies.
   (p. 154)
8. the transitional yet inchoate matrix of death and
   becoming. (p. 142)
9. the seething cauldron of dark world will and
   psyche. (p. 142)

What immediately emerges is the identification of the
fourth area of experience with the source of poetic intuition, which is hardly surprising since Ogun is himself the
god of creativity. Thus, "the numinous area of transition"
is the home of the tragic muse. "Tragic music," says
Soyinka, "is an echo from that void," and he goes on:

> The source of the possessed lyricist chanting hitherto
> unknown mythopoeic strains whose antiphonal re-
> frain is however immediately recognised and thrust
> with all its terror and awesomeness into the night by
> swaying votaries, this source is residual in the numi-
> nous area of transition. (pp. 148–149)

Still, there is a metaphysical edge to the meaning of the
fourth stage. It is a connecting link (a passage) between
the three areas of existence defined by Yoruba ontology as
the world of the ancestor, the living, and the unborn. A
diagrammatical representation of this ontological universe
presents the following picture. The gulf of transition is a
symbol of continuity: it permits free traffic through the

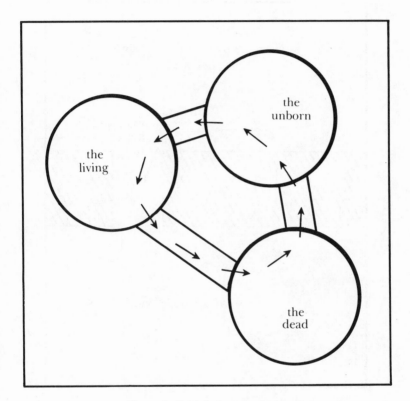

Figure 1. Soyinka's cosmology.

three areas of existence, and, as Ogun's pathway, establishes Ogun's primacy as the god of the "road."

Soyinka's essay endorses a tragic view of artistic creativity that maintains that all the great poems of the world have their foundations fixed in agony. Both Yeats and the Nigerian poet Okigbo uphold the notion of tragic creativity whose metaphoric summation is contained in Yeats's observation that "the poet has made his home in the serpent's mouth."[21] Both Soyinka and Ogun are tragic artists. Ogun immersed himself into the seething cauldron of the

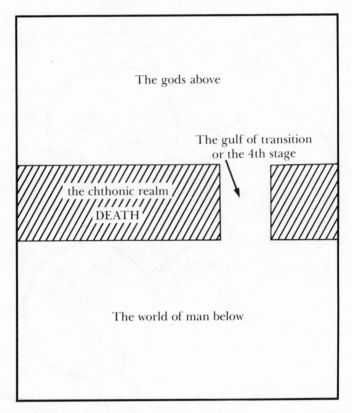

Figure 2. Soyinka's cosmology in three dimensions.

dark-world will to forge a bridge for both men and gods. For his courage he was rewarded with the appellations: "primogenitor of the artist as creative human," and "forerunner and ancestor of palactechnic man" (p. 150). When we transfer Ogun's action to its artistic complement, we have the following statement:

> To act, the Promethean instinct of rebellion, channels anguish into a creative purpose which releases man

from a totally destructive despair, releasing from within him the most energetic, deeply combative inventions which, without usurping the territory of the infernal gulf, bridges it with visionary hopes. Only the battle of the will is thus primarily creative; from its spiritual stress springs the soul's despairing cry which proves its own solace, which alone reverberating within the cosmic vaults usurps . . . the power of the abyss. (p. 146)

The soul's despairing cry, "which proves its own solace, which alone . . . usurps . . . the power of the abyss," is poetry.

Soyinka's essay is insightful about hubris. Soyinka's master, Nietzsche, sees hubris as a tragic necessity at the root of every tragic myth; for, as he says, "How should man force nature to yield up her secrets but by successfully resisting her, that is to say, by unnatural acts?"[22] Wisdom, Nietzsche goes on, is a crime committed against the gods, for it equips the sage with divine secrets. But the acquisition of such rare wisdom is accompanied by an attendant penalty. This, says Nietzsche, is the inexorable logic of the law of karma:

Whoever, in pride of knowledge, hurls nature into the abyss of destruction, must himself experience nature's disintegration.[23]

Soyinka applied the insights from Nietzsche to Ogun's act of hubris, his defiance of the cosmic forces that lay guardian to the yet inchoate matrix of being and non-being. His hubris is in the very nature of Ogun's destiny and of tragedy in general.

Tragic fate is the repetitive cycle of the taboo in nature, the karmic act of hubris, willing or unwilling into which the demonic will within man constantly compels him. Powerful tragic drama follows upon the act of hubris, and myth exacts this attendant penalty from the hero where he has actually emerged victor of a conflict. (p. 156)

But Soyinka changes the idea of hubris as he weaves the
concept into the fabric of the Yoruba worldview. In this
context, hubris is a factor in the cyclic resolution of man's
metaphysical situation. It triggers a chain reaction which
"hurts" and "benefits" nature. The whirlpool of transition
requires occasional hubristic invasions for its continuous
regeneration. The role of hubris as a mechanism for guar-
anteeing the continuity of cosmic balance and harmony is
stressed in the passage that follows:

> Offences even against nature may in fact be part of the
> exaction by deeper nature from humanity of acts
> which alone can open up the deeper springs of man
> and bring about a constant rejuvenation of the human
> spirit. Nature, in turn, benefits by such broken taboos,
> just as the cosmos by the demand made upon its will
> by man's cosmic affront. Such acts of hubris compel
> the cosmos to delve deeper into its essence to meet the
> human challenge. Penance and retribution are not
> therefore aspects of punishment for crime but the first
> acts of a resumed awareness, an invocation of the
> principle of cosmic adjustment. (p. 156)

And because restitution in the natural order is possible
through the act of hubris, hubris itself becomes an essential
element in the Yoruba concept of morality; for morality for
the Yoruba is what creates harmony in the cosmos.

The issue of morality is taken up more fully in the
second ritual essay, "Morality and Aesthetics in the Ritual
Archetype." The operative words in the title of this essay
are "ritual archetype." The term must be understood in its
specific meaning and in its original Jungian sense. "Ritual
archetype" is here synonymous with "the drama of the
gods." This drama is essentially a ritual (and a rite of
passage), and the gods themselves are the first actors in the
drama; the drama is, therefore, primal or primordial, that
is, archetypal. Human enactments of the drama of the gods
are imitations of the archetypal original. Soyinka uses the
words "ritual" and "drama" interchangeably in the essay.
In his view, there can be no legitimate dividing line between ritual and drama. Ritual is drama and drama is

ritual. Experts in dramatic literature and criticism would, of course, argue, but they do agree (especially Anthony Graham-White) that "the distinction between ritual and dramatic performances is not often made in traditional African societies."[24] And when Soyinka equates ritual with drama, he has traditional African drama in mind. After pp. 34–35, the words "ritual archetype" reverts to their original Jungian meaning as the primordial inhabitants of the "collective unconscious," or, as Soyinka renders the term, "the hinterland of transition." Soyinka quarrels with Jung for including dream images and psychotic exhalations and deliriums in the category of archetypes. These, says Soyinka, are not archetypes but mere emanations from the ephemeral and transient portions of the human psyche, whereas archetypes *proceed* from the congealed substrata of the psyche which are constantly enriched by the moral and historic experience of man. In spite of Soyinka's criticism of Jung, his understanding of myth has been enriched by Jungian psychology.

Soyinka proceeds to illustrate the issue of morality and aesthetics in the drama of the gods by using examples from the myths of his favorite deities—Sango, Obatala, and Ogun. His basic argument is that the gods are conceived among the Yoruba within the context of human fallibility. They are prone to error, which disrupts nature, in expiation of which they must do penance. Their penance restores order in the world of man and in the cosmos. Morality in Yoruba worldview is bound up with the mandatory compensations of nature. It is predicated on the dialectics of challenge and response, on action and counteraction, on the hubristic infractions of nature, which, in turn, compel countermeasures for the reassertion of totality. The drama that develops from the history of these gods is a rite of passage distinguished by the three-part structure basic to all rites of passage; ordeal and ritual death, followed by rebirth.

This ritual dialectic has wider implications; it is linked to the cyclical dynamics of nature, that is, to the alternating cycles of death and life, dearth and plenty, drought and rain. The ordeal of the gods is nature's mechanism for renewal. These gods are vegetation deities to a certain ex-

tent, for they possess affinities with such nature deities as
Osiris, Ishtar, and Thammuz.

Sango's destiny at the positive end of the dialectical axis
is apotheosis, aptly defined by Soyinka as "the joining of
energies in cosmic continuity" (p. 11). As the god of
thunder and lightning, Sango is the "cosmic instrument
of swift retributive justice" (p. 8). Sango's history is the
history of an anthropomorphic deity. A one-time tyrant of
the ancient kingdom of Oyo, Sango became the victim of
his own cunning. He had conspired with some of his
henchmen to eliminate two of the most powerful warlords
in his kingdom, Gbonka and Timi. The first strategy,
which failed, was to expose them to the risk of death in a
war with an external aggressor. The second, which succeeded, was to force them to fight in single combat. The
stronger of the two warlords, Gbonka, defeated his rival
and emerged from the combat wiser. He confronted Sango
with his machinations and demanded his throne. Sango
considered the challenge an affront to his royal dignity,
and in a fit of rage he slaughtered his own subjects, thereby
committing a sacrilege for which he had to atone by exile
and suicide. But after his death by hanging, his subjects,
who had abandoned their king at his moment of trial,
praised the dead king for his courage to dare the abyss of
transition through ritual suicide and proclaimed him a
god. Sango's slaughter of his own people was the consequence of his hubristic neglect of the virtues of self-control.

Obatala's own error resulted from his addiction to palm
wine. He was drunk as he performed the divine duty of
molding human shapes out of clay, for he was the god of
creation. His craftsman's fingers faltered from his intake
of alcohol, and he molded albinos, hunchbacks, and cripples. He sinned against the aesthetics of creation. Nemesis
caught up with Obatala when he visited his old friend
Sango at Oyo. Suspected of trying to steal Sango's horse,
Obatala was clamped into prison, and creation came to a
standstill because the god who turns blood into children
was languishing in jail. The imprisonment of Obatala
disrupted harmony in the cosmos and in the world of man,
which was restored after the god's release. We have here an
anomalous situation in which the crimes of the gods are

visited upon mankind. This cannot be otherwise, says
Soyinka, because "the relationship between man and god
(embodiment of nature and cosmic principles) cannot be
seen in any other terms but in those of naturalness" (p. 15).

As for Ogun, we are already familiar with his hubristic
invasion of the whirlpools of transition. The cosmic forces
that guard the pool postponed Ogun's penalty till the
fateful moment at the battle of Ire, when, under the influence of alcohol, Ogun massacred his own men. For that
unwitting error, Ogun is compelled to visit earth annually
in atonement. His visit to earth means harvest, and his
withdrawal implies drought and scarcity. The alternating
cycles of harvest and scarcity represent the god's descent to
earth and his subsequent withdrawal. This myth is the
subject of *Idanre*:

> He comes, who scrapes no earth dung from his feet
> He comes again in Harvest, the first of reapers
> Night is our tryst when sounds are clear
> And silences ring pure tones as the pause
> Of iron bells.[25]

The African gods retain the importance ascribed to them
in their home grounds, but those that survive in the Americas have lost that position assigned in the popular imagination. In Brazil, for example, the Yoruba god Obatala is
known as Oxala. Soyinka used the example of the changes
in the essence of Obatala (Oxala) through his syncretic
associations with Christian gods in the Americas to illustrate the relevance of the second keyword (aesthetics) in the
title of the second ritual essay. A comparison of two versions of the Obatala passion play, one by a Nigerian playwright and the other by a Brazilian, helped Soyinka to
advance his argument. As a result of association with the
Christian saints, the African gods in the Americas have
taken on the Western conception of deity as Olympian
archetypes. This view of the gods is the direct heritage of
the Platonic-Christian tradition, which has encouraged the
gradual erosion of Earth in the Western metaphysical universe. It runs counter to the geocentric dispositions of the
gods themselves, which have brought them within the

sphere of human fallibility in the African worldview. In
the play *The Imprisonment of Obatala*, the gods assert
their *humanity*. They dine, drink wine, and chat with men
and are prone to human foibles and weaknesses. In Zora
Zeljan's play, on the other hand, *The Story of Oxala*, the
African gods are transcendental deities, inhabiting a separate sphere from the humans. It is this different attitude to
the gods in the two versions of the Obatala tragedy, that is,
the contrast between Obatala's earthiness in the original
play and Oxala's ethereal incorporeality in Zora Zeljan's
version, that Soyinka seeks to convey with the term "aesthetics." In the Brazilian play, the gods' reality is defined
by the "aesthetics of estrangement" (p. 25). Soyinka holds
that the gods are remote in the Brazilian play because over
there in the Americas they have inherited the "attenuation
of terrestrialism . . . brought upon by the encounter of the
gods with Christian saints" (p. 24). And when this happens
the moral imperatives of complementarity become meaningless:

> When ritual archetypes acquire new aesthetic charac-
> teristics, we may expect re-adjustments of the moral
> imperatives that brought them into existence in the
> first place, at the centre of man's effort to order the
> universe. (p. 25)

But one wonders, however, whether the word "aesthetics" has been properly employed in Soyinka's essay. Is it
not, indeed, possible that Soyinka is merely attracted by the
rhythmic resonance of the word "aesthetics" for its own
sake in a title that reads like a line of verse? But the term
"aesthetics," though not specifically illustrated in Soyinka's essay, also implies the staging of the drama of the gods,
the mode of presentation, the details of space, music, poetry
and the producer's consciousness of the need to elicit from
ritual archetypes "the emotive progression which leads to a
communal ecstasy or catharsis" (pp. 5–6).

The third ritual essay, "Drama and the African World-
View," has two main thrusts. The first focus is on the
symbolic function of space in ritual theatre. In the second
part of the essay, Soyinka discusses two plays, J. P. Clark's
Song of a Goat (1964) and Duro Ladipo's *Oba Koso* (1964),

as being good examples of the way drama can reflect the African worldview.

First, what are the main features of Soyinka's pet concept, the African worldview? They may be summarized as the union of divine and human essences in man and god, the replenishment and continuance of which guarantees unity of being in both. In the world of nature, Soyinka sees this union as "animist interfusion of all matter and consciousness" (p. 145). Cosmic balance is a function of the healthy interaction of the spiritual, the human and the natural forces. Hubris is nature's mechanistic device for its own regeneration. Without the challenge of the cosmic status quo through hubris, cosmic equilibrium would risk sterile harmony. Add to all these the movement of transition between the world of the ancestors, the living, and the unborn, and the reality of the fourth space acting as a channel for transition.

What emerges is a homogeneous worldview in which the elements are interrelated and inseparable from one another. This view of the universe is not peculiar to the African mind. Elements of it can be observed in other cultures and in other periods of history. There are, for instance, affinities between this worldview and the ordered hierarchy of the Elizabethans.

Two plays illustrate aspects of this point of view: *Song of a Goat* and *Oba Koso*. *Oba Koso* has already been discussed: Sango's self-sacrifice is a heroic gesture in spite of the crime against nature that motivated it, his apotheosis benefits the community. As a tyrant and a murderer Sango was an abnormal growth on the body of nature. Nature can only be returned to harmony through a total excision of the abnormal outgrowth. Sango wins the reader's sympathy through his courage to dare the abyss. The play is reminiscent of 'the universe of *Song of a Goat*, in which man's bonds with nature are visceral. Timi, one of the protagonists, was encouraged by his consciousness of this union of man and nature to summon nature to his aid in his own rites of passage:

> I come this day to Ede town
> It is the gentle wind that says,
> blow towards me

Spirits of swarming termites say,
swarm towards me
Two hundred rafters support the house
Two hundred lizards support the wall
Let all hands be raised to sustain me. (p. 59)

The tragedy in *Song of a Goat* lies not in the crime of incest
but in Zifa's impotence and his sterile pride that threatens
the breakdown in moral order. Soyinka explains:

> Where society lives in a close inter-relation with Na-
> ture, regulates its existence by natural phenomena
> within the observable processes of continuity—ebb
> and tide, waxing and waning of the moon, rain and
> drought, planting and harvest—the highest moral
> order is seen as that which guarantees a parallel conti-
> nuity of the species. (p. 52)

The theoretical focus of the third ritual essay deals with
the metaphysical implications of the ritual theatre. These
implications were enumerated early in the essay on "ritual
archetypes." The stage, says Soyinka, is "a microcosmic
copy of the chthonic realm, which requires the presence of
a challenger, a human representative to breach it periodically on behalf of the well-being of the community" (p. 3).
Soyinka made this statement with special reference to the
drama of the gods; but he maintains that even for the so-
called realistic or literary drama, this view of the stage still
holds. But the ritual theatre and its metaphysical implications exercise the greatest fascination for Soyinka. In its
metaphysical context, Soyinka's stage is a symbolic representation of earth and the cosmos, and the actor is a human
challenger reenacting man's existential predicament. The
stage is one arena in which man has attempted to come to
terms with the spatial phenomenon of his being. Soyinka
returns again and again to the cosmic definition of the stage.
Two more representative citations might suffice:

> The concern of ritual theatre in this process of spatial
> definition . . . must be seen as an integral part of
> man's constant efforts to master the immensity of the
> cosmos with his minuscule self. (p. 40)

And again:

> Ritual theatre establishes the spatial medium not
> merely as a physical area for simulated events but as
> a manageable contraction of the cosmic envelope
> within which man . . . fearfully exists. (p. 41)

The insight revealed in these ritual essays shows Soyinka
to be an accomplished critic of the ritual stage who has
made original contributions to dramatic theory and criticism.

IDEOLOGY OR SOCIAL VISION?

Two essays concern us here, essays that outline the religious and secular dimensions of Soyinka's statments on
works of social vision. These essays are further clarifica-
tions of Soyinka's position on the issue of ideological
(Marxist) commitment in works of literature. Although
Soyinka stretches the meaning of ideology to embrace such
literary movements as Expressionism, Surrealism, and *Negritude*, the term "ideology" in the essays under consideration is used in a Marxist sense. This prejudice is understandable considering Soyinka's own "passage" through
the Marxist circles at the Universities of Ibadan and Ife,
where he has been found to be ideologically wanting.
Soyinka has, thus, a reason to restate and redefine his
position in the context of the on-going debate on literature
and ideology. He says "yes" to a social vision and "no" to a
literary ideology because the latter limits and imposes
upon the free operations of the creative spirit. Works of
literature, says Soyinka, are "essentially fluid operations of
the creative mind upon social and natural phenomena"
(p. 61). In a literary ideology this fluidity yields to rigidity,
and the creative imagination is compelled to follow the
routes mapped out by ideological manifestos. The choice
for a social vision is determined, therefore, by Soyinka's
regard for the integrity and autonomy of the creative artist,
but autonomy does not preclude social relevance. The artist
does not live in an ivory tower; his visionary imaginings
have the good of society as their goal. A prime function of
art in its social context, says Soyinka, is "the visionary

reconstruction of the past for the purpose of a social direction" (p. 106). This definition of literature's social role is a
carry-over from Soyinka's earlier view of the role of a writer
in a modern African state. In the essay on that subject
published in 1967, Soyinka charges the African writer with
a deplorable lack of "vision." The African writer is urged
in that essay to abandon the "historic" vision inherent in
Negritude so as to more easily fix his gaze on the immediate
realities of society. Only through the acquisition of a realist
vision, says Soyinka, could the writer express the real essence of himself as "the record of the mores and experience
of his society and as the voice of vision in his own time."[26]
The writer's capacity to combine the gains of historic and
realist visions into a constructive program for the future is
what might amount to a social vision. The very conception
of the writer's social program as being attainable only in
the future renders that image of society a visionary projection.

Soyinka is at pains to define exactly what he means by
the term "social vision." We have several tentative offerings:

a. The reflection of experience is only one of the functions of literature. . . . And when that experience is
   social we move into areas of ideological projection,
   the social vision. (p. 64)

b. A creative concern which conceptualises or extends
   actuality beyond the purely narrative, making it
   reveal realities beyond the immediately attainable,
   a concern which upsets orthodox acceptances in an
   effort to free society of historical or other superstitions, these are qualities possessed by literature of a
   social vision. (p. 66)

c. A re-statement of the values of past or present in
   integrated perspectives of a future potential. (p. 98)

The continuous search for definition is necessary because Soyinka insists on making a distinction between a
social vision and a socialist (revolutionary) vision. If the
distinction must be maintained, it follows that a socialist

revolutionary fiction might belong to the category of social vision, whereas not all works of a social vision are transposable to the socialist revolutionary category. The problem is compounded by the religious factor in Soyinka's work of a social vision. The way out of the dilemma is to again qualify his definition of social vision in terms of its relationship to a socialist revolutionary fiction:

> Revolutionary writing is generally of this kind (the category of a social vision), though whether or not much of the writing which aspires to the label is always literature is another question. (p. 66)

Most revolutionary writings do not qualify as literature, so Soyinka prefers the expression "social vision" to the term "socialist revolutionary vision." This term enables him to bring a wide spectrum of fiction under the label.

The practical illustration of his thesis is easier for Soyinka than his theoretical definitions. Since he draws his example from works of fiction we can distinguish three categories of fiction:

a) social realist fiction
b) socialist realist fiction
c) social visionary fiction.

Social realist fiction is generally novels of disillusionment. Soyinka's first novel, *The Interpreter* (1965), belongs to this group. Others include Alex La Guma's *A Walk in the Night* (1964), Achebe's *A Man of the People* (1966), and Armah's *The Beautyful Ones Are Not Yet Born* (1969), to name only a few examples. Social realist fiction makes no pretensions to a social vision although Armah's *The Beautyful Ones* moves from the social realist level to a social visionary plane at the end of the novel when Armah envisions the symbolic, solitary flower positioned in the center of the elegiac inscription "The beautyful ones are not yet born." The birth of the "beautyful ones" is forecast in the image of the beautiful flower and fulfilled in Armah's third novel *Two Thousand Seasons* (1973).

Under the second category we include Soyinka's own

novel *Season of Anomy* (1973), Senbene Ousmane's *God's Bits of Wood* (1970), Armah's *Two Thousand Seasons* (1973), and Ngugi's *Petals of Blood* (1977). Only two of these novels (*God's Bits of Wood* and *Two Thousand Seasons*) are discussed in Soyinka's essay. They are works of social vision because they speculate on the nature of the evolving society.

Social visionary novels project an image of the ideal society. This vision is similar to that in socialist realist novels, but the novelist need not, in this case, embody his dreams in revolutionary terms. Soyinka is thinking here of the visions of ideal society entertained by a great many African novelists that are derived either from a religious/ salvationist or other (secular) ethos. Iconoclastic literature (which may not necessarily be socialist) belongs to the category of social vision. The positive values of the author may be inferred from the negative values he destroys. This is particularly true of Ouologuem's *Bound to Violence* (1971), which "upsets orthodox acceptances in an effort to free society of historical or other superstitions" (p. 66). The superstition in this case is the Arab-Islamic colonization of Black Africa. Ouologuem, Soyinka believes, has deliberately countered Hamidou Kane's claim in *The Ambiguous Adventure* (1972) that Islam is "one religion whose ethics, philosophy, and form of worship reconciles races and encourages universal fraternalism" (p. 77).

In the face of such examples as Camara Laye's novels *The Dark Child* (1955) and *The Radiance of the King* (1956), Soyinka's thesis falters a little. The secular vision in these works is not necessarily social. If we insist on Soyinka's other definition of social vision as "a re-statement of the values of the past or present in integrated perspective of a future potential," Laye's *Radiance of the King* does not embody a social vision. It restates the values of the past (the African worldview) but offers no projections for the future. *The Radiance* is best appreciated for its vindication of the authenticity of the African worldview, just as that worldview is best illustrated in drama by *Song of a Goat* and *Oba Koso*.

It is Achebe's rather ambivalent attitude to that worldview in his third novel *Arrow of God* (1964) that makes it difficult (in Soyinka's view) to determine the role of the gods in that novel. The supernatural and the mystical lack the sustained dignity they have in Achebe's other novels. His attitude to the divine is here cavalier, sometimes irreverent and often determined by political rather than spiritual considerations. The imprisonment of Ezeulu, the half-man, half-spirit, would have been a good opportunity for the writer in the mythic mode to explore the cosmic implications of that hubristic breach on nature, but, curiously, Achebe avoids the spiritual dimensions of the priest's experience of exile. In the earlier essay "From A Common Back Cloth," Soyinka commends Achebe for according the mystical its rightful place in the order of things in his first novel *Things Fall Apart* (1958). That novel has "a pattern of understated mysteries, of psychical influences on daily routine, of a man's personal *Chi*, of initiations, of guilt and purifications whose ethics are not those of a court of law but of the forces of Nature cycle, of the living and the dead."[27] In *Arrow of God*, the story is different:

> Considerations of the authenticity of spiritual inspiration, or of manifestations which may be considered supernatural, or at the least, ominous coincidences, are given alternative (secular) explications in the casual reflections of members of his (Achebe's) Igbo community, coloured as always by individual problems or positions taken in sectional confrontations. In short, coloured by their *humanity*. (p. 87)

These remarks underscore the difference between the temperament and imagination of the two writers. It is the difference between the mythic imagination (Soyinka) and the historical imagination (Achebe).

Soyinka's reading of Achebe's novel from a mythic perspective is innovative, being so different from the general concerns of Achebe criticism. Most critics have tended to situate Achebe's novels merely in their historical and cultural contexts, but Soyinka's approach is refreshening.

Soyinka holds that religious factors may also influence a writer's views about the nature of society. He is thinking here of two main religions: Christianity and Islam. In cases

where an author's religious background has influenced the
resolution of the plot, the result is often to weaken the
novels concerned. Such interference from a religious ideology is comparable, in the secular realm, to a forced resolution by a socialist ideology. In both William Conton's
novel *The African* (1960) and in the play *The Rhythm of
Violence* (1964) by Lewis Nkosi, the logical progression of
the plot is distorted by a Christian salvationist ethic that
pretends that a fraternal understanding between races can
be brought about through the affirmation of Christian
values. In Conton the value asserted is forgiveness, and in
Nkosi, it is love. "These," says Soyinka, "are the ethical
lines on which an envisioned regeneration of society will
be based" (p. 70), hence the author's social vision. Other
writers ensnared by the illusions of the Christian vision are
Alan Paton and Peter Abrahams: They were reprimanded
in the earlier essay "From a Common Back Cloth" (1963).
Nearly two decades later Soyinka has cause to return to
them with his first judgments still unchanged.

The Islamic vision is represented by Hamidou Kane's
novel *The Ambiguous Adventure.* The summation of the
Islamic viewpoint is contained in Soyinka's preliminary
observations to his discussion of this novel:

> In colonial societies which constantly seek a world-
> view to challenge the inherent iniquities of any phi-
> losophy which can be associated with the colonial
> intrusion, we naturally encounter works which make
> a point of claiming that Islam is one religion whose
> ethics, philosophy and form of worship reconciles
> races and encourages universal fraternalism. (p. 77)

In Kane's hands, the Islamic vision is shown to be less
harmful to the creative imagination than William Conton
or Lewis Nkosi's handling of the Christian message of love
and forgiveness in their works. The Islamic vision is not
reduced to the level of propaganda in Kane's novel, and the
novel achieves a satisfying resolution of its conflicts
through the author's evocation of his religious background
instead of the mechanical imposition of Christian values as
on *The African* and *Rhythm of Violence.* Death is the

logical outcome of Samba Diallo's apostasy. The doctrine of death, the standpoint of the grand master of the Word, the Teacher, makes the final determination in the novel's conflicts, not the traditional Diallobe society nor the West, which was responsible for the weakening of Diallo's spiritual roots (p. 85).

The closing paragraphs of the essay restate Soyinka's long-standing objections to *Negritude*. Three key issues are at stake here. The first (the Cartesian fallacy) is the naivete of the founding fathers of the *Negritude* movement, a naivete that manifested itself in their uncritical acceptance of Eurocentric prejudices and racist ideologies. Descartes had said, "I think, therefore I am"; and that supreme Cartesian, Senghor, came up with the variant: "I feel, therefore I am." Soyinka wonders why an anti-European intellectual movement should borrow its self-characterizing definition from a European system of thought: "Negritude's reference points took far too much colouring from European ideas even while its messiahs pronounced themselves fanatically African" (p. 127).

The second objection (the aesthetic fallacy) is *Negritude*'s attitude to creativity, its defeatist, self-justifying aesthetic stance, which breeds a poetry of self-contemplation rather than a poetry of action. Soyinka's euphemism for the poetry of self-contemplation is "narcissism." Soyinka recalls the points made in the earlier essay "And After the Narcissist?" in one important statement: One of the unfortunate by-products of *Negritude* was "a mounting narcissism which involved contemplation of the contrived self in the supposed tragic grandeur of the cultural dilemma" (p. 130).

The third objection (the dialectical fallacy) was the fallacy of the dialectical self-resolution predicted by Sartre for *Negritude*. *Negritude*, says Sartre, occupies a middle position in the three-stage movement of an inexorable dialectical progression. The first movement (the thesis) is the assertion of white supremacy, which gave birth to *Negritude* in the first instance; the second stage (the antithesis) is the countering of this supremacist ideology by *Negritude*, that is, the birth of *Negritude*; the third stage (the synthesis) will resolve itself in the ultimate cancellation of the racial concepts in both the thesis and the antithesis. This stage will witness the union of all the workers of the world (both white and black) in a proletarian struggle for the establishment of a raceless society. Soyinka commends Sartre and his dialectical ancestor, Descartes, for their logic: They are white creatures in pith-helmets in an African jungle who think, but their thinking should have opened their eyes to the reality of *Negritude*—it was the property of a bourgeois intellectual elite, and as such it cannot integrate itself in the destiny of the working classes.

Although all these objections are interrelated, the most important, because it concerns the theme of creativity, is the second objection. And this brings us back to the subject of the essays in this section, the question of ideology and literature. *Negritude* tended to channel its creative energies through a particular artistic expression—the contemplative narcissistic mode. This bending of the natural disposition of the creative mind to accommodate certain preconceived ideas is the bane of all literary ideologies. The principles of creativity cannot be legislated. "The practical effects," writes Soyinka, "of literary ideology on the creative process lead to predictability, imaginative constraint, and thematic excisions" (p. 65).

All this does not mean that there is no fallacy in Soyinka's own argument. The definition of *Negritude* in terms of the Cartesian proposition runs into the same dilemma as does the act of writing African literature or Soyinka's literary criticism, in a European language. We cannot accept the view which asserts that "the writer is far more preoccupied with visionary projection of society than with specific projection on the nature of literature." The writer in fact is concerned with both. Most great writers, Matthew Arnold, Yeats, and Eliot, for example, have indeed speculated on the nature of literature and of its relation to society. Nor can we accept the reasoning that relegates the question of literary ideology to the province of the critic. Ngugi, Armah, and Sembene have steered their art according to consciously formulated ideological convictions. "It is only in the socialist context," wrote Ngugi in 1968, on the issue of ideological program for African literature, "that a look at yesterday can be meaningful in illuminating today and tomorrow."[28] Nine years later, Armah echoes this view: "In my people's world revolution would be the only art, revolutionaries the only creators. All else is part of Africa's destruction."[29] We have noted, in the chapter on *Season of Anomy*, how these convictions have shaped their art in at least one of their respective works.

The arguments of the two essays on ideology and social vision carry further the points made by Soyinka in a lecture delivered at the University of Washington's faculty seminar in 1973. The lecture, "Drama and the Revolutionary Ideal," focused on the pitfalls of ideological commitment in drama. Soyinka concluded that ideological interests were bound to weaken drama's integrity as an art form because drama is by its very nature a revolutionary medium. It is the art form most vulnerable to ideological manipulation. To superimpose an ideology on an art form that is intrinsically revolutionary is to overburden the form. The insertion of an ideology into drama's structure could, however, be adroitly managed by a gifted dramatist through the medium of ritual. In lesser hands, however, the result is frequently melodrama. The dramas of Arnold Wesker (*Roots*) or Edward Albee (*Who's Afraid of Virginia Woolf?*) and the social visionary plays written of Lewis Nkosi (*Rhythm of Violence*) and Alton Kumalo (*Themba*) suffer from contrived anguish and enforced resolution. Soyinka reaffirms the point we have already made that literary ideology (usually the concern of the critic rather than the writer) has the tendency to "dam up the creative paths natural to the writer's peculiar genius and lead him toward an artificial concept of proletarian art."[30] Since revolutionary tendencies are built in the dramatic mode itself, the less consciously ideological the dramatist appears to be, the more effectively would the subversive intent of his message be disseminated:

> The creative ideal in revolutionary theatre is not a self-conscious pandering to any proletarian illusion on any level whatever, be it the spiritual level or the social-revolutionary level, because . . . the matrix of

creativity, most especially in the dramatic mode, embraces at all times—both in individual and communal
affectiveness—the regenerative potential of society.[31]

Rituals function as vectors of social or revolutionary
message through the medium of audience participation.
This is the secret of Ben Caldwell's achievement in *The
Fanatic* or Imamu Baraka's play, *The Slave Ship*. In these
plays, the revolutionary message is effectively disguised
under the ritual idiom of audience participation.

If we were to arrive at a summary of the essays discussed
in this section, one would suggest that Soyinka is firmly
opposed to a conscious injection of ideological motives
into works of imaginative literature. This attitude appears
to be a self-defensive posture, intended to justify the kind of
literature Soyinka himself produces. But whether this attitude should lead to a denial of literary ideology in itself as
well as of the achievement of writers with obvious ideological motivations, is another matter. Also, Soyinka's essays
suffer from weak theoretical definition. He is unable to
convincingly separate the term "literary ideology" from
what he calls "social vision." However, Soyinka's evaluation of the authors discussed in the essays is unquestionably insightful.

CONTROVERSIES

Soyinka has come under attack as a writer by two radical
schools of criticism. The most outspoken, though perhaps
less well known, is the Marxist school led by Biodun Jeyifo,
Femi Osofisan and others of the Ibadan–Ife leftist critics.
The other radical voice in Soyinka criticism is the school of
neo-*Negritudist* apologetics for traditional African aesthetics led by Chinweizu and his group. The uncompromising
posture struck by these two schools in their evaluation of
Soyinka's work has drawn Soyinka into controversial polemics, which are not strictly literary criticism but which
nevertheless contain insights that further clarify Soyinka's
conception of the nature of art. The Marxist school of
critics approaches a work of art from the materialist-historical perspective. Leon Trotsky has outlined[32] some key

issues in the materialist-historical theory of art. These include such fundamental questions as the following:

a. To what order of feelings does a given artistic work correspond in all its peculiarities?
b. What are the social conditions of these thoughts and feelings?
c. What place do they occupy in the historic development of a society and of a class?
d. Under the influence of what historic impulse and conditions has the work been produced and in what ways have those conditions and contradictions been reflected in the work?

The Nigerian Marxist critics indict Soyinka for his supreme indifference to the responsibilities of the artist. It is the function of art, in the materialist-historical aesthetic, to reflect the historical processes at work in society at a given historical moment together with their internal contradictions and tensions (that is, their dialectics). To the Nigerian Marxians every work of the imagination that dares an independent existence outside the framework of "historical materialism"[33] is open to the charge of deliberate falsification of experience and reality. Other metaphors for falsification are "distortion," "romanticizing," "mythifying," "mystifying," and "prettifying." Soyinka's natural predilection for a mythic exploration of experience obviously exposed him to the Marxist notions of falsification. Every utterance of the Nigerian Marxists echoes the view that Soyinka's perception of history is static, mythic, and, therefore, unrealistic. In a reading of Soyinka's tragedy, *Death and the King's Horseman* (1975), Biodun Jeyifo criticizes Soyinca for his "mythopoeic attitude to history, his constant penchant for transforming experience into metaphysical, trans-historical, mythic dimensions."[34] Femi Osofisan, in the essay "Drama and the New Exotic," ridicules the "new exotic" stage of such playwrights as Soyinka and Ola Rotimi, peopled by animist gods and utterly indifferent to the logic of "historical contradictions in the dialectics of flux."[35] Omafume Onoge and G. G. Darah make the same point in their paper "The Retrospective Stage: Some

Reflections on the Mythopoeic Tradition at Ibadan." They dismiss as "mythic" and "retrogressive" a dramatized historiography of the past where antagonistic contradictions do not exist.[36] "It is this undialectical approach," they affirm, "plus the pre-eminence of the supernatural in the artistic representations of the past that we have termed mythopoeic."[37] Applying the materialist theory to *Death and the King's Horseman*, Jeyifo finds the play guilty of mispresenting and misinterpreting the real identity of the indigenous society. The play, says Jeyifo, did not attempt to highlight the real objective differences between conflicting groups and classes in the indigenous society. What we have, instead, is a rationalization of "the rule of the dazzling FEW over the deceived MANY."[38] In an earlier essay on Soyinka's *The Road*, Jeyifo concedes to Soyinka some awareness of the dialectical processes of history but that awareness, he felt, is subverted by Soyinka's mythopoeic imagination, which has led to a deliberate mystification or reification of a natural instrument of labor, the road, so that we have in that play a "hidden" class war rather than an open one:

> The reification of the road . . . is a mystification: the road (and the vehicles which ply it) is a product of man's labour, a specific item in the ensemble of the forces of production; it is not a manifest destiny unto itself.

> *The Road* is imbued with the heavy atmosphere of death, is obsessed by the deaths and "dangerous employment" on the road because it penetrates the "natural," normal aspects of a mode of production in which the relationship between the instruments and tools of labour and the labouring classes is distorted, mythified.

Several years before the New Marxist radicals began to articulate their objections to Soyinka's works, the Kenyan novelist and critic, Ngugi Wa Thiong'o, had expressed a similar dissatisfaction with Soyinka's writings. We quote

Ngugi in full as an illustration of a Marxist criticism that is sober, levelheaded, pedestrian, and bereft of linguistic mystifications:

> Although Soyinka exposes his society in breadth, the picture he draws is static, for he fails to see the present in the historical perspective of conflict and struggle. It is not enough for the African artist, standing aloof, to view society and highlight its weaknesses. He must try to go beyond this, to seek out the sources, the causes and the trends of a revolutionary struggle which has already destroyed the traditional power-map drawn up by the colonialist nations.[40]

Soyinka's reply to his Marxist critics is contained in the paper "Who's Afraid of Elesin Oba?" delivered to the Conference on Radical Perspectives on African Literature held at Ibadan in 1977, and in the Inaugural Lecture he delivered at Ife in November 1980, entitled "The Critic and Society," The point of view in these essays is identical, and a detailed analysis would be repetitive. Soyinka reaffirms in these essays the points he had already made in the essay on ideology and social vision. Soyinka insists on the autonomy of the creative imagination; its operations on social and natural phenomena cannot be legislated. Criticism evaluates works of imagination only in terms of the works' own aesthetic universe. The criticism that seeks in every work of art a causal and historical and socioeconomic network of society is reductionist and arbitrary—it imposes extra burdens on art. "Criticism—dealing with general principles and theories of creativity—has gone beyond its competence and dared to enlarge upon the legitimate purlieu of imaginative projection.[41]

On his addiction to myth and ritual, Soyinka believes, as did Joyce, Eliot, and Jung, that both myth and ritual are relevant to the spritual needs of modern man. It is only the Western University-educated sceptics who would repudiate the element of mystery in the contemporary setting. Myth may be viewed as the spiritual dimension of the very historical processes which the Nigerian radicals accuse Soyinka of ignoring. The Nigerian critic, Stanley Macebuh, has noted that myth and history complement one another in Soyinka's works:

> To the extent that myth and history are complementary, it may be suggested that Soyinka's persistent meditation on myth is an attempt to reveal the primal foundations of African culture, and therefore of history.[42]

Soyinka himself has affirmed his confidence in the mutual interdependence of myth and history.

> My social temperament is not without its complementary objective study of the society we live in and the societies we do not live in but which do impinge on our immediate society.[43]

The message of the two essays is summed up in the epigrammatic statement:

> When art ceases to imitate life: it does not thereby aspire to imitate ideology; while criticism which fails to emulate life ends up as an imitation of art.[44]

Soyinka does not give up easily in intellectual debates. His intellect appears to be stimulated by polemics as is evident from the witty, pungent, and incisive replies he metes out to his critics. He tries to use the logic of the Marxist critics to defeat their own arguments. Marxist criticism, says Soyinka, tends very often to reduce art to an economic commodity. It treats art as bourgeois capitalists treat labor: "The work of art is the product of intellectual labour which, without any self-criticism, the critic appropriates to ends other than the ends for which the work is produced and marketed."[45] This capitalist attitude to art shows up in the language of the Marxist critic himself. In spite of his supposed sympathy for the proletariat, the critic's language is not proletarian. It is a "seminarist language replete with its infinite discursiveness submerging, distorting and finally appropriating the original commodity in its quotational garrulity."[46]

The next radical voice in Soyinka criticism is the school of critics led by Chinweizu. These critics examined, among other things, the attitudes and tendencies of modern Nigerian poetry between the 1960s and the early 1970s. The poets whose works were scrutinized are J. P. Clark, Christopher Okigbo, Michael Echeruo, Wole Soyinka, Romanus Egudu, and Okogbule Wonodi. These poets, in the opinion of the Chinweizu critics, are lacking in craft and are guilty of the following faults:

  a. old-fashioned, craggy, unmusical language
  b. obscure and inaccessible diction
  c. a plethora of imported imagery
  d. a divorce from African oral poetic tradition.

The poet most guilty of these charges is probably Soyinka. Of Soyinka's *Idanre*, the Chinweizu critics delivered this verdict:

> The imagery is imprecise and opaque and lacking in evocative power. All we can decipher are the names of the various deities: Ogun, Sango, Ajantala, Esu, Orunmila, Orishanla (sic). But in this narrative poem it is never clear who does what to whom and with what consequences. It is often difficult to tell who the many pronouns—*he, she, we, us,*—refer to. We are shut off from the experience on both the intellectual and emotional levels. The language is a formidable barrier; and even after you have hacked your way through it, you still cannot understand what, if anything, is supposed to be going on.[47]

There is merit in these observations; for if, as Soyinka himself has claimed, works of literature are "fluid operations of the creative mind upon social and natural phenomena," his own works have not always been so. He injects studied metaphysical strains into the free operation of the creative intuition upon social and natural phenom-

ena. Critic Roderick Wilson had earlier complained of
complexity and confusion in Soyinka's poetry.[48] The Chinweizu endorsement of these charges lends them the weight
of authority.

Soyinka replied to the Chinweizu critics in two essays:
"Neo-Tarzanism: The Poetics of Pseudo-Tradition" (1975)
and "Neo-Tarzanism: The Aesthetic Illusion" (1976). The
argument of these two essays is similar although their tones
differ. Soyinka defends the disposition of his imagination
as a creative artist in these essays. What he calls "selective
eclecticism"[49] is the technical approach that rewards his
imagination, enriching his sensibilities as a poet. As a
creative artist, his imagination is not limited to considerations of local color only (the flora and fauna of the African
poetic landscape recommended by the Chinweizu critics)
but transcends these to assimilate new experiences from
other cultures and traditions. And so the "plethora of imported imagery" cannot but be persistent. Even his attitude
to that local environment itself is more complex than
usual:

> My African world is a little more intricate and em-
> braces precision machinery, oil rigs, hydro-electricity,
> my typewriter, railway trains (not iron snakes), ma-
> chine guns, bronze sculpture, etc., plus an ontological
> relationship with the universe including the above
> listed pumpkins and iron bells. This may result in a
> subtle *complication* in the "narration, reflection and
> resolution" of these phenomena but emphatically de-
> nies the deliberate *complication* of them.[50]

But in spite of his eclectic sensibility, it is still necessary
to distinguish between the true poet and the imitative poet.
The true poet assimilates disparate experiences only to
transform them into a new mintage. The great poets of the
world both dead and living form part of the cultural inheritance of every other poet regardless of his background.
What distinguishes the genuine poet from the imitative
poet is their attitude to that cultural heritage. The mind of

the true poet transforms what it borrows into a new whole, whereas the imitative poet merely echos his master's voice:

> A distinct universal quality in all great poets does . . . exercise ghostly influences on other writers—however different in background—at moments when a similarity of the particularized experience is shared. For the genuine creative mind, this need not be a cause for self-flagellation. The resulting work is easily judged by its capacity to move one step further, or sidewise; a conceptual variant or sleight-of-thought, by the naturalness of the influence, the thoroughness of ingestion within a new organic mould, its felicitous re-emergence and by the original strength of the new organic entity.[51]

These essays help us to understand Soyinka's views about the nature of poetry. Poetry for him is that metrical composition that is "visceral and sensuous" and "engages the imagination."[52] Indeed the "principle of imaginative challenge is one of the functions of poetry."[53] Also we have gained an insight from the essays into Soyinka's concept of image or symbol. What determines his choice of image is its peculiar potential to spark off "a dynamic relationship which consists of an internalized dialectic of phenomenon and perception."[54]

Because the Chinweizu critics advocate a return to tradition, Soyinka unkindly labels them with the stigma "Neo-Tarzanists" and calls them "advocates of a noble-savage school of poetics." Tradition, he affirms in a different context, does not mean raffia skirts or menstrual loin cloths.[55]

Of the two essays Soyinka wrote in reply to the Neo-Tarzanists, "Neo-Tarzanism: The Aesthetic Illusion"[56] is more sober, more weighty, less polemical, and more emotionally controlled than the essay "Neo-Tarzanism: The Poetics of Pseudo-Tradition." The published paper might have been written on the spur of the moment. Soyinka appears to have been too emotionally involved with his subject for the essay to have been objective. His judgment in the unpublished essay is more mature and more aesthetically distanced from its immediate target and therefore more effective as a literary polemic.

This chapter has not exhausted all that is to be said about Soyinka's criticism, it has only attempted to analyze the major critical essays so as to gain a fuller understanding of Soyinka's mind and art. For Soyinka's critical writings illuminate his own works. Soyinka has always urged upon the African writer the philosophy of self-acceptance: The acceptance of the true image of the African. The philosophy of acceptance is the inspiration behind the Incidental Essays. Soyinka has quarrelled with Senghor and the others of the *Negritude* school for distorting Africa's true literary image in their writings. This denial of the authentic image is at the root of Soyinka's criticism of Negritude.

The Ritual Essays transport us into the world of Yoruba mythology, exploring the origin and nature of Yoruba tragedy and the role of hubris in the drama of the gods. Tragedy originates from Ogun's sacrifice of his being in the first archetypal stage (the fourth space). Taking their cue from Ogun's example, the other ritual archetypes— Sango and Obatala—have learnt to face tragedy as a reparation for a previous act of error. It is in the principle of challenge and restitution that (ritual) drama can be related to the African worldview.

These essays are written with Soyinka's own work in mind, for he is a writer in the mythic mode as distinct from one whose imagination is historical. It is here (his mythic imagination) that Soyinka falls short of the expectations of Marxist critics. Indeed his essays on ideology and social vision reflect the dilemma of the mythic imagination in a world of pragmatic ideology. This is the argument of his literary polemics where they do not concern themselves with the problems of poetics. The mythic imagination can hardly consort with ideology in the Marxist sense, but it can make projections. This projection into the future is what Soyinka means by "social vision" in both its religious and secular dimensions.

When illustrating his theories with practical examples, Soyinka is an accomplished critic; in the formulation of these theories, however, he is not so clear and precise. This is understandable for Soyinka is primarily a creative writer, not a literary theorist.

Notes

1. Hugh Holman et al., *A Handbook to Literature* (New York: The Odyssey Press, 1960), p. 298.

2. Holman, p. 299.

3. Bernth Lindfors, "The Early Writings of Wole Soyinka," *Journal of African Studies*, Vol. 2 No. 1 (Spring 1975), p. 85.

4. Lindfors, "The Early Writings of Wole Soyinka," p. 86, and Martin Banham, "The Beginnings of a Nigerian Literature in English," *Review of English Literature*, 3 (1962), p. 90.

5. Wole Soyinka, "From a Common Back Cloth: A Reassessment of the African Literary Image," *American Scholar*, No. 32 (1963), p. 393.

6. *Ibid.*, p. 394.

7. *Ibid.*, p. 391.

8. *Ibid.*, p. 392.

9. Wole Soyinka, "And After the Narcissist?" *African Forum*, Vol. 1, No. 4 (Spring 1961), p. 62.

10. Cited from Erich Heller, *The Artist's Journey into the Interior and Other Essays* (New York: Random House, 1965), p. 103.

11. "And After the Narcissist?," p. 53.

12. *Ibid.*, p. 59.

13. *Ibid.*, p. 60.

14. Wole Soyinka, *Myth, Literature and the African World* (Cambridge: Cambridge University Press, 1976), p. 150. Subsequent references are to essays in this book.

15. "And After the Narcissist?," p. 59.

16. Communications of the University of Ife Newsletter, June 11, 1980.

17. Soyinka's essay first appeared in *The Morality of Art* dedicated to G. Wilson Knight and edited by D. W. Jefferson (London: Routledge and Kegan Paul, 1968), pp. 119–34.

18. *Myth and Literature*, p. 19.

19. Friedrich Nietzsche, *The Birth of Tragedy*, trans. Francis Golffing (New York: Doubleday, 1956), p. 99.

20. *The Birth of Tragedy*, p. 97.

21. W. B. Yeats, *Essays and Introductions* (London: Macmillan, 1961), p. 288.

22. *The Birth of Tragedy*, p. 61.

23. *Ibid.*

24. Anthony Graham-White, *The Drama of Black Africa* (New York: Samuel French, 1974), p. 22.

25. Wole Soyinka, *Idanre and Other Poems* (London: Methuen, 1967), p. 62.

26. Wole Soyinka, "The Writer in a Modern African State," in Per Wasberg, *The Writer in Modern Africa* (New York: Africana Publishing Corporation, 1969), p. 21.

27. "From a Common Back Cloth," p. 393.

28. Ngugi Wa Thiong'o, "The Writer and His Past," in *Homecoming* (London: Heinemann, 1978), p. 46.

29. Ayi Kwei Armah, *Why Are We So Blest?* (London: Heinemann, 1974), p. 231.

30. Wole Soyinka, "Drama and the Revolutionary Ideal," in *In Person: Achebe Awoonor, and Soyinka*, ed. Karen L. Morell (Seattle: University of Washington, Institute for Comparative and Foreign Area Studies, 1975).

31. *Ibid.*

32. Leon Trotsky, "The Formalist School of Poetry and

Marxism," in *Marxists on Literature*, ed. David Craig (Harmondsworth: Penguin, 1977), p. 368.

33. For more information on "historical materialism," see Ernst Fischer. *Marx in His Own Words*, trans. Anna Bostock (London: Penguin, 1970), pp. 80–93.

34. Biodun Jeyifo, "Tragedy, History and Ideology: Notes Toward a Query on Tragic Epistemology," paper presented at a Department of Modern European Language Seminar, University of Ife, 1977, p. 6. A later version of this paper appears in Jeyifo's *The Truthful Lie: Essays in a Sociology of African Drama* (London and Port of Spain: New Beacon Books, 1985), p. 27.

35. Femi Osofisan, "Drama and the New Exotic: The Paradox of Form in Modern African Theatre," paper presented at a Department of Modern European Languages Seminar, University of Ife, 1978, p. 7.

36. Omafume Onoge and G. G. Darah, "The Retrospective Stage: Some Reflections on the Mythopoeic Tradition at Ibadan," *Chindaba*, No. 1, Vol. 3 (October-December 1977), p. 55.

37. "The Retrospective Stage," p. 53.

38. Biodun Jeyifo, "Tragedy, History, and Ideology: Notes Towards a Query on Tragic Epistemology," p. 15.

39. Biodun Jeyifo, "The 'Hidden' Class War in *The Road*," paper presented to the First Ibadan Annual Literature Conference, University of Ibadan, 1976, pp. 12 and 13. Also available in Jeyifo's *The Truthful Lie*, pp. 11–22.

40. Ngugi Wa Thiong'o, "Wole Soyinka, T. M. Aluko and the Satiric Voice," in *Homecoming* (London: Heinemann, 1978), pp. 65–66.

41. Wole Soyinka, "Who's Afraid of Elesin Oba," paper presented at the Conference of Radical Perspective on African Literature, Ibadan, 1977, p. 23.

42. Stanley Macebuh, "Poetics and the Mythic Imagination," in *Critical Perspectives on Wole Soyinka*, ed. James

Gibbs (Washington, D.C.: Three Continents Press, 1980), p. 201.

43. Wole Soyinka, "Who's Afraid of Elesin Oba?," p. 10.

44. "Who's Afraid of Elesin Oba?," p. 16.

45. Wole Soyinka, *The Critic and Society* (University of Ife Inaugural Lectures Series 49, 1982), p. 9.

46. *The Critic and Society*, p. 8.

47. Chinweizu *et al.*, "Towards the Decolonization of African Literature," *Transition*, 48 (April-June 1975), p. 32.

48. Roderick Wilson, "Complexity and Confusion in Soyinka's Shorter Poems," *Critical Perspectives on Wole Soyinka*, pp. 158–169.

49. Wole Soyinka, "Neo-Tarzanism: The Poetics of Pseudo-Tradition," *Transition*, 48 (April-June 1975), p. 44.

50. "Neo-Tarzanism: The Poetics of Pseudo-Tradition," p. 38.

51. Wole Soyinka, "Neo-Tarzanism: The Aesthetic Illusion," Mimeograph (Philadelphia, 1976), p. 15. This essay was later published as "Aesthetic Illusion: Prescriptions for the Suicide of Poetry," *Third Press Review*, 1 (1975), 30–31, 65–68.

52. "Neo-Tarzanism: The Poetics of Pseudo-Tradition," p. 40.

53. "Neo-Tarzanism: The Poetics of Pseudo-Tradition," p. 43.

54. "Neo-Tarzanism: The Aesthetic Illusion," p. 20.

55. John Agetua, p. 46, and "From A Common Back-Cloth," p. 390.

56. This essay, I am told, has appeared in one of the numbers of *Third Press Review*.

CONCLUSION

SOYINKA AND THE FUTURE OF AFRICAN LITERATURE

African literature has come of age: It is now assured a
place in the comity of world literature. One of the
writers whose works has won for African literature the
current international recognition it enjoys is Wole
Soyinka. He has sophisticated technique, depth and complexity of meaning, intellectual appeal, and universal relevance. Soyinka has produced works that are capable of
engaging the attention of the scholar. One way by which he
has strengthened African literature is by his possessed utterance. The Yorubas regard the artist as a man possessed. As
a poet, novelist, dramatist, critic and essayist Soyinka performs under demonic possession. The demon is of course
his god, Ogun. In a possessed utterance, language is highly
charged, symbolic and mytho-embryonic. The possessed
utterance is what is generally referred to as Soyinka's addiction to a compact language, whose features include a cryptic syntactical structure, multi-valent and mythopoeic images, the latter investing Soyinka's language with such
unseen *personae* as the primordial beings Sekoni sees in the
passage on his technological schemes for his country or
Ofeyi's vision of the monsters of the deep at the worksite at
Shage. In every work of Soyinka's the poet's alter-ego typi-
fies this possession. This acute sensitivity for language is a
personal idiosyncracy, something he owes to his patron
saint, Ogun, the god of puzzles.

But there is an experimental angle to Soyinka's use of language. As a modern writer open to Western influences, especially the modernist influence, Soyinka discards the descriptive attitude to language in favor of the poetic approach. In the poetic approach, moods and rhythms are suggested through images and symbols, rather than by direct declamation. This strategy is what Soyinka means when he sees himself as belonging to the elliptical style of writing.[1] The third factor that has influenced Soyinka in his use of language is his Yoruba background. Language in traditional usage, he tells us, is not declamatory but "a densely packed matrix of reference."[2] Whatever innovations Soyinka has brought to his handling of poetry, fiction and drama owe their origin to one or more of the three factors mentioned above, that is, his personal temperament as a protagonist of change, his role as a neo-modernist, and his destiny as a Yoruba writer. Whether the change is a flashback, the disruption of the linear structure in favor of a cyclical one, or the fusion of the Yoruba traditional idioms with the conventions of a modern theatre, it is all traceable to our three-fold hypothesis.

Another feature of Soyinka's technique is his use of myth. Myth for Soyinka is much more than the integration of mythological personages into the structure of his plots. Myth takes into consideration the realities of his own people's worldview of known and unknown areas of existence. For James Joyce and T. S. Eliot, myth underscores the parallel between antiquity and contemporaneity. Myth reflects also the contrast or similarity between the past and the present in Soyinka, but there is another dimension to his interest in myth. His use of myth is reminiscent, too, of the way W. B. Yeats has used it to reflect the reality of the world we see and the world we do not see. In Soyinka's poem, "In Memory of Segun Awolowo," the death of a dear one is mourned both by the living and the dead. The dead, called "the grey presences of head and hand," are said to "make complaint" and "wander still/Adrift from understanding." What distinguishes Soyinka from other Yoruba writers who use the same traditional material is his personal interpretation of the myth of Ogun, the Yoruba god of contradictions.

The compact language and the use of myth are the elements of Soyinka's style that can be called "metaphysical." The metaphysical style of Soyinka's poetry has been criticized in some quarters for its easy tendency toward obscurity. Others have found it exciting, excusing it on the ground that it is the rightful inheritance of the mythic imagination.[3] This style has of course strengthened Soyinka's work. It is, indeed, what has made his writings unique. Each of Soyinka's two novels, for example, mark a major advance in the development of the African fiction. Both *The Interpreters* and *Season of Anomy* signify the advent of the full-fledged novel (the novel with depth and complexity) on the African literary scene. A critic in the *Times Literary Supplement,* discussing *The Interpreters'* complex imagery and subtle organization, called it "a work of great distinction and wide influence."[4] We are sure of the distinction but not quite certain of the influence. In his review of *Season of Anomy* Edgar Wright noted that a novel with a similar depth and breadth as Soyinka's novel was yet to emerge in Africa.[5] Other African writers are, however, beginning to come up with profound works of fiction.

Can there be another Soyinka on the African literary scene? This is a difficult question to answer now. What is significant is that his kind of technique is one that requires industry. We are yet to have a writer who is a man of many parts such as Soyinka himself is. His work is more admired than imitated. He has a following among some young Nigerian poets such as Odia Ofeimun and Fumso Aiyejina, and in the area of drama we include Ola Rotimi and Femi Osofisan. The young poets have been enabled by Soyinka's self-confidence to develop their own voice, but the dramatists who look up to Soyinka have yet to attain the master's level of competence in technique.

Soyinka's influence is more keenly felt in the direction he gave to African literature in the famous Afro-Scandinavian Writers' Conference in which he urged the African writer to break with the past and attend to assessing the present. From that time onward, Soyinka's own works moved from private experience to purposeful commentary. This is the current stage of much of African literature today. But the preoccupation with the present is fraught with its own aesthetic problems. Would the writer distance himself sufficiently from the events of his time to be able to view them objectively and thus come forth with an enduring commentary? The features of Soyinka's style are his means for mediating between experience and art. Each writer working with contemporary material must forge his own mediatory medium if he is to outlive his time.

Notes

1. John Agetua, *Six Nigerian Writers* (Benin: Bendel Newspaper Corporation, n.d.), p. 45.

2. Wole Soyinka, "Neo-Tanzanism: The Poetics of Pseudo-Tradition," *Transition* 48 (April-June 1975), p. 39.

3. This countering view is held by Stanley Macebuh in his "Poetics and the Mythic Imagination"; see *Critical Perspectives on Wole Soyinka*, ed. James Gibbs (Washington: Three Continents Press, 1980), pp. 200-212.

4. Cited from John Wakeman, ed., *World Authors 1950-1970: A Companion Volume to Twentieth Century Authors* (New York: H. H. Wilson Co., 1975), p. 101.

5. Edgar Wright, "Review of Wole Soyinka's *Season of Anomy*," *African Literature Today*, 8 (1976), p. 120.

BIBLIOGRAPHY

NOVELS BY SOYINKA

The Interpreters. London: Andre Deutsch, 1965.

Season of Anomy. London: Rex Collings, 1973.

POETRY BY SOYINKA

Idanre and Other Poems. London: Methuen, 1967.

A Shuttle in the Crypt. New York: Hill & Wang, 1972.

Ogun Abibiman. London and Ibadan: Rex Collings, 1976.

PLAYS BY SOYINKA

A Dance of the Forests, The Road, The Bacchae of Euripedes in *Collected Plays, Vol. 1.* London: Oxford University Press, 1973.

Madmen and Specialists, in *Collected Plays, Vol. 2.* London: Oxford University Press, 1974.

Death and the King's Horseman. London: Methuen; New York: Norton, 1975.

NONFICTIONAL PROSE OF SOYINKA

The Man Died: Prison Notes of Wole Soyinka. London: Rex Collings, 1972.

Ake: The Years of Childhood. London: Rex Collings, 1981.

CRITICAL WORKS

"From a Common Backcloth." *The American Scholar*, 32 (1963).

"And After the Narcissist?" *African Forum*, 1 (Spring 1966).

"The Writer in a Modern African State." *The Writer in Modern Africa, African-Scandinavian Writers' Conference, Stockholm, 1967*, ed. Per Wastberg. Uppsala, Scandinavian Institute of African Studies, 1968.

"Neo-Tarzanism: The Poetics of Pseudo-Tradition." *Transition*, 48 (April–June 1975).

"Drama and the Revolutionary Ideal." *In Person: Achebe, Awocnor, and Soyinka*, ed. Karen L. Morell. Seattle: Institute for Comparative Foreign Area Studies, 1975.

"Neo-Tarzanism: Aesthetic Illusion." Mimeograph, 1976; also in *Third Press Review*, 1 (1975).

Myth, Literature and the African World. London: Cambridge University Press, 1976.

"Who is Afraid of Elesin Oba?" Mimeograph, 1977.

The Critic and Society. University of Ife Inaugural Lectures Series, 49 (1980).

BOOKS CONSULTED

Abimbola, Wande. *Ifa: An Exposition of Ifa Literary Corpus*. Ibadan: Oxford University Press, 1976.

Agetua, John. *When the Man Died*. Benin City: Bendel Newspapers Corporation, 1975.

———. *Six Nigerian Writers*. Benin City: Bendel Newspapers Corporation, n.d.

Beier, Ulli (ed.). *Introduction to African Literature*. London: Longmans, 1967.

Booth, James. *Writers and Politics in Nigeria.* London, 1981.

Gakwandi, Shatto Arthur. *The Novel and Contemporary Experience in Africa.* New York: Africana, 1977.

Gibbs, James (ed.). *Critical Perspectives on Wole Soyinka.* Washington: Three Continents Press, 1980.

Graham-White, Anthony. *The Drama of Black Africa.* New York: Samuel French, 1974.

Heller, Eric. *The Artist's Journey into the Interior and Other Essays.* New York: Random House, 1965.

Idowu, Bolaji. *Olodumare: God in Yorubu Belief.* London: Longmans, 1977.

Jones, Eldred. *The Writing of Wole Soyinka.* London: Heinemann, 1973.

Killam, G. D. *African Writers on African Writing.* London, 1972.

Larson, Charles R. *The Emergence of African Fiction.* London, 1978.

Laurence, Margaret. *Long Drum and Cannons*: Nigerian Dramatists and Novelists, 1952–1966. London: Macmillan, 1968.

Mayerson, Philip. *Classical Mythology in Literature, Art and Music.* Lexington: Lexington Xerox College Publishing, 1971.

McNamara, Eugene. *The Interior Landscape: The Literary Criticism of Marshall McLuhan.* Toronto: McGraw-Hill, 1969.

Moore, Gerald. *Wole Soyinka.* London: Evans, 1976.

Morell, Karen L. (ed.). *In Person: Achebe, Awonoor, and Soyinka.* Seattle: Institute for Comparative and Foreign Area Studies, 1975.

Ngugi Wa Thiong'o. *Homecoming.* London: Heinemann, 1978.

Nietzsche, Friedrich. *The Birth of Tragedy.* New York: Doubleday, 1950.

Nkosi, Lewis. *Tasks and Masks.* Burnt Mill: Longmans, 1981.

Ogunba, Oyin. *The Movement of Transition.* Ibadan: Ibadan University Press, 1975.

Ogunba, Oyin, and Abiola Irele (eds.). *Theatre in Africa.* Ibadan: Ibadan University Press, 1978.

Olney, James. *Tell Me Africa: An Approach to African Literature.* Princeton: Princeton University Press, 1973.

Palmer, Eustace. *An Introduction to the African Novel.* London: Heinemann, 1972.

——. *The Growth of the African Novel.* London: Heinemann, 1979.

Roscoe, Adrian. *Mother Is Gold: A Study in West African Literature.* London: Oxford University Press, 1969.

Spears, Monroe K. *Dionysus and the City.* London: Oxford University Press, 1970.

Strauss, Walter A. *Descent and Return: The Orphic Theme in Modern Literature.* Cambridge: Harvard University Press, 1971.

Thomson, George. *Aeschylus and Athens.* New York: Grosset and Dunlop, 1968.

Wright, Edgar (ed.). *The Critical Evaluation of African Literature.* London: Heinemann, 1973.

ARTICLES AND ESSAYS

Asgill, E. J. "African Adaptations of Greek Tragedies." *African Literature Today,* 11 (1980).

Chinweizu and Onwuchekwa Jemie and Iheahukwu Madubuike. "Towards the Decolonization of African Literature." *Transition,* 48 (April–June, 1975).

Davis, Ann B. "Dramatic Theory of Wole Soyinka." *Critical Perspectives on Wole Soyinka*, ed. James Gibbs. Washington: Three Continents Press, 1980.

Eliot, T. S. "The Use of Poetry and the Use of Criticism." *Selected Prose of T. S. Eliot*, ed. Frank Kermode. London: Faber and Faber, rept., 1975.

Enekwe, Ossie Onuora. "Wole Soyinka as Novelist." *Okike*, 9 (December 1975).

Fletcher, John, and James McFarlane. "Modernist Drama: Origins and Patterns." *Modernism*, eds. Malcolm Bradbury and James McFarlane. Harmondsworth: Penguin, 1976.

Friedman, Alan. "The Novel." *The Twentieth Century Mind, Vol. 1*, eds. C. B. Cox and A. E. Dyson. London, 1972.

Gibbs, James. *Study Aid to Kongi's Harvest*. London: Rex Collings, 1972.

——. "The Origins of *A Dance of the Forests*." *African Literature Today*, 8 (1976).

——. "My Roots Have Come out in the Other World: Soyinka's Search for Theatrical Form up to the End of 1960." Mimeograph, 1981.

Hollington, Michael. "Suevo, Joyce and Modernist Time." *Modernism*, eds. Malcolm Bradbury and James McFarlane. Harmondsworth: Penguin, 1976.

Izevbaye, D. S. "Language and Meaning in *The Road*. *African Literature Today*, 8 (1971).

——. "Mediation in Soyinka: The Case of the King's Horseman." *Critical Perspectives on Wole Soyinka*, ed. James Gibbs. Washington: Three Continents Press, 1980.

——. "Soyinka's Black Orpheus." *Critical Perspectives on Wole Soyinka*, ed. James Gibbs. Washington: Three Continents Press, 1980.

Jeyifo, Biodun. "Wole Soyinka: An Interview." *Transition*, 42 (1973).

———. "The Hidden Class War in *The Road*." Mimeograph, 1976.

———. "Tragedy, History and Ideology: Notes Towards a Query on Tragic Epistemology." Mimeograph, 1977.

Jones, Eldred. "Wole Soyinka: Critical Approaches." *The Critical Evaluation of African Literature*, ed. Edgar Wright. London: Heinemann, 1973.

Lindfors, Bernth. "The Early Writings of Wole Soyinka." *Critical Perspectives on Wole Soyinka*, ed. James Gibbs. Washington: Three Continents Press, 1980.

Macebuh, Stanley. "Poetics and the Mythic Imagination." *Critical Perspectives on Wole Soyinka*, ed. James Gibbs. Washington: Three Continents Press, 1980.

Maduakor, Obi. "Conquering the Abyss of the Crypt: Survival Imperative in Soyinka's Shuttle." *World Literature Written in English*, 16 (1977).

———. "Soyinka's *Season of Anomy*: Ofeyi's Quest." *International Fiction Review*, 7 (1980).

———. "Soyinka's Animystic Poetics." *African Studies Review*, 25 (1982).

Nkosi, Lewis. "Fiction by Black South Africans." *An Introduction to African Literature*, ed. Ulli Beier. London: Longmans, 1967.

Ogunba, Oyin. "The Agemo Cult in Ijebu-Land." *Nigeria Magazine*, 86 (1965).

Ogundipe-Leslie, Omolara. "A Comment on *Ogun Abibiman*." *Critical Perspectives on Wole Soyinka*, ed. James Gibbs. Washington: Three Continents Press, 1980.

Okonkwo, Juliet I. "The Essential Unity of Soyinka's *The Interpreters* and *Season of Anomy*." *African Literature Today*, 11 (1980).

Onoge, Omafume F. "The Crisis of Consciousness in Modern African Literature: A Survey." *Canadian Journal of African Studies*, 8 (1974).

Onoge, Omafume, with G. G. Darah. "The Retrospective Stage: Some Reflection on the Mythopoeic Tradition at Ibadan." *Chindaba*, 3 (October–December 1977).

Osofisan, Femi. "Tiger on Stage: Wole Soyinka and Nigerian Theatre." *Theatre in Africa*, eds. Oyin Ogunba and Abiola Irele. Ibadan: Ibadan University Press, 1978.

———. "Drama and the New Exotica." Mimeograph, 1978.

Osundare, Niyi. "Words of Iron, Sentences of Thunder: Soyinka's Prose Style." *African Literature Today*, 13 (1983).

Senanu, K. E. "The Exigencies of Adaptation: The Case of Soyinka's *Bacchae*." *Critical Perspectives on Wole Soyinka*, ed. James Gibbs. Washington: Three Continents Press, 1980.

Tighe, C. "In Detentio Preventione in Aeternum: Soyinka's *A Shuttle in the Crypt*." *Critical Perspectives on Wole Soyinka*, ed. James Gibbs. Washington: Three Continents Press, 1980.

Wilkinson, Nick. "Demoke's Choice in Soyinka's *A Dance of the Forests*." *Critical Perspectives on Wole Soyinka*, ed. James Gibbs. Washington: Three Continents Press, 1980.

Wilson, Roderick. "Complexity and Confusion in Soyinka's Shorter Poems." *Critical Perspectives on Wole Soyinka*, ed. James Gibbs. Washington: Three Continents Press, 1980.